# DoD Supply Chain Management Implementation Guide

Logistics Management Institute
McLean, VA USA

**Deputy Under Secretary of Defense
(Logistics and Materiel Readiness)**

Office of Supply Chain Integration

ISBN: 0-9661916-3-3 (hardcover)


Library of Congress Catalog Card Number: 00-134067

Printed in the United States of America.

# Table of Contents

# Figures

# Tables

# Foreword

Department of Defense logistics managers have a long tradition of being in the forefront of implementation of new programs and innovative approaches to providing the best possible materiel and services support to the nation's warfighters. The transition to a new and challenging environment following the end of the Cold War period has been particularly difficult.

The world is different: Technology, access to information, and military deployments have all significantly changed over the past decade. New operational concepts have built on combat agility, information dominance, surgical precision, and focused logistics. These concepts (the Joint Staff's Joint Vision 2020 and the military departments' Army After Next, Forward From the Sea, Operational Maneuver From the Sea, and Air Expeditionary Force) mandate implicit operational logistics requirements. For the logistics community, the challenge is to improve our processes by introducing and adopting those supply chain management skill sets needed to provide the best possible support to the customer within the bounds of available personnel and financial resources. Defense logistics must use these new tools to transform itself to attain greater efficiencies, borrowing best practices from successful organizations and applying them to our own requirements.

Supply chain management is one of the key practices developed in the private sector over the past two decades. This concept, which involves significant process change, holds great promise for improving military logistics support. Making successful use of this concept requires the proper mix of commercial practices, modern technologies, and consideration of DoD's unique logistics characteristics.

The *DoD Supply Chain Management Implementation Guide* is published as a tool to assist DoD logistics personnel at all organizational levels who want to improve materiel support and service to customers. Implementing supply chain management concepts in the context of the military environment will create significant public value and enhance the successful achievement of the logistics mission.

James T. Eccleston
Assistant Deputy Under Secretary of Defense, Supply Chain Integration

# Preface

The *DoD Supply Chain Management Implementation Guide* is a tool to assist logistics personnel who are responsible for implementing supply chain management. To personnel in DoD who already have embarked on this journey, this *Guide* should be a useful supplement to your own ideas and plans. The experience of world-class companies in the private sector clearly indicates that applying the principles and management approaches outlined in this document can produce dramatic results in logistics process performance and corresponding degrees of improved customer satisfaction.

The purpose of this *Guide* is not to provide an in-depth description of the workings of a supply chain management process. Covering all aspects of the mechanics of the process would require volumes of information. Throughout the *Guide*, we have provided numerous references to detailed information the supply chain implementation team will need to pursue its task.

This document is intended to serve as a roadmap for individuals and organizations seeking day-to-day direction for implementing supply chain management in a DoD environment. To the extent possible, we have used DoD terminology and points of reference to outline required concepts and actions. In some cases, alternative implementation strategies or different sequences of actions may be more effective. No single document can corner the market on good ideas.

In preparing this *Guide*, we performed an in-depth review of a broad spectrum of successful efforts. This *Guide* presents the key principles and implementation strategies we found, compiled into a structured and workable approach for achieving progress toward fully incorporating supply chain management into the DoD logistics process.


James H. Reay
Logistics Management Institute

# Chapter 1
# Introduction

Change is the law of life. Any attempt to contain it guarantees an explosion down the road; the more rigid the adherence to the status quo, the more violent the ultimate outcome will be.

Henry Kissinger

As DoD enters a new century, it bears the burden of a logistics system that is designed to fight the wars of the past. Earlier conflicts often focused national attention on the war and required the American people to make personal sacrifices as resources were diverted to support the war effort. The nation willingly tolerated logistical inefficiencies and applied virtually unlimited resources in order to "win." America's attitudes were best summarized by President John F. Kennedy in his inaugural address:

Let every nation know, whether it wishes us well or ill, that we shall pay any price, bear any burden, meet any hardship, oppose any foe, in order to assure the survival and the success of liberty. This much we pledge—and more.

The American public's attitude toward the cost of armed conflict has changed, however. America no longer faces direct threats from fascism or an "evil empire." During the last decade of the 20th century, America's armed conflicts were much shorter in duration and more regionally confined than they were earlier in the century. Although the American public continues to support a military presence throughout the world, they are no longer willing to pay any price for it. The challenge for the DoD logistics community, then, is to provide the best possible materiel and services support to the operational warfighter within the bounds of available personnel and financial resources. Therefore, Defense logistics must strive for greater efficiencies, borrowing best practices and enabling technologies from successful activities and applying them to DoD. In spite of its past successes, DoD must embrace change.

In an article in *Logistics Management and Distribution Report,* Senior Editor Toby Gooley summarized the fundamentals of change management in large organizations.[1] He first discussed the reasons for change and then summarized several critical considerations.

> Change, then, is part and parcel of today's logistics environment. But those who passively accept change instead of managing it often become its victim, losing control and influence over their environment or even losing their jobs, say the experts. Instead, logistics managers should become "change leaders" who motivate their organizations to seize the opportunities for improvements that change offers.

A mere desire to lead change is not enough, however; there must be a well-conceived plan to effect the required specific actions. This *Department of Defense (DoD) Supply Chain Management Implementation Guide* offers a perspective in some detail on how DoD logistics organizations, as well as other government activities and supporting contractors, might approach the challenge of going beyond rhetoric and good intentions and pursuing a structured approach to implementing modern supply chain management (SCM) processes.

Gooley further outlines several essential change management considerations that are particularly applicable to the DoD environment:[2]

- ◆ *Understand the psychology of change.* Know why people resist change and anticipate the resulting behaviors that can sabotage implementation.

- ◆ *Prove beyond doubt that change is needed.* Any plan to change the way people carry out their responsibilities will need full cooperation and support from every participant.

- ◆ *Communicate, communicate, and communicate!* Communicating the goals, progress, and impact of planned changes to every participant is absolutely critical.

- ◆ *Help others handle change successfully.* It's important to provide training that gives employees the skills they will need to carry out their new responsibilities.

- ◆ *Be a good role model.* It's critical that managers behave in a way that's consistent with their statements.

---

[1] Toby B. Gooley, "Take Charge of Change," *Logistics Management and Distribution Report,* August 1, 1999.

[2] Ibid.

◆ *Don't take on more change than your organization can handle.* Some organizations try to make long technological leaps in order to adopt industry best practices. Use a building block strategy to attain results.

◆ *Focus on people's work processes, not on technical issues.* Technologies are only solutions if they enable process improvements or more efficient use of resources.

In developing the *DoD Supply Chain Management Implementation Guide*, the foregoing criteria played an important part in focusing the document's content on creating a plan of action for applying SCM in DoD. This *Guide* is designed as a practical reference tool for individuals and organizations who are responsible for learning how the private sector has formulated a new way of accomplishing logistics tasks and significantly transitioning the current DoD logistics process to this new paradigm.

The challenges to successful implementation of SCM in DoD are formidable in any environment. In 1997 two leading supply chain experts, Robert Monczka and James Morgan, outlined the resistance factors that must be overcome. Although they were discussing resistance in a private-sector context, the factors they identified are equally applicable to today's DoD environment:[3]

◆ Fragmentation in the way supply chain management is understood and applied.

◆ Failure of organizations to develop true integration of the processes used to achieve supply chain management.

◆ Organizational resistance to the concept.

◆ Lack of buy-in by many top managers.

◆ Lack of and/or slow development of needed measurement systems.

---

[3] Robert M. Monczka and James P. Morgan, "What's Wrong with Supply Chain Management?" *Purchasing*, January 16, 1997.

◆ Lack of good and sufficient information, including integrated information systems and electronic commerce linking participants in the supply chain.

◆ Failure of management thinking to look beyond the bounds of individual organizations.

These factors are all too familiar to many DoD logistics practitioners. A central objective of the *DoD Supply Chain Management Implementation Guide* is to meet these challenges head-on and offer a roadmap through these impediments toward a transformation of the Department's logistics processes in keeping with SCM precepts.

Clearly, no single publication will contain all of the answers in a field as complex as SCM. Hundreds of academic and commercial sources are available in published and electronic form to add greater detail and perspective to this *Guide*. Seminars and conferences on SCM abound. Furthermore, as many DoD personnel have recognized, the military logistics environment differs significantly from the private-sector environment in purpose, objectives, and procedures. Although some of these differences are largely semantic or superficial, others are real and substantial.

Since the end of the Cold War, DoD's military and civilian leadership have struggled to redefine the Department's role in the context of a New World military paradigm. As a major entity within the Department, the logistics community has faced this same dilemma in dealing with political, economic, and technological changes. At the same time, the dramatic reduction of in-house civilian and military logistics expertise has resulted in a drain of knowledge that has left the community ill-prepared to transition to the new environment.

A 1999 corporate study concluded, "An enterprise's model of the world resides primarily in the minds of its employees and in its software applications. One of the most painful and costly incongruences in large, modern enterprises is the difference between the mental models of its employees (which reflect the real world they deal with) and the implementation of business processes in its software applications."[4] The *DoD Supply Chain Management Implementation Guide* is intended as one mechanism to help the logistics community focus its collective wisdom and resources in support of a timely,

---

[4] Proforma Corporation, "Enterprise Application Modeling, Concept to Code," White Paper, 1999.

effective, and thorough adaptation of changes required in the logistics process of the 21st century. Throughout this *Guide,* we recognize that a DoD team that is responsible for supply chain implementation must make its own interpretation and selection of the manifestation of SCM that is appropriate for DoD application.

In addressing the application of the SCM concept in DoD, the scope of this *Guide* is simple and straightforward. The DoD supply chain process encompasses all government and private-sector organizations, processes, and systems that individually or collectively play a role in planning for, acquiring, maintaining, or delivering material resources for military or other operations conducted in support of the United States' national Defense interests.

The *DoD Supply Chain Management Implementation Guide* is intended to be a working reference tool for individuals and organizations within and outside DoD who are executing the Department's efforts to adapt the SCM concept to the military logistics process. The structure of the *Guide* covers the principal elements that must be addressed in a successful implementation of SCM. Together, these elements provide the basis for a series of actions that can lead to successful implementation of SCM in DoD organizations. In summary, these elements are as follows:

- ◆ Determination of guiding principles to focus and validate required actions

- ◆ Establishment of a team-based, coordinated organizational structure to complete or oversee required implementation actions

- ◆ Development, publication, and management approval of a comprehensive implementation strategy

- ◆ Identification and implementation of selected applicable best business practices to support DoD transition to the supply chain concept

- ◆ Identification and application of enabling methods and technologies

- ◆ Management of the future process through enterprise-wide performance measures.

Collectively, these elements provide the basis for structural changes that are necessary to accomplish the transition to an SCM way of doing business in

DoD. Figure 1-1 portrays these "pillars of success" in the SCM implementation process.

*Figure 1-1. Pillars of Success*

The remaining sections of this *Guide* are organized as follows:

- ◆ *Chapter 2*—A discussion of fundamental supply chain management principles as applicable to DoD

- ◆ *Chapter 3*—A description of the six-step high-level strategy for SCM implementation

- ◆ *Chapter 4*—A suggested organizational approach for getting started on SCM implementation

- ◆ *Chapter 5*—An overall perspective on developing an SCM implementation strategy, including performance measurement for DoD activities

- ◆ *Chapter 6*—Capabilities and actions required to design and evaluate a supply chain structure in a DoD environment

- *Chapter 7*—A compendium of "best" business practice improvements with potential for application in DoD supply chains

- *Chapter 8*—Use of available technology enablers in supply chain implementation

- *Chapter 9*—A high-level approach for management oversight of operational DoD supply chains

- *Appendix A*—Principles for managing the supply chain implementation program

- *Appendix B*—Supply chain capabilities required in support of "focused logistics"

- *Appendix C*—An outline of DoD logistics functional process elements

- *Appendix D*—Supply Chain Operational Reference (SCOR) model descriptive materials.

- *Appendix E*—Current Supply Chain Management Applications.

- *Appendix F*—Abbreviations.

This *Guide* should be used as a "cookbook" rather than an encyclopedia. There are many variations, of course, to the supply chain "recipe" presented in these pages. Supply chain practitioners are free, as always, to embellish, omit, substitute, or garnish as required.

# Chapter 2
# Supply Chain Management Principles for DoD

## Why Use A Supply Chain Strategy for DoD?

Providing logistics support to America's fighting forces at home and over-seas has always been a significant part of the military mission. Beginning with the American Revolution, providing the necessary material to support the fighting capability and well-being of our troops has occupied a large por-tion of the military establishment's time and resources. The evolution of the military logistics process culminated during World War II (WWII) with the most massive production and delivery of military supplies and equipment in history.

During the period of the Cold War with the Soviet Union (1947–1989), the requirement to support large numbers of personnel and equipment at widely dispersed locations continued. The wartime scenarios of this period dictated a logistics strategy of massive inventories and great delivery capacity to be used against an enemy with superior numbers of personnel and weapons. Fixed material pipelines between continental United States (CONUS) sources of supply and the planned theater locations in Europe and Northeast Asia were lengthy and expansive.

During the protracted war in Vietnam, this same logistics capability was used to pour millions of tons of material into the Southeast Asia war zone. Mili-tary strategists believed that using America's superior production and deliv-ery capacity to overwhelm the enemy with an avalanche of material and equipment would produce the desired results, as it had successfully in WWII. Many of today's military leaders and strategists had their defining wartime experience in Vietnam. That experience—coupled with the demise of an en-emy with large numbers of personnel and equipment—has generated a new strategy of flexibility and agility. In addition, different military missions have emerged in the form of smaller-scale regional conflicts and peacekeeping and humanitarian roles. The new warfighting concepts for the 21st century are documented in the *Joint Vision 2010* (*JV2010*), *Joint Vision 2020* (*JV2020*), and *Focused Logistics* publications.[1]

The logistics process that developed during WWII and generally continued during the Cold War and Vietnam eras essentially was a "one-size-fits-all" process. The material support process as implemented in the military services and the Defense Logistics Agency (DLA) was based universally on the concept that government-operated organizations would acquire material from manufacturers and distributors in the private sector, compute projected quantities of items for use by military customers, store inventory in government-operated warehouses, accomplish repair and overhaul as required, and manage the delivery of goods to authorized users. DoD policies directed the Department's logistics organizations to operate a "stock, store, and issue" process in accordance with standard procedures. During most of the 50 years after WWII, this approach worked well. In fact, DoD logistics managers were regarded as national leaders in operating efficiency and management innovation. During this same time, DoD budgets were sufficiently large to support the tried-and-true military logistics process.

By the end of the 1980s, however, events caused DoD to reexamine its long-standing approach to providing military logistics support. The following separate but ultimately interrelated events have caused DoD to revisit its approach to logistics management:

◆ The end of the Cold War, which resulted in a new set of military threat scenarios and responsibilities

◆ Significant downsizing of DoD in terms of personnel and available budget resources

◆ Emergence of a competitive global economy and subsequent advances in logistics process improvement and related technologies in the private sector.

For DoD logistics managers, the combined effects of these three influences have been dramatic. The significant changes in potential combat scenarios

---

[1] U.S. Department of Defense, Chairman of the Joint Chiefs of Staff, *Joint Vision 2010*, 1996.

U.S. Department of Defense, Chairman of the Joint Chiefs of Staff, *Joint Vision 2020*, 2000.

Joint Staff, Director for Logistics, *Joint Vision 2010, Focused Logistics, A Joint Logistics Roadmap*, August 1, 1997.

now mandate a substantially more flexible and more responsive logistics process. The previous stock, store, and issue system simply cannot satisfy the varied materiel and service requirements of the modern warfighter. Nor are the process cycle-time standards that are inherent in current processes acceptable in the "short-notice" environment of today's military operations. Furthermore, because of major reductions in logistics personnel and budgets, managers no longer can rely on the application of large amounts of manual force and generous infusions of funds to compensate for system sluggishness and inflexibility during periods of crisis.

Concurrent with the evolving transition of the combat and operational responsibilities of the armed forces, the corresponding changes required to accomplish logistics responsibilities must be different in the future. The *2000 DoD Logistics Strategic Plan* states the logistics mission as follows: "To provide responsive and cost-effective support to ensure readiness and sustainability for the total force across the spectrum of military operations."[2] Although the fundamental mission of the logistics process is relatively unchanged, specific strategies to accomplish that mission will change significantly. Some implications for the future logistics process are shown in Table 2-1.

*Table 2-1. Exemplary Future Logistics Requirements*

| JV2010 | Operating strategy | Logistics strategy | Logistics requirements |
|---|---|---|---|
| Dominant maneuver | Position and employ widely dispersed joint air, land, and sea forces to gain positional advantage and use decisive speed and tempo to apply decisive force against enemy centers of gravity | Increase mobility of assets to provide logistics support commensurate with speed and tempo of operational units | • Smaller in-theatre footprint<br>• Continuous replenishment<br>• Full asset visibility<br>• Rapid transportation<br>• Flexible combat service support |

[2] U.S. Department of Defense, Deputy Under Secretary of Defense (Logistics), *DoD Logistics Strategic Plan*, 2000 edition, August 1999.

*Table 2-1. Exemplary Future Logistics Requirements (Continued)*

| JV2010 | Operating strategy | Logistics strategy | Logistics requirements |
|---|---|---|---|
| Precision engagement | Use integrated systems to coordinate employment of all Defense capabilities to provide greater assurance of delivering desired effect, lessen risk to U.S. forces, and minimize collateral damage | Increase customization of logistics packages tailored to unique and diverse requirements of operating units | • Rapid and precise requirements planning <br><br> • Real-time decision-support tools <br><br> • Competitive sourcing <br><br> • Flexible load configurations <br><br> • Precise delivery of support |
| Full dimensional protection | Ensure that forces and facilities are protected from enemy attacks, thereby maintaining freedom of deployment, maneuver, and engagement | Increase survivability of logistics lines and lines of communication | • Greater dispersion of logistics assets <br><br> • Greater use of "virtual" logistics chains |

Source: *Joint Vision 2010.*

During the past several years, DoD management has initiated several efforts to outline the direction for widespread process improvement in all phases of Department activity. In 1997, the Secretary of Defense promulgated his Defense Reform Initiative (DRI)[3] to define the Department's future direction. The DRI builds on previous efforts and presents a strategy for transforming the Defense structure of the Cold War era into a streamlined but effective force for the 21st century. The thrust of the DRI is particularly applicable to Defense logistics. The following four action areas are highlighted in the DRI:[4]

♦ *Reengineering*—Adopting modern business practices to achieve world-class standards of performance

♦ *Consolidation*—Streamlining to remove redundancy and maximize synergy

---

[3] Secretary of Defense, *Defense Reform Initiative Report,* November 1997.

[4] Ibid., p. iii.

◆ *Competition*—Applying market mechanisms to improve quality, reduce costs, and respond to customer needs

◆ *Elimination*—Reducing excess support structures and focusing on core competencies.

Each approach can be applied effectively in Defense logistics, but on balance, all are required to achieve the significant improvements in performance and efficiency envisioned by the Secretary's initiative.

## The Future DoD Logistics Vision

DoD's high-level logistics managers have formulated a vision of the future that reflects a composite view of the direction of change in the first decade of the 21st century. The 2000 edition of the *DoD Logistics Strategic Plan* provides the following statement of the future DoD logistics vision:

> By 2010, the logistics process will be an efficient, integrated supply chain of private sector and organic providers that ensures full customer-oriented support to personnel and weapon systems.[5]

This official vision of the future of the DoD logistics process presupposes the Department's ability and commitment to implementation of substantial logistics process changes that are necessary to apply SCM concepts developed in the private sector to the DoD environment.

For Defense logistics, the process improvement requirements of the DRI and the *DoD Logistics Strategic Plan* are analogous to similar initiatives that originated in the private sector and continue there today. In fact, one of the general premises of the DRI and subsequent related publications is that the transformation of DoD can be facilitated and accelerated through large-scale adoption of proven private-sector business practices by DoD business-like activities. We discuss this premise later in this chapter. For now, this narrative focuses on one of the most far-reaching and influential of these concepts—"supply chain management."

In discussing the potential application of SCM to DoD logistics, it is easy to make the mistake of assuming that because DoD already has multiple organizations and processes for the acquisition and distribution of material

---

[5] U.S. Department of Defense, Deputy Under Secretary of Defense (Logistics), *DoD Logistics Strategic Plan*, 2000 edition, August 1999.

from suppliers to consumers (i.e., a supply chain) that some form of SCM already is in place. Such assumptions are analogous to believing that the Wright brothers' biplane at Kitty Hawk, North Carolina and Boeing's 747 are essentially the same. For DoD logistics, the danger of this assumption arises when responsible managers conclude that implementation of SCM in DoD will be primarily an effort to streamline, modernize, and speed up current logistics functions, mainly through large doses of new technologies. Although this approach may result in some process improvement—and may be better than nothing—it will not achieve the performance and cost savings that true implementation of the private sector's actual SCM concept can generate.

At the same time, however, personnel who are responsible for implementation of SCM in DoD must not take the equally erroneous path of assuming that a cost-effective supply chain process can be purchased "off-the-shelf" like any one of thousands of commercially available software or hardware packages. DoD logistics does have real differences from commercial logistics processes that must be recognized and accommodated in the implementation strategy. As a first step toward supply chain implementation, we need to develop a common definition that is appropriate for the DoD. Research indicates that associations, academics, and companies in the private sector have adopted their own definitions of SCM, tailored to their particular perspective or circumstances. Although these definitions often are similar in scope and meaning, if not specifically in terminology, citing a litany of organization-specific definitions could be more confusing than educational. Therefore, as a starting point, we rely on the efforts of two prominent industry associations for their definitions of SCM:

- ♦ *Council of Logistics Management.* "The management of all internal and external processes or functions necessary to satisfy a customer's order (from raw materials through conversion/manufacturer through shipment)."

- ♦ *Supply Chain Council.* "The management of internal logistics functions and the relationships between your enterprise and its customers and suppliers."

These two definitions capture the essence of the SCM concept from the private-sector perspective. Some organizations, companies, and individuals have modified these basic statements by adding more elements, such as customer satisfaction or cost constraints. The fundamental premise of SCM remains the operation of a continuous, unbroken, comprehensive, and all-inclusive logistics process, from initial customer order for material or services to the ultimate satisfaction of the customer requirement. In formulating a working definition for DoD activities, several influencing elements should be considered:

◆ Mission responsibilities

◆ Legal requirements imposed by statute

◆ Acquisition regulations

◆ Organizational arrangements

◆ Management policies.

Implementation of SCM in DoD can be accomplished within the parameters put forth by the foregoing elements. The structured implementation approach in this document attempts to balance the requirements of these influencing factors with the need to accelerate adoption of the SCM concept across DoD components.

The definition of SCM in the DoD context must focus on the primary mission of logistics: providing materiel and related service support to the operational customer. Therefore, we propose the following definition:

> DoD supply chain management is an integrated process that begins with planning the acquisition of customer-driven requirements for material and services and ends with the delivery of material to the operational customer, including the material returns segment of the process and the flow of required information in both directions among suppliers, logistics managers, and customers.

Management of the supply chain also entails a fully coordinated set of related process cycles—including planning, procurement, repair, and delivery—that are collectively optimized to ensure that materiel and service requirements are efficiently planned for and executed to the satisfaction of the customer. DoD supply chain management focuses principally on satisfying customer requirements and secondarily on meeting these requirements at the lowest total process cost.[6]

A new perspective on the scope of the supply chain is the idea of exercising management responsibility for providing continuity of materiel and services

---

[6] U.S. Department of Defense, Deputy Under Secretary of Defense (Logistics), *Logistics Functional Requirements Guide*, August 1998, p. 7-1.

support over the life cycle of the logistics product. In this context, processes such as configuration management, reliability improvement, management of hazardous waste byproducts, and other long-term functions become integral parts of the supply chain manager's scope of responsibility even after delivery of the product or service to the customer. Such concepts further strengthen the requirement for long-term relationships among suppliers, customers, and supply chain participants.

Implementation of SCM in DoD cannot focus only on individual functions within an organization. It must concentrate on the end-to-end process of ensuring that warfighting and other operational requirements are consistently satisfied at the point of need. Because of its comprehensive nature, DoD supply chain management is not limited to single organizations; it requires coordinated efforts by all organizations with some responsibility for the end-to-end process. Managers and organizational entities must work together to optimize process management, business decisions, and resource allocations. Decisions must be made on the basis of total enterprise-wide cost and performance objectives rather than the performance of an individual function, organization, or echelon of support. The "best value" is obtained from logistics resources when functions are fully integrated to perform as part of a single logistics process. SCM must include the full scope of DoD logistics activities and interfaces, as well as commercial sources that provide products and services to the customer.[7]

## Principles of Supply Chain Management

In the foregoing definition, we are beginning to discover what SCM is. In addition, we must determine how it works—or should work—and ultimately commit to transforming the current DoD logistics process to a true supply chain-oriented approach. Implementation of SCM in DoD, however, will not be simply a matter of adopting the best practices as they are purported to exist in the commercial world. There are significant differences between DoD logistics and systems employed by Wal-Mart, 3M, General Motors, and others. Therefore, an initial step toward implementation of SCM in DoD logistics is articulation of the basic principles under which DoD can successfully attain improved performance and related benefits of SCM and still accomplish its fundamental mission responsibilities. By stating some fundamental principles for SCM implementation in DoD, we establish the basic

---

[7] Ibid., p. 7-1.

"how" of the process and set some benchmark guidelines for measuring our progress toward implementation.

To begin development of SCM principles for DoD application, let's look at the principles used in the private sector as a starting point. Of course, SCM experts have written volumes on this subject. Therefore, we need a composite of the vast amount of information currently available. Fortunately, such an aggregation already exists. In 1997, senior analysts at Andersen Consulting Corporation developed a list of seven principles that appear to capture, in summary form, most of the fundamental characteristics of the SCM concept:[8]

♦ *Segment customers based on service needs.* Companies traditionally have grouped customers by industry, product, or trade channel and then provided the same level of service to everyone within a segment. Effective SCM, by contrast, groups customers by distinct service needs—regardless of industry—and then tailors services to those particular segments.

♦ *Customize the logistics network.* In designing their logistics networks, companies should focus intensely on the service requirements and profitability of customer segments identified. The conventional approach of creating a monolithic logistics network runs counter to successful SCM.

♦ *Listen to signals of market demand and plan accordingly.* Sales and operations planning must span the entire chain to detect early warning signals of changing demand in ordering patterns, customer promotions, and so forth. This demand-intensive approach leads to more consistent forecasts and optimal resource allocation.

♦ *Differentiate product closer to the customer.* Companies today no longer can afford to stockpile inventory to compensate for possible forecasting errors. Instead, they need to postpone product differentiation in the manufacturing process closer to actual consumer demand.

♦ *Strategically manage sources of supply.* By working closely with their key suppliers to reduce the overall costs of owning materials and services, SCM leaders enhance margins for themselves and for

---

[8] David L. Anderson, Frank E. Britt, and Donavon J. Favre, "The Seven Principles of Supply Chain Management," *Supply Chain Management Review,* Spring 1997.

their suppliers. Beating multiple suppliers over the head for the lowest price is out, Andersen advises. "Gain sharing" is in.

◆ *Develop a supply chain-wide technology strategy.* As one of the cornerstones of successful SCM, information technology must support multiple levels of decision making. It also should afford a clear view of the flow of products, services, and information.

◆ *Adopt channel-spanning performance measures.* Excellent supply chain measurement systems do more than just monitor internal functions. They adopt measures that apply to every link in the supply chain. Importantly, these measurement systems embrace service and financial metrics, such as each account's true profitability.

The analysis that identified the foregoing principles also included an overall assessment of private-sector efforts to address supply chain process improvement. That assessment has equal applicability to DoD. Andersen Consulting's research found that "successful initiatives that have contributed to profitable growth share several themes. They are typically broad efforts, combining both strategic and tactical change. They also reflect a holistic approach, viewing the supply chain from end to end and orchestrating efforts so that the whole improvement achieved—in revenue, costs, and asset utilization—is greater than the sum of its parts. Unsuccessful efforts likewise have a consistent profile. They tend to be functionally defined, narrowly focused, and lacking in sustaining infrastructure. Uncoordinated change activity erupts in every department and function and puts the company in grave danger of 'dying the death of a thousand initiatives.' The source of failure is seldom management's difficulty in identifying what needs fixing. The issue is determining how to develop and execute a supply chain transformation plan that can move multiple, complex operating entities (internal and external) in the same direction."[9]

These comments go to the heart of DoD's requirement to accomplish a process-wide transformation of the military logistics process. Like their counterparts in the private sector, DoD logistics managers require a fundamental set of guiding principles or business rules for developing future DoD logistics policies, procedures, and information systems. Once these principles have been developed, they also will provide a rationale for selecting and prioritizing functional process improvements and technological enhancements to achieve the logistics vision. At the same time, they will become targets of

---

[9] Ibid.

achievement to which management and operating personnel can jointly commit.

For DoD logistics activities, the applicable guiding principles must be oriented foremost to satisfying the logistics support requirements of the military operating forces and, as a corollary, making the best use of available personnel, financial, and infrastructure resources. For persons charged with SCM implementation, commitment to these principles is the essential first step toward success. For the DoD logistics process, SCM guiding principles are as follows:[10]

| DoD Logistics SCM Guiding Principles |
|---|
| 1. Structure logistics procedures and systems to provide an agile response during crises and joint operations. |
| 2. Focus on satisfying warfighter requirements at the point of need. |
| 3. Link customers directly to the source of materiel and services support. |
| 4. Balance the use of all available logistics resource elements to deliver customer requirements at the lowest cost. |
| 5. Measure total supply chain performance, based on effective delivery of products and services to customers. |
| 6. Make maximum, effective use of competitive, global commercial capabilities. |
| 7. Accomplish common requirements cooperatively. |
| 8. Provide a consistent structure, content, and presentation of logistics information, particularly when supporting common interfaces among the military services, Defense agencies, and international partners. |
| 9. Address logistics requirements and related costs early in the acquisition cycle and continue to the end of the life-cycle support period. |
| 10. Include all logistics requirements and costs in the program baseline and develop them initially without any internally or externally imposed financial constraints. |
| 11. Replace the practice of information ownership with a concept of information stewardship (e.g., shared data). |
| 12. Provide effective training and supporting technology to logistics personnel. |

As progress is made toward SCM implementation, logistics managers should constantly refer back to these principles. Individually and collectively,

---

[10] U.S. Department of Defense, Deputy Under Secretary of Defense (Logistics), *Logistics Functional Requirements Guide*, August 1998, p. 3-1.

these principles should be the benchmarks for measuring progress toward implementation.

Assessment of individual process improvement initiatives or technology insertions should first be accomplished in the context of their support for the foregoing DoD SCM principles. Therefore, SCM implementers should use the principles collectively as an initial evaluation checklist for selecting and prioritizing process changes, best practices, and technologies.

Another useful evaluation tool is the customer service pyramid (CSP).[11] The CSP is a graphical approach to help categorize or segment suppliers, internal processes, and improvement initiatives into logical groupings that identify the degree to which these elements contribute to the overall effectiveness of the supply chain—and ultimately to customer satisfaction. The list of operating principles and the CSP give DoD managers two easily understood tools to aid in defining and assessing the relative value and potential contributions of process improvement initiatives, actions, and technologies as part of the supply chain implementation process. By establishing and using operating principles and the CSP gauge, management can communicate to all personnel its basic intent and direction from process operation and customer focus perspectives. Furthermore, by establishing use of these tools early in the implementation process, management can reinforce its commitment to the implementation of a meaningful SCM program. The CSP helps further differentiate the relative potential contribution of individual changes toward improving customer service.

Figure 2-1 illustrates the basic concept of the CSP. This framework establishes a hierarchy that can be used to segment proposed capabilities into three tiers: reliability, flexibility, and creativity (or innovation). As changes are proposed to implement SCM, they may be categorized in one of the three tiers. The bottom tier, reliability, represents capabilities or changes that are fundamental to customer service. Effective performance in these areas is mandatory to providing minimally acceptable customer service. Failure to perform satisfactorily in these areas is likely to significantly degrade current levels of customer satisfaction. Capabilities or changes at the second tier, flexibility, will permit the organization to maintain customer satisfaction at current levels. Changes at this level may be a basis or starting point toward SCM implementation. Process changes or innovations at the third tier, creativity, are building blocks for implementing a world-class supply chain.

---

[11] William C. Copacino, *Supply Chain Management, The Basics and Beyond,* Boca Raton, Florida: St. Lucie Press, 1997, pp. 74–75.

## Figure 2-1. Customer Service Pyramid

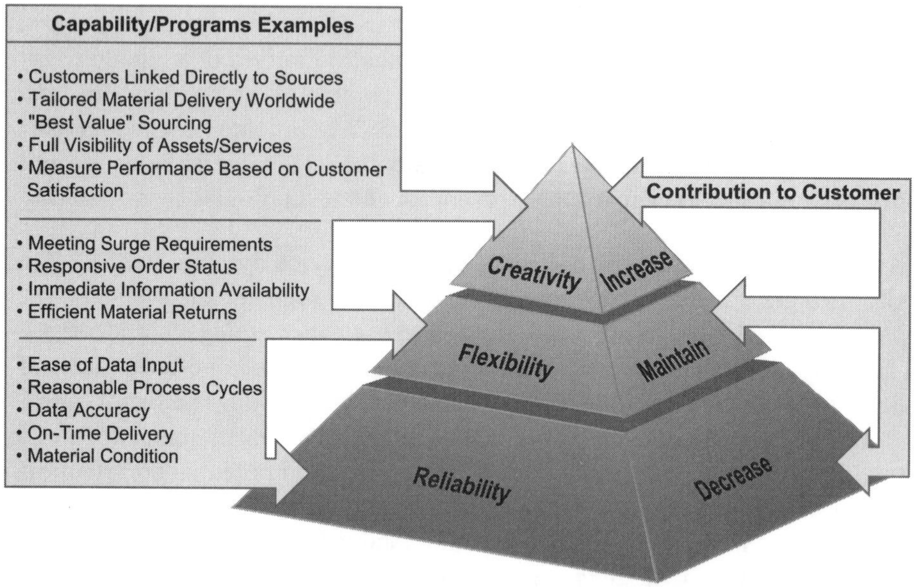

**Capability/Programs Examples**

- Customers Linked Directly to Sources
- Tailored Material Delivery Worldwide
- "Best Value" Sourcing
- Full Visibility of Assets/Services
- Measure Performance Based on Customer Satisfaction

- Meeting Surge Requirements
- Responsive Order Status
- Immediate Information Availability
- Efficient Material Returns

- Ease of Data Input
- Reasonable Process Cycles
- Data Accuracy
- On-Time Delivery
- Material Condition

*Creativity* *Increase*

*Flexibility* *Maintain*

*Reliability* *Decrease*

**Contribution to Customer**

Organizations must implement changes at all three tiers; to ensure achieve-ment of significant improvement in customer satisfaction, however, value-added changes at the second and third tiers must be accomplished. By using the CSP during the implementation process as a standard gauge for assessing proposed process and technology changes, SCM managers can identify inno-vations that can best contribute to a successful SCM program and may decide to postpone or eliminate other changes that may not significantly contribute to customer satisfaction or other primary objectives.

In Chapter 3, we present a six-step, high-level program that can be used as the overall team approach for implementation of SCM in DoD. We envision that the SCM implementation team will use this guideline to develop an implementation program tailored to specific organizational needs and circumstances.

# Chapter 3
# Six Steps to Implement Supply Chain Management

If you don't know where you are going, any path will take you there.

From *The Peter Principle* (1969)

The idea in the foregoing quote often seems to apply to logistics planners and managers. In their enthusiasm to accelerate change and quickly implement new solutions, even before an end objective has been determined or a workable plan of action has been adopted, they may lose sight of the end target. Furthermore, no single plan is sufficient for setting achievable goals and objectives or describing implementation actions for the diverse range of organizations under the umbrella of the DoD logistics community. The *2000 DoD Logistics Strategic Plan* sets the *overall* direction for the military logistics process for the 21st century. *JV2010, JV2020,* and *Focused Logistics* establish a warfighter perspective for the future. Collectively, these documents provide a high-level framework for the implementation of SCM as one of the key tools to meet DoD's military responsibilities. Successful implementation of SCM in DoD, however, requires that organizations responsible for this implementation develop and follow a tailored, disciplined plan of action.

To assist DoD organizations in developing their supply chain initiatives, this chapter outlines a basic six-step implementation approach that builds on the experiences of successful private-sector companies and takes into account the special characteristics of the DoD environment. Although each organization should tailor its implementation approach to its own particular circumstances, the steps outlined in this chapter provide a good model to use as a point of departure. In subsequent chapters, we drill down further into the specifics of required approaches and actions.

## Step One: Establish Your Implementation Team

Building an effective team to implement SCM is as important as having a credible and feasible implementation strategy. Clearly, these elements go hand in hand to ensure success. Within DoD, the implementation team cannot simply be directed by the company president or chief operating officer to "make SCM happen." Of course, this approach rarely works even in private companies. In DoD, however, implementing SCM will require crossing organizational boundaries. The "stovepiped" organizational structure within the Department's logistics community is legendary. Furthermore, successful SCM implementation must cross over to the domain of the operational customer and even outside DoD to commercial providers of goods and services. Moving from a highly segmented functional approach to a cross-functional team orientation is a significant challenge to the SCM implementation initiative, largely because of natural organizational resistance to change and formal organizational barriers inherent in the DoD culture.

Early in the implementation process, the SCM team must identify the key group of high-level executives who are the principal decision makers with individual or collective signature authority to make decisions and commit resources to successfully accomplish SCM implementation. Ideally, one or more key executives will be early proponents of the SCM initiative. Often, one in particular will be the implementation team's overall sponsor. The SCM effort must have the full support of upper management. Surveys of SCM implementations in the private sector invariably place responsibility for success or failure on the degree of top management support.[1] Management must continually reinforce the common goal of teamwork, reminding team members that they are all part of the same effort and have common goals. Perhaps most important, key executives must take a leadership role in informing and involving all major supply chain participants, including outside suppliers and customers.

In today's DoD logistics community, most high-level managers have been exposed to the basic concepts of SCM as it has been applied in the private sector. Although DoD logistics managers accept SCM (to varying degrees) for potential application in DoD, they often are unfamiliar with the specifics of the changes required under SCM and usually have not progressed beyond endorsing the principle in concept. In virtually all successful private-sector implementations of SCM, a cross-functional team approach has been employed. Integration across functional processes is at the very heart of the SCM concept. Supply chain teams are required to cut across organizational and process barriers and embrace all parties responsible for acquiring and moving products and services to the end-use customer. The question then becomes, "Who should be on the team?" In DoD, a corollary question is, "Who should lead the team?"

---

[1] William C. Copacino, *Supply Chain Management, The Basics and Beyond,* Boca Raton, Florida: St. Lucie Press, 1997, p. 8.

Let's address the second question first. One myth regarding SCM in DoD is that it is essentially a supply process. This misconception stems from the word *supply*—a specific term that DoD traditionally has applied primarily to functions relating to materiel management and distribution. In the DoD culture, the larger function is called *logistics;* logistics has three primary subfunctions: supply, maintenance, and transportation. Let's accept the traditional semantics for now, with the caveat that when we say *supply* chain management, we really are saying *logistics* chain management. Terminology notwithstanding, each military service organization and DLA must establish an implementation focal point to coordinate and integrate the SCM initiative.

Historically, this cross-functional interface has been accomplished by supply (materiel) management functional organizations because supply managers generally have the most interfunctional interfaces with the procurement, engineering, technical, financial, and operational communities. Within logistics, the supply function also tends to be the interfacing process between maintenance and transportation. At the same time, the SCM implementation focal point must be positioned close enough to the actual operations of the supply chain to have current practical expertise with the process and, conversely, to have sufficient interaction with—and the confidence of—higher-level authority.

Therefore, indications are that leadership of the SCM implementation team logically should reside at the various DoD logistics command organizations (i.e., Army Materiel Command, Naval Supply Systems Command, Marine Corp Installations and Logistics, and Air Force Materiel Command.) For DLA, leadership of the SCM implementation team may be appropriate at DLA headquarters or at a designated supply center. Of course, the decision on leadership responsibility rests with the appropriate component management. Regardless of the team leadership assignment, sufficient resources must be provided to accomplish team responsibilities.

Once the SCM implementation team organizational focal point is established, principal core team members should be selected. Ideally, core team members are assigned full time to SCM implementation, although they may not necessarily be reassigned permanently to a single organization.

The core SCM team must understand the difficulty of achieving the cross-functional and organizational integration necessary for successful SCM implementation. In an article in *Logistics Management and Distribution Report,*

Francis J. Quinn outlines several perspectives on the organizational impediments to beginning an SCM implementation initiative.[2] As Quinn observes,

> The process of capitalizing on the potential of SCM and initiating the design process begins internally. Before an organization can design and implement a collaborative supply chain that embraces the outside partners—suppliers, contract manufacturers, logistics services providers, and customers—it needs to get its own house in order. Put simply, functional silos need to give way to seamless integration of people and processes.

"Functional 'intragration' must occur within the organization before integration can occur throughout the entire supply chain," according to Richard H. Thompson, a partner in the Chicago office of Ernst & Young LLP. Included in that intragration effort should be all logistics-related functions, such as inbound and outbound transportation, distribution, warehousing, and fleet management. Supply management activities such as sourcing, vendor selection, and purchasing also are critical elements. Manufacturing-related activities—such as production planning, scheduling, and packaging—must be part of the intragration effort as well—and don't forget information technology.

Throughout the internal design process, keep in mind who has the power in the organization, says Bruce C. Arntzen, president of Global Supply Chain Associates in Maynard, Massachusetts. "In most companies," Arntzen explains, "the power lies in manufacturing or marketing. A lot of attempts by logistics professionals to integrate the supply chain cross-functionally hit a wall because they don't have the support of key functional areas. The biggest challenge is getting these bigger, more powerful organizations to cooperate with you." Arntzen suggests a couple of ways to obtain the necessary cooperation. One is for logistics people to present a persuasive argument to other departments that shows how integrated SCM would benefit the overall organization, specifically addressing potential benefits for each function. "An even better way," he adds, "is to build a solid rapport with all participating organizations. In essence, position yourself as being part of their team."

Internal walls invariably are toughest to scale. Consultants who have worked on the problem say that top management must give full and visible support to dismantling barriers. Managers can accelerate the process by linking measures and rewards to overall supply chain goals, rather than focusing narrowly on individual functional performance. Resource constraints (money and people) remain powerful motivators.

---

[2] Francis J. Quinn, "Building a World Class Supply Chain," *Logistics Management and Distribution Report*, June 1998.

The next step in the design process is to integrate the internal organization with the external partners—the suppliers, customers, and logistics service-providers who will work with you up and down the pipeline. Forging partnerships does not come easily to most organizations. The traditional model is to look out for your own best interests and let the other guy do the same. Being a partner, on the other hand, means sharing—sharing information about upcoming production plans, sharing promotions, sharing new product introductions, and even sharing certain financial data.

That need to share is particularly important in the relationship between a logistics organization and its material/services providers. James P. Fields, Vice President of Business Development at Menlo Logistics, explains:

> For the partnership between the customer and the logistics-services provider to reach its full potential, customers must openly share accurate information on their business, their customers, their suppliers, and any other relevant information about the operating environment. This helps the logistics provider build a supply chain strategy that supports the business strategy.

The same basic integration strategy clearly has application in DoD. Thus, an important initial step toward SCM implementation is to build a team that represents organizations that are essential to an integrated supply chain. Table 3-1 is a starting point for DoD organizations that are planning to designate core membership on an SCM implementation team.

Table 3-1 depicts a minimum level of participation and expertise required to begin the SCM implementation process. Specific numbers of personnel will be at the discretion of management, however. Substantive representation across these basic organizational areas is a critical element of success. Additional personnel and supporting resources will be required from other organizations as the implementation process progresses. Ultimately, personnel from supporting areas such as cataloging, technical data management, engineering, and packaging must be brought into the SCM design process. The team should be composed of knowledgeable personnel representing every link in the supply chain, from the initial suppliers of material and services—within and outside the government—to the ultimate customer of the chain. These basic personnel and financial resource requirements must be clearly described as part of the implementation strategy plan prepared in step one. High-level management must fully understand the commitment in resources required to successfully implement SCM.

*Table 3-1. The DoD Supply Chain Management
Core Implementation Team*

| Organization | Purpose |
|---|---|
| Representatives from component command headquarters | Provide policy guidance and interface with senior management officials |
| Logistics command supply management staff | Provide core team leadership and staff support for the SCM initiative; provide materiel management and distribution expertise |
| Logistics command maintenance staff | Provide staff support for SCM initiative and maintenance expertise |
| Component transportation staff | Provide staff support for SCM initiative and transportation expertise |
| Component operational commands | Provide staff support for SCM initiative and logistics expertise for field-level supply and maintenance processes; provide customer perspective |
| Procurement organization | Provide staff support for SCM initiative and acquisition process expertise |
| Comptroller organization | Provide staff support for SCM initiative and financial management/budget expertise |
| Information technology organization | Provide staff support for SCM initiative and IT/communications expertise |
| Contract support (as required) | Provide SCM process and technical support expertise |

Note: IT = information technology.

Finally, a few words about leadership and teamwork are in order. In an article in *Purchasing* magazine, Brian Milligan focuses on the need for organizational cooperation and communication as critical elements of the SCM implementation effort.[3] Milligan writes, "Teamwork is something just about every organization strives for, but few achieve." Most professionals agree that cooperation and communication are the best mechanisms for getting different functions to work together. They also point out that neither attribute exists naturally in a large organizational setting.

In DoD, fragmentation of responsibilities for different segments of the logistics process has been the tradition for many years—in some cases for several hundred years. Yet for supply chain management to work, communication

---

[3] Brian Milligan, "Despite attempts to break them, functional silos live on," *Purchasing,* November 4, 1999.

and integration of processes is an essential element. In the private sector, high-level management sometimes can mandate the requirement to work together. In DoD, the fundamental challenge to the SCM implementation team is to accomplish process integration and teamwork despite the impediments of organizational barriers.

## Step Two: Develop Your Own Supply Chain Implementation Strategy

This step prescribes the need to develop, obtain approval for, and publish your SCM implementation plan. This plan must be a formal document. It should be well organized, easily understood, and credible to management, your supply chain implementation team, and your customers. A comprehensive and systematic master plan is required to manage a large-scale effort such as supply chain implementation. The plan also must encompass the full supply chain, from initial product suppliers to final customers. Chapter 2 presents a series of guiding principles derived from private-sector experience but tailored to DoD requirements. These principles should provide the general conceptual direction for preparation of an implementation strategy document for your organization's needs. They represent the minimum requirement for effecting the spirit and substance of the modern SCM concept. Implementation of additional changes may be necessary or advantageous.

Strategic documents vary widely in scope, format, and level of detail. Use the format that best meets your needs, but bear in mind the requirement for credibility and ease of understanding by all potential readers. Avoid glittering generalities, and concentrate on detailing specific courses of action whenever possible. The strategic plan outline prescribed by the 1993 Government Performance and Results Act (GPRA)[4] may provide a good starting format for your SCM plan. GPRA suggests the following structure:

1. A comprehensive mission statement covering major SCM functions and operations of the activity

2. General goals and objectives, including outcome-related goals and objectives, for major functions to be covered by SCM

3. A description of how goals and objectives are to be achieved, including a general description of operational processes, skills, and

---

[4] Chapter 3, Title 5, United States Code, Sec. 306.

technology, as well as human, capital, information, and other resources required to meet those goals and objectives

4.  Descriptions of how performance goals included in this plan are related to the general goals and objectives of SCM

5.  Identification of key factors external to your organization and beyond your organization's control that could significantly affect achievement of general goals and objectives

6.  A description of the program evaluation process to be used in managing and evaluating progress

7.  A plan of action and milestones (may be developed over time).

Your SCM implementation plan may differ from the format suggested above. However, a formal SCM implementation plan must be fully staffed and approved by appropriate levels of management prior to initiation of further implementation actions. After management approval, the plan also should be "sold" to major process customers and stakeholders.

An effective SCM implementation plan balances scope, clarity, and level of detail. The plan of action and milestones portion of the plan may be the most critical element. This portion of the plan describes supply chain implementation as a phased effort with manageable stages. Rockford Consulting has developed a model that suggests an incremental approach to the SCM master plan.[5] This model proposes a "closed loop" development effort that includes four stages: diagnostics and concept development, detailed action planning, capability building, and results measurement.

♦   *Diagnostics and Concept Development.* This stage involves assessment of the organization's supply chain "competitiveness." For DoD organizations, competitiveness means the ability of the supply chain to meet performance requirements, as driven by military customer requirements. The evaluation begins with a diagnosis and comparison of desired process capabilities against existing capabilities and performance. A vision is developed for where the organization should be with respect to performance objectives. Ideally, initial

---

[5] Rockford Consulting, *Inducing World Class Performance for the 21st Century*, Rockford, Illinois: Rockford Consulting, 1998.

high-level performance objectives are established and approved at this point.

♦ *Detailed Action Planning.* This stage further develops the master plan by expanding on the details of initial phases. The long-term supply chain structure is developed by identifying component elements of the supply chain and determining new process and information technologies, organizational changes, or related improvements required to effect desired performance objectives. Concurrently, implementation resources are identified and the process for programming these resources is initiated. This stage focuses on documenting a structured approach to improving the performance drivers of responsiveness, flexibility, quality, cost, and service.

♦ *Capability Building.* This stage includes execution of plans documented in stages 1 and 2. Using the detailed documentation outlined above, the implementation team manages a time-phased implementation of process changes, technology insertion, organizational realignments, interorganizational arrangements, and facilities changes. Clearly, this stage is highly dependent on the availability of implementation resources.

♦ *Results Measurement.* As the changes executed in stage 3 are put in place, performance measurement of desired results can begin. Because SCM is not a project but a continuous process, performance measurement against the plan results in a return to stage 1 for further diagnosis and reassessment, and the development effort begins again. This iterative process enables the organization to focus initially on high-payback areas and selectively bring other elements into the process later.

You can use the Rockford model as a template for constructing your organization's supply chain implementation strategy. Regardless of the particular planning approach, however, the initial strategy-planning step must be completed prior to proceeding with further SCM development. Of particular importance, appropriate decision makers must understand and support the SCM implementation initiative. We discuss specific implementation strategies in greater detail in Chapter 5.

# Step Three: Measure Performance

Steps one and two outline the requirements to provide the proper team resources to accomplish SCM implementation and to prepare and obtain approval for a credible and feasible implementation plan. These two initial steps often are accomplished concurrently. That is, a small core staff may develop the implementation plan while resources for the full implementation team are being identified, approved, and put into position. Beginning additional steps, however, is foolhardy until the two initial steps have been completed. In effect, the first two steps are the foundation of the SCM effort. Proceeding further without completing these steps is a waste of time and resources. Once you have assembled your SCM team and formalized the implementation plan by documenting a course of action and obtaining management approval to proceed, you are ready to begin step three.

Customers of the DoD logistics system are demanding improved performance in the areas of reliability, flexibility, and responsiveness. At the same time, logistics providers are being challenged to reduce logistics costs to make funds available for modernization. The military services and the Office of the Secretary of Defense (OSD) have numerous initiatives to reduce logistics costs and improve overall supply chain performance. Performance measures, or "metrics," are required to monitor the progress of supply chain improvement initiatives. A consensus in DoD, however, considers the metrics currently available to senior DoD managers to be inadequate or lacking the depth to measure effectiveness and efficiency across the DoD supply chain. These existing metrics are not "balanced" across customer service, cost, and readiness and sustainability performance objectives.

The lack of correct and comprehensive supply chain metrics in DoD is echoed in most private-sector companies. According to Dale Rogers of the University of Nevada (quoted by James Aaron Cooke[6]), many companies today are using measures that don't reflect 21st century conditions. In fact, Rogers believes that many problems that surface in large corporations arise from managers' attempts to use accounting systems developed in the 18th century to assess the performance of today's supply chain. Traditional financial measures, for example, rate warehouses by assessing the value and amount of inventory held. "But warehouses are not just designed to store product," Rogers says. "They're set up to move product quickly. You want to measure a warehouse as a product replenishment facility." Furthermore, he

---

[6] James Aaron Cooke, "Measure for Measure," *Logistics Management and Distribution Report*, July 1, 1999.

notes, traditional accounting systems tend to measure variance from a standard. This approach forces companies to suboptimize performance; in other words, companies measure parts of the supply chain rather than the entire process. Businesses typically grade the manufacturing operation, for example, on cost of production rather than by measuring the supply chain's ability to manufacture and deliver a product to a customer. The problem of suboptimization is further compounded when one trading partner in an extended supply chain lowers its costs at the expense of another trading partner. Rogers says companies have failed to grasp that measurements themselves have life cycles and that old yardsticks don't apply to supply chain management. He believes that the business community must develop a new set of metrics for evaluating the supply chain's effectiveness in delivering value to a customer.

What should these new supply chain metrics measure? As a starting point, the DoD SCM implementation team should consider as a baseline of measurement factors metrics that are based on the 10 dimensions of service quality identified by Valerie Zeithaml, A. "Parsu" Parasuraman, and Leonard Berry in their book *Delivering Quality Service.*[7]

- *Tangibles.* The first factor an organization should evaluate is the appearance of its facilities, equipment, personnel, and even its marketing brochures. Organizations may wish to develop a grading scale for evaluating appearance and then conduct a survey to see where their operations fall short. A manager rating a warehouse's appearance, for example, might subtract points for material left in the aisles or for sloppily dressed personnel.

- *Reliability.* The second service quality criterion reflects the ability to keep promises. A logistics operation could measure whether it fills orders correctly and whether its carriers keep their delivery appointments with customers.

- *Responsiveness.* An organization's willingness to help customers and provide prompt service constitutes the third dimension of service quality. Time is the variable that should be measured here. An activity should measure how quickly it fills and ships orders or how quickly its customer-service personnel pick up the phone.

---

[7] Valerie Zeithaml, Leonard Berry, and A. Parasuraman, *Delivering Quality Service, Balancing Customer Perceptions and Expectations*, New York: Simon and Schuster Trade, 1990.

◆ *Competence.* Competence refers to workers' mastery of the skills and knowledge required to perform specified services. Organizations too often mistakenly assume that their managers and workers have the knowledge and skills to do their jobs. They would do better to require workers and managers to hold certification in certain areas and then keep tabs on whether they obtain those certifications.

◆ *Courtesy.* The fifth criterion rates the politeness, respect, consideration, and friendliness the company's contact personnel show to customers. Although this dimension of service quality can be difficult to calibrate, organizations should try keeping track of complaints or adopt a policy of having a supervisor monitor conversations between its employees and customers.

◆ *Credibility.* The sixth area to monitor is the business' credibility—how well it delivers on promises to customers. Organizations can assess performance in this area by measuring whether they meet delivery dates or service dates. Unlike some of the other service dimensions, this one's fairly easy to calculate.

◆ *Security.* Security—freedom from danger, risk, and conflict—makes up the seventh service-quality dimension. To grade performance in this area, activities should look at the amount of pilferage and other losses they experience. As part of this exercise, organizations should make an effort to identify anything in their distribution operations that might adversely affect a customer's business.

◆ *Access.* The eighth dimension of service quality consists of approachability and ease of contact with members of the organization. Companies should measure how quickly a customer can find a customer-service representative when he or she contacts the organization. When someone tries to find the senior guy or just a live voice, can they do it? Put yourself in the customer's shoes when there's a breakdown in service.

◆ *Communication.* The ninth standard for evaluation centers on communication—a commitment to keeping customers informed in language they can understand, as well as a commitment to listen to them. As you move into a partnership or alliance with a trading partner, you have to keep everyone informed. Because quality of communication is difficult to gauge, companies often measure the frequency of communication with customers.

◆ *Understanding the customer.* The final service-quality element is how well the company understands its customers. Organizations need to ask themselves whether they truly know their customers' needs. Conducting a survey of customers that asks them to name their five most important issues may be appropriate. The business then should test its own managers and ask them whether they can name the same five issues their customers identified.

As difficult as the task might be, organizations will have to find ways to incorporate some of the foregoing elements into their supply chain measurement programs. Measurements built around the total supply chain are critical. The SCM implementation team must identify or develop metrics for their supply chain if they are to succeed. Development of applicable metrics should be started early in the implementation process because knowledge of key measures of performance will help determine the optimal supply chain design. Substantial work already has been accomplished in DoD along these lines. In Chapters 5 and 9, we discuss more specific proposals for ways to satisfy DoD logistics activities' metrics requirements.

## Step Four: Designing Your Supply Chain

This step focuses on describing the supply chain (or chains) by developing a graphical description of the end-to-end process required to obtain material from initial government or commercial sources and deliver the material or services to the ultimate military customer. In many cases, this step begins concurrently with step three. Early identification of at least preliminary performance metrics will enable the team to be in position to proceed quickly with validation of the "to-be" supply chain design as it develops.

Creating the baseline description of a future supply chain structure requires a creative approach to describing the various processes that constitute the chain; it also entails avoiding the temptation to merely document the current way of doing business. A further challenge is to avoid being bogged down in details of the many functions that, taken together, make up the overall supply chain process. At this point, let's clarify some important terminology.

◆ *Processes*—Processes are groupings of activities (functions) that, taken together, result in a fully completed action in support of a customer.

◆ *Functions*—Functions are identifiable activities that are grouped together because of common characteristics or interfaces. Functions are synonymous with process elements.

For example, a supply chain is a process. Maintenance is a function. Processes are made up of functions that are linked together by people, communication mechanisms, or physical bonds, with the objective of providing added value, products, or services to customers. As the supply chain design develops, the process and the function must be distinct. The completed design must comprehend the end-to-end supply chain process; the functions that constitute the chain are subject to change through process improvement, technology enhancement, alternative sourcing, or even elimination.

Since the advent of the personal computer, numerous computer-aided techniques for developing process descriptions have been developed. These techniques range from simple automated flow chart programs to relatively complex process modeling tools, such as integrated definition modeling. Other methods of graphically describing processes include process reference models or simulation models. Numerous variations of these and related tools are readily available. For the purposes of constructing the initial supply chain design, however, we recommend that the SCM team use a relatively simple approach to capture the functions and relationships of the supply chain.

A good approach to developing the initial supply chain graphical description has been published by the Command, Control, Communications, Computers, Intelligence, Surveillance, and Reconnaissance (C4ISR) Architecture Working Group (AWG) Framework, Panel, whose members included representatives from the Joint Staff, the services, OSD, and Defense agencies. The product of this panel's work is the *C4ISR Architecture Framework, Version 2.0.*[8] The *Architecture Framework* prescribes in detail the process of creating a DoD architecture for military processes. At this point, we suggest that the implementation team focus on the portion of the architectural development process that relates to preparing the initial process design documents. We recommend two of these documents, in particular, as models for the initial SCM design.

The first document is the Operation View-1, High-Level Operational Concept Graphic (OV-1). Completion of this document will give the SCM team a

---

[8] Assistant Secretary of Defense (Command, Control, Communications, and Intelligence [C3I]), *C4ISR Architectural Framework Version 2.0*, December 18, 1997. Additional information on DoD architectures and activity models is available at http://www.c3i.osd.mil/org/cio/i3/AWG_Digital_Library/index.htm.

high-level graphical description of the operational concept (high-level organizations, missions, geographic configuration, connectivity, etc.) of the supply chain. Figure 3-1 provides an example of a high-level operational concept graphic.

*Figure 3-1. Operation View-1, High-Level Operational Concept Graphic (OV-1)—Theater Air Defense Example*

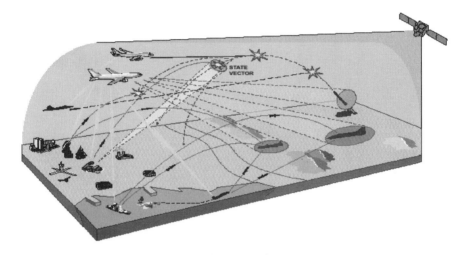

The high-level concept graphic provides a visual overview of the process being depicted. In subsequent chapters, we present a representative high-level graphic of a DoD supply chain. The SCM implementation team should prepare such a graphic representation, tailored to the organization, to assist in ensuring that management, process participants, suppliers, and customers have a common understanding of the scope of the specific supply chain.

The second recommended graphical representation of the supply chain is the Operational View-2, Operational Node Connectivity Description (OV-2). The main features of this product are operational nodes and elements, the relationship lines between them, and the characteristics of the information exchanged.

## Figure 3-2. Operational View-2, Operational Node Connectivity Description (OV-2) Diagram (Example)

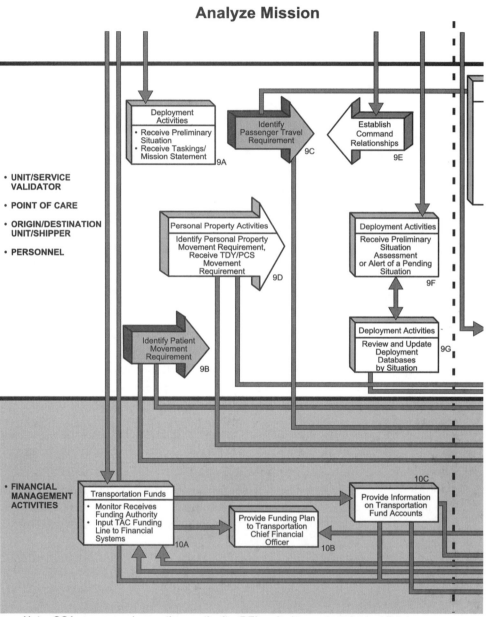

**Analyze Mission**

Note: COA = command operations authority; DEL = deployment equipment list; JOPES = joint operational planning and execution system; PCS = permanent change of station; TAC = transportation account code; TDY = temporary duty; TPFDD = time-phased force and deployment data; UBT = unit base table; ULN = unit line number.

## Structure Force

## Refine Deployment Data

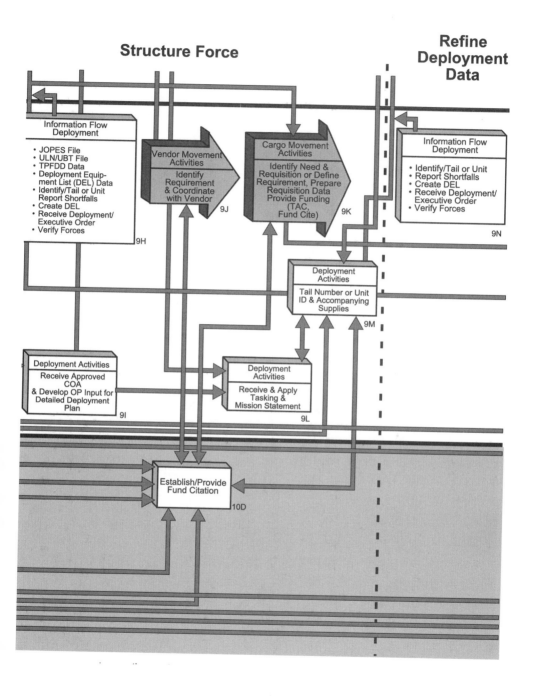

**Information Flow Deployment**

- JOPES File
- ULN/UBT File
- TPFDD Data
- Deployment Equipment List (DEL) Data
- Identify/Tail or Unit Report Shortfalls
- Create DEL
- Receive Deployment/ Executive Order
- Verify Forces

9H

**Vendor Movement Activities**

Identify Requirement & Coordinate with Vendor

9J

**Cargo Movement Activities**

Identify Need & Requisition or Define Requirement, Prepare Requisition Data Provide Funding (TAC, Fund Cite)

9K

**Information Flow Deployment**

- Identify/Tail or Unit
- Report Shortfalls
- Create DEL
- Receive Deployment/ Executive Order
- Verify Forces

9N

**Deployment Activities**

Tail Number or Unit ID & Accompanying Supplies

9M

**Deployment Activities**

Receive Approved COA & Develop OP Input for Detailed Deployment Plan

9I

**Deployment Activities**

Receive & Apply Tasking & Mission Statement

9L

Establish/Provide Fund Citation

10D

OV-2 diagrams should be constructed to show end-to-end process connectivity for the organization's major commodity, end item, weapon system, or service responsibility. For example, a diagram could show process nodes for providing spare parts support for a tank, aircraft, major ship component, communications ship, or consumable commodity. Operational nodes represent each process activity that supports acquisition of spare parts through delivery to the supply chain customer. Each information, service, or physical material product exchange is represented by an arrow (indicating the direction of information or material flow); each arrow is annotated to describe the information-exchange characteristics of the data or information (e.g., its substantive content and media: voice, imagery, text and message format). Volume requirements, security or classification level, timeliness, and requirements for information system interoperability also may be annotated.

What constitutes an operational node can vary from one organization to another. An operational node may represent a role (e.g., Air Operations Commander), an organization (e.g., U.S. Air Force), an operational facility (e.g., Joint Intelligence Center), and so on. The notion of "node" likewise will vary, depending on the level of detail addressed by the architecture design effort. In the past, many organizations have represented some operational nodes in physical (and locational) terms if these nodes were intended to remain constant in the architecture analysis (e.g., determine the most cost-effective communication options between an in-garrison commander-in-chief [CINC] and a joint task force [JTF] commander located at X, Y, or Z). On the other hand, organizations have tended to represent operational nodes much more generically, or notionally, if they were analyzing the entire business practice from scratch, with no constraints (e.g., current facilities) confronting the architect.[9] In building the connectivity nodes diagram for the SCM design, nodes generally should represent functional activities or points of information exchange rather than specific organizations. Figure 3-2 is an example of an operational node connectivity diagram for a portion of the DoD transportation system.

These two types of process descriptive diagrams demonstrate the kind of graphical representations that are needed in the SCM implementation design phase. There are hundreds of graphically oriented ways to present a high-level description of the supply chain process and the various elements of functional activity and connectivity. Likewise, many computer graphics tools are available to assist in this step of the SCM implementation effort.

---

[9] Ibid., pp. 4–11.

Preparation of the descriptive documents as suggested above will enable the SCM implementation team to proceed with development of the more detailed supply chain design effort. Figure 3-3 lays out the basic actions required for the design process.

*Figure 3-3. Supply Chain Design Process*

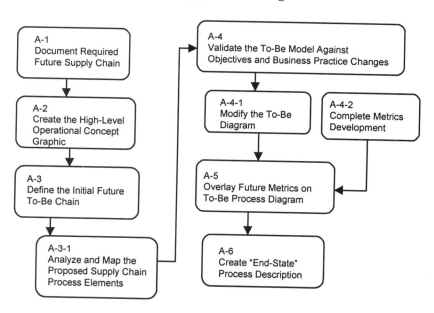

The methodology pictured in Figure 3-3 was adapted from an approach developed by Fred Kuglin in his book, *Customer-Centered Supply Chain Management*.[10] Unlike a traditional "as-is" to "to-be" development approach, this methodology begins by establishing the initial baseline structure, characteristics, and related metrics of the future supply chain and then proceeds to apply specific business practice changes and metrics to the to-be baseline, ultimately creating the to-be process description. This sequence of actions requires the implementation team to focus early on end-state results and reduces the danger that it will become bogged down in the detailed characteristics of the current process. We discuss the future supply chain design process in greater detail in subsequent chapters of this guide.

---

[10] Fred A. Kuglin, *Customer-Centered Supply Chain Management*, New York: American Management Association, 1998, p. 156.

# Step Five: Selecting and Applying Best Practices and Technologies

Since the beginning of the modern computer age in the 1950s, most managers—particularly those in the DoD logistics community—have believed in the power of technological advance as a driving force in improving process performance and reducing resource requirements. No discussion of supply chain design can be complete without focusing on the information technology (IT) component. As Donald Bowersox of Michigan State University has pointed out,

> Technology serves as the primary enabler to facilitate supply-chain-wide integration while simultaneously allowing key business relationships to be conducted on an exclusive enterprise-to-enterprise basis. Ranging from advanced Internet to more traditional [electronic data interchange] and hardwired communications, such cross-enterprise technology linkage provides the backbone of successful supply-chain strategy.

Current and future technology requirements clearly must be factored into the supply chain design equation. According to AMR—a Boston-based market analysis firm that specializes in supply chain technology—options in the supply chain space abound. By the end of 1997, the SCM software market alone had hit $2 billion in revenue. Analysts project that this amount will increase exponentially. Available software now covers virtually all aspects of the SCM process, according to AMR, enabling all participants to communicate more effectively and make better-informed management decisions.[11]

Although technology and business process improvements clearly are key enablers of progress, many billions of dollars and years of time have been expended on failed applications of new technology and process improvement solutions that turned out to be more fad than reality. The SCM implementation team must address the apparent contradiction: technology, savior, or roadblock? An article in *Logistics Management and Distribution Report* explored some of the myths and misconceptions of logistics.[12] For example:

> Corporate America, like most institutions throughout history, has created myths to explain its customs, beliefs and phenomena. The myth, "The customer is always right," explains why some companies cripple themselves by trying to serve an unprofitable customer base. Another myth argues that "logistics best practices depend on technology." No one would

---

[11] Francis J. Quinn, "Building a World Class Supply Chain," *Logistics Management and Distribution Report,* June 1998.

[12] "Business Issues," *Logistics Management and Distribution Report*, May 1, 1999.

argue that logistics owes an enormous debt to advances in information and communications systems. However, applications of new technologies have sometimes done more harm than good. An example is the Overnite Transportation Company's use of an automated voice response system to provide shipping status to customers. After significant adverse customer reaction, Overnite replaced their automated system with human operators. They realized a good lesson that technology doesn't work when it comes before customer needs. Technology also doesn't work when it is implemented over an ineffective process.

In DoD logistics, there are numerous examples of initiatives to acquire new technologies before functional requirements are clearly determined. Barcoding, automatic identification technology (AIT), and technical data digitization are good examples of very useful technologies that have not fully attained payback for investment costs, largely because of inadequate planning and assessment of functional needs for these technologies. More alarming are the billions of dollars already spent by the DoD logistics community on computer systems modernization, with only limited benefits.

Because of the less-than-successful track record for cost-effective technology application in the logistics community, the SCM implementation team must be highly disciplined in its selection and application of technology solutions for supply chain management. In Chapter 2, we discuss seven principles of SCM as articulated by Andersen Consulting Corporation. Principle six specifically addresses the requirement for the SCM team to develop a supply chain-wide technology strategy. Fundamentally, this strategy should assure that IT supports multiple levels of decision making. It also should afford a clear and comprehensive view of the flow of products, services, and information.

In support of the supply chain implementation, technology enablers are required that integrate three kinds of essential capabilities. For the short term, the system must be able to handle day-to-day transactions and electronic commerce across the supply chain and thus help align supply and demand by sharing information on orders and daily scheduling. From a mid-term perspective, acquired technologies must facilitate logistics process planning and decision-making, supporting the demand and shipment planning and master production scheduling needed to allocate resources efficiently. To add long-term value, the system must enable strategic analysis by providing tools, such as an integrated network model, that synthesize data for use in high-level "what-if" scenario planning to help managers evaluate plants, distribution centers, suppliers, and third-party service alternatives. Electronic connectivity creates opportunities to change the supply chain fundamentally—from slashing transaction costs through electronic handling of orders, invoices, and payments to shrinking inventories through vendor-managed inventory programs.[13]

Despite making huge investments in technology, few DoD logistics organizations are acquiring this full complement of capabilities. Today's computer systems remain function-bound, unable to share across the supply chain information that channel partners must have to achieve mutual success. Ironically, the information most organizations urgently require to enhance SCM resides outside their own systems, and few organizations are adequately connected to obtain the necessary information.

The SCM team must recognize the requirement to select and apply only technology enablers that can be linked to the attainment of total supply chain performance and cost objectives. At a minimum, technology-based solutions should be cross-referenced to specific elements of the supply chain design in the context of their planned contribution to satisfying supply chain performance objectives. The application of technology should support redesigned processes, including enhanced communications across functions and organizations. The objective is to acquire only the technology needed to implement the to-be supply chain process and to attain desired levels of performance. Therefore, we should proceed with assessment and acquisition of new technologies only after the functional elements of the new process are substantially determined and the process performance targets have been identified. Often—as shown in Figure 3-4—a design, measure, and implement sequence of events is a prudent approach to constructing the segments of the chain. This perspective on effective use of technology enablers helps prevent the phenomenon of "technologies in search of applications." Furthermore, by viewing technology selection and application as a circular process, we can readily envision a continuing reassessment of new technologies in the context of their impact on and relevance to effective supply chain design and performance improvement.

---

[13] David L. Anderson, Frank E. Britt, and Donavon J. Favre, "The Seven Principles of Supply Chain Management," *Supply Chain Management Review,* Spring 1997.

*Figure 3-4. A Design, Measure, Implement Strategy*

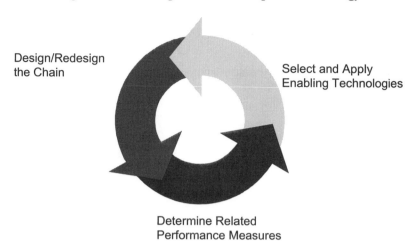

Design/Redesign
the Chain

Select and Apply
Enabling Technologies

Determine Related
Performance Measures

## Step Six: Managing Supply Chain Implementation

The first five steps toward SCM implementation focus principally on developing the elements of the changed process to be implemented. Managing the sequence of events required to put an operational version of a modernized supply chain in place is a matter of effectively accomplishing the first five steps and then arranging the necessary organizational, procedural, and technical changes required to permit implementation of the newly designed capabilities.

After successfully completing steps one through five, the implementation team is ready to begin the final push toward operational implementation. The SCM team can begin preparing for the implementation phase very early in the process, however. Part of this preparation is ensuring that the team clearly understands the elements of SCM and fully recognizes why SCM implementation is a good thing. Managing SCM implementation in DoD will involve keeping the team's focus on the principles of the SCM concept and the ultimate objective. SCM implementation is—and should be—one of the principal goals of logistics transformation for the 21st century.

The key objective for the SCM team should be balancing the unique requirements of Defense logistics with the rapid adoption of supply chain concepts. In simple terms, the objective of the DoD logistics process, now and for the foreseeable future, can be stated in the form of the well-known seven R's of customer satisfaction:[14]

- ◆ The Right product

- ◆ Delivered to the Right place

- ◆ In the Right condition and packaging

- ◆ In the Right quantity

- ◆ At the Right cost

- ◆ To the Right customer

- ◆ At the Right time.

Most DoD logisticians recognize these seven elements as a high-level statement of the basic functions of logistics. In the past, DoD has accomplished these functions somewhat independently through disparate organizations, such as materiel management, maintenance, or transportation. As we proceed with SCM implementation, we should see the process and organizational barriers between functional categories blur, and the process should take on a significantly more integrated character.

Implementation of SCM in DoD will continue to be aimed at the most effective and efficient accomplishment of these seven elements. SCM also must result, however, in significantly greater integration of the entire end-to-end process, with primary focus on satisfying the logistics requirements of the "customer"—that is, the personnel, organizations, weapon systems, or equipment at the end of the supply chain: the users of material and services. In building the integrated supply chain for DoD logistics, the organizational barriers that inhibit teamwork must be overcome. Speaking at the annual meeting of the Council of Logistics Management, Gary Sease and David

---

[14] Kuglin, *Customer-Centered Supply Chain Management*, p. 72.

Frentzel summarized management recommendations to accomplish the integration objective:[15]

♦ Obtain senior management's commitment and support to address existing barriers and their underlying organizational support structures.

♦ Deemphasize functions and focus instead on core processes.

♦ Assign leaders, goals, milestones, measures, and rewards to processes rather than functions.

♦ Combine processes into an effective supply chain with linked objectives.

♦ Align milestones, measures, and rewards to achieve process and supply-chain goals.

♦ Use the linked objectives and aligned measures to inspire supply-chain participants to communicate and take individual responsibility.

♦ Provide individuals with the training and resources needed to prosper in the new environment.

These guidelines provide the implementation team with an overall working strategy for successfully obtaining approval and accomplishing SCM execution milestones. Team members should regularly refer back to this overall approach as SCM implementation proceeds.

Early in the process, the SCM team should establish a structured and comprehensive approach to proceeding with supply chain implementation. Because SCM is multi-functional and cross-organizational by definition, once the team has constructed the overall supply chain design (step four), it should decide how to subdivide the implementation effort into logical, doable, and complementary segments. Great care should be taken to avoid falling back into the traditional supply, maintenance, transportation, functional systems, and wholesale-retail stovepipes.

---

[15] Francis J. Quinn, "Building a World Class Supply Chain," quoting Gary Sease and David Frentzel, "Six Ways to Bring Down the Walls," *Logistics Management and Distribution Report,* June 1998.

The goal of supply chain management is to optimize the entire supply chain. This requires "systems thinking," a business discipline derived from general systems theory. Most workers involved in supply chain management today, however, are not trained to think of optimizing the whole system, just the parts encompassed by their assigned responsibilities and organizations. Optimizing the functional sub-elements of the chain does not optimize the overall system—these are lessons learned from a decade of business process reengineering.[16]

Many current initiatives to implement SCM have adopted a linear perspective regarding their efforts. The Supply Chain Council—an organization that comprises many private-sector corporations and public organizations—focuses on supply chain practices, representing the elements of supply chains as four processes: plan, source, make/maintain, and deliver. Because of the analogy of the supply *chain*, a linear (linked) perspective is logical and understandable. In fact, we use many tenets of the Supply Chain Council's analytical process in subsequent chapters to help construct our DoD version of the chain. A more holistic or "organic" view of the supply chain process may be more appropriate for our purposes, however. Let's envision our DoD supply chain process as an organism, with several primary subsystems (analogous to circulatory, nervous, or similar systems in a living organism). Each system or chain may work separately in different ways, but with a common objective: to support the activities of the total organism—in our case, the DoD military mission.

In our supply chain organism, we have shared processes, overlapping physical boundaries, and common use of information and decision processes. As we begin to manage implementation of the SCM concept in DoD, we should identify the fundamental elements of our supply chains and develop required plans of action and milestones for each area. Each implementation team may develop its own categorization of these elements. These comprehensive groupings, however, should address the required processes and provide interaction among the segments to accomplish the customer-driven objectives of the total logistics process. Table 3-2 is a representative list of supply chain process areas that may be a starting point for developing and managing the SCM implementation effort.

---

[16] Peter Finger, "Transforming the Supply Chain," Supplement to *Logistics Management and Distribution Report*, April 1, 2000.

*Table 3-2. SCM Implementation Team Process Areas*

| Process area | Purpose |
|---|---|
| Integration team | To ensure compliance with team strategy and tracking of POA&Ms. |
| Supplier development and management | To develop and oversee collaborative management of SC suppliers. |
| Decision tools | To identify and oversee implementation of SCM required decision tools. |
| Organizational development and training | To develop and recommend organizational changes to facilitate SCM implementation and identify training requirements. |
| Information access and exchange | To identify and coordinate overall SCM information sources and exchange requirements. |
| Customer requirements and interaction | To identify customers and their information, supply chain performance, material, and service requirements. |

Note: POA&M = plan of action and milestones; SC = supply chain.

The categorization outlined in Table 3-2 represents an approach to subdividing the SCM team into focused working-level groups and to organizing the SCM implementation effort into logical elements. This type of grouping also can assist the team in its detailed work of using SCM analytical tools such as the Supply Chain Council's Supply Chain Operational Reference (SCOR) model. Such categorizations permit a more credible approach for tasking of actions, management oversight, and division of available workforce.

In the following chapters, we begin to further elaborate on more specific actions required to pursue the six-step approach for implementing SCM in DoD.

# Chapter 4
# Getting Started

In Chapter 3 we outline a proposed membership for the SCM implementation team. Our recommendation is based on an ideal team composition that considers the stakeholders, suppliers, participants, and customers in a DoD supply chain. In reality, however, management may not provide the initial SCM implementation team with the full range of personnel and related resources needed to accomplish the implementation task. In this case, the initial SCM team members should begin a "start-up" effort that makes maximum use of available resources and sets the groundwork for future progress. The SCM team should obtain senior management's commitment and support for the team's plans as early as possible. Such commitment must be verified early because future success is highly dependent on management's support. In this chapter, we outline a plan of action to get the SCM team started on the path to SCM implementation.

## Assess Available Resources and Organize the Team

If the initial implementation team is composed only of government personnel, the first step should be to document an internal plan of action. The sections of this chapter describe recommended actions for inclusion in the team's basic plan. Initially, the plan can be a simple one-page outline of responsibility assignments and planned products or a graphical action/milestone chart. Team members must understand their respective responsibilities, however, and strive to meet deadline dates for assigned products.

If the team has contractor support, ensuring that the contractor fully understands its tasks and the importance of meeting deliverable dates is even more essential. Contractor support personnel should always be given specific assignments and deliverables. An open-ended tasking to support contractors (i.e., "Give us proposals on what you should be doing") is a formula for disaster and wasted resources. If contractor personnel are the team's principal resource for understanding the DoD logistics process or the SCM concept, the government's team manager should require the contractor to prepare and submit a personnel responsibility list, projected milestones, and an outline of products very early in the process. Regardless of the team's composition, the initial effort should be the creation of a team concept document.

# Create a Team Concept Document

To obtain management's full commitment to the SCM implementation effort and to ensure a common and credible understanding of the supply chain approach as it applies to DoD, the team must create a basic document that succinctly provides fundamental information about the SCM effort. This document serves several purposes:

◆ It provides the layperson with a basic, understandable SCM implementation project description.

◆ It is a vehicle to reinforce management's support of the SCM initiative.

◆ It helps explain the project to process stakeholders, customers, and outside activities (e.g., budget reviewers and General Accounting Office reviewers).

◆ It helps institutionalize the project.

◆ It is the first step to creating other documents, including a more detailed strategy and a plan of action and milestones.

We recommend that the initial informational document be created in a brochure-type format of 3–10 pages and that it include, at a minimum, the following basic information:

◆ A statement from the appropriate level of management expressing support for the SCM implementation project and its importance to the component's logistics process

◆ A copy of the DoD SCM guiding principles (see Chapter 2) or similar material

◆ A brief description of the SCM concept in terms of your specific DoD organization

◆ The high-level SCM operational concept graphic, if available (see Chapter 3)

◆ A brief narrative description of the SCM implementation team's mission and objectives

◆ A list of initial organizations and resources involved in the project

◆ A brief description of potential SCM performance and cost benefits to the organization, with quantitative examples (if available).

Once the basic SCM team brochure has been created, it can be used as an informational tool to advertise the supply chain initiative. We suggest that this document be widely disseminated to gain support among potential participants in the implementation process. Development of an implementation team Internet site also is a good way of maintaining channels of communication among team participants, the supplier community, customers, and management. Basic Web site information may include the following:

◆ Project descriptions

◆ Strategy documents

◆ Draft and final products

◆ Plans of action and milestones

◆ Training materials

◆ Reference documents

◆ Points-of-contact information.

## Obtain Basic Supply Chain Management Training

In concert with the team's efforts to advertise and promote the SCM project, government and contract personnel on the team must be thoroughly familiar with the fundamental tenets of SCM as espoused by academic experts and practiced by "world-class" private-sector companies and other government organizations. Implementation of SCM in DoD activities will be different in some respects from implementation to the private sector; many of the practices associated with SCM in business and the strategies used to implement these practices will be applicable to the military environment, however.

Several avenues are available for obtaining basic SCM training. One basic starting point is to review the available literature. A good method for locating current reference material is to search on supply chain management at commercial book-selling sites on the Internet (e.g., amazon.com or barnesandnoble.com). Dozens of basic works are available in libraries or for purchase. Excellent references include the following books:

- Donald J. Bowersox and David J. Closs, *Logistical Management: The Integrated Supply Chain Process*

- William C. Copacino, *Supply Chain Management: The Basics and Beyond*

- Robert B. Handfield et al., *Introduction to Supply Chain Management*

- Fred A. Kuglin, *Customer-Centered Supply Chain Management*

- Robert M. Monczka et al., *Purchasing and Supply Chain Management*

- Charles C. Poirier, *Advanced Supply Chain Management*

- David Simchi-Levi, *Designing and Managing the Supply Chain*

- James A. Tompkins, *No Boundaries: Moving Beyond Supply Chain Management.*

These books provide a good introduction to the principles and practices of SCM as viewed by the academic community and private-sector SCM practitioners. Another good source of basic SCM reference materials in periodical form is http://www.manufacturing.net/search.htm. This Web site contains a wealth of information for manufacturing and related functional professionals in an easily accessible format. It includes up-to-date references to magazine articles from more than 20 periodicals, product information, economic statistics, and industry-specific news and research. This site is a service of Cahners Business Information.[1] Its purpose is to provide essential business information to users in its various markets. Cahners' objective is to deliver this information in a form that is most effective for business people to use in making business decisions. Researchers should use the search capability at the site for the SCM community. Another excellent Internet reference for current SCM information is the Web site of the Achieving Supply Chain Excellence through Technology (ASCET) project sponsored by Andersen

---

[1] Cahners Business Information is not associated with DoD, nor is this reference an endorsement by DoD.

Consulting and supported by other supply chain-oriented companies. The ASCET address is http://www.ascet.com/ascet2/index.html. This site is more commercially oriented to providing users with information on supply chain technology solutions.

For organizations desiring additional academic training in SCM, more formal educational opportunities are available from several outstanding colleges and universities. For example, programs/courses in supply chain management are available at the following institutions:

- Arizona State University
- Tennessee State University
- Georgia Institute of Technology
- Northwestern University
- Michigan State University
- Harvard Business School
- North Florida University
- University of Tennessee
- North Carolina State University
- University of Maryland
- Ohio State University
- Northeastern University
- Pennsylvania State University
- Stanford University
- Syracuse University
- University of Wisconsin
- Massachusetts Institute of Technology

This listing represents outstanding academic programs in SCM. Other colleges and universities throughout the country may have similar programs. Further information on specific training offerings may be obtained from the Web sites of specific educational institutions.

In addition to formal academic training for SCM, dozens of private-sector consulting firms offer SCM training. In many cases, this training can be tailored to the specific needs of the DoD organization and made available at government sites. An Internet search for supply chain management training will yield numerous such training opportunities. In addition, the Supply Chain Council's Web site at http://www.supply-chain.org/includes an excellent list of solution providers and supply chain consultants.

We encourage organizations and personnel who are interested in maintaining currency regarding SCM issues and applications to become members of the

Supply Chain Council. The Council was incorporated in June 1997 as a not-for-profit trade association. The Council offers members an opportunity to improve the effectiveness of supply chain relationships from the supplier's supplier to the customer's customer. A nominal fee is charged to government activities for Council membership. In addition to providing collaborative technical support in the form of the SCOR model and performance benchmarking information, the Council sponsors numerous meetings, conferences, seminars, and training programs where members and industry-leading practitioners discuss supply chain issues.

Another excellent professional association for logistics managers is the Council of Logistics Management (CLM). CLM is a not-for-profit organization of business personnel who are interested in improving their logistics management skills. CLM works in cooperation with private industry and various organizations to further the understanding and development of the logistics concept. CLM accomplishes this goal through a continuing program of organized activities, publications, research, and meetings designed to develop the theory and understanding of the logistics process, promote the art and science of managing logistics systems, and foster professional dialogue among logistics practitioners and developers within the profession. Although CLM does not focus exclusively on SCM, it is a valuable educational and research resource for many logistics-related areas. The CLM Web site is at http://www.clm1.org/.

## Identify Initial Target Areas of Opportunity

Rome wasn't built in a day.

Implementation of SCM is a massive undertaking with profound impact on processes, organizations, and resource allocations. Because this effort will not pay off overnight, management must carefully balance its long-term promise against more immediate business needs.

The complexity of the supply chain can make it difficult to envision the whole, from end to end. But successful supply chain managers realize the need to invest time and effort up front in developing this total perspective and using it to form a blueprint for change that maps linkages among initiatives and a well-thought-out implementation sequence. This blueprint also must coordinate the change initiatives with ongoing day-to-day operations and must cross-organizational boundaries. The blueprint requires rigorous assessment of the entire supply chain—from supplier relationships to internal operations to the end customer. Current practices must be ruthlessly weighed against best practices to determine the size of the gap prioritizing and sequencing initiatives, establishing resources and people requirements, and getting a complete picture of the organization's supply chain—before, during, and after implementation.[2]

As part of the long-term implementation strategy, the SCM team should follow the six-step approach described in Chapter 3 to formulate the future supply chain design and select process and technology tools that are appropriate to attaining the design vision. As part of the "getting started" phase, however, we recommend that the team establish a preliminary set of targets of opportunity or focus areas to permit the earliest possible achievement of results. This strategy will help develop credibility and direction for the long-term effort.

The initial areas selected should be key enablers of the future implementation of the fully integrated supply chain. In Chapter 2, we suggest 12 guiding principles for SCM in DoD. Implementation of these principles ultimately will be the yardstick by which a successful SCM program will be measured.

The SCM implementation team must approach the overall task of implementing the full range of guiding principles, recognizing that success can be achieved only through a "building block" strategy. This strategy requires early establishment of a foundation of essential capabilities on which the supply chain can be built.

Although each team should identify its own particular initial targets of opportunity, the 12 guiding principles suggest some obvious choices. In addition, in a survey of high-level logistics managers from the military services, several key issue areas to SCM success were identified.[3] Using these two sources, we created a list of initial SCM implementation focus areas (Table 4-1).

The SCM implementation team should keep in mind that the selection of applicable best practices and supporting technologies should not be simply a matter of picking and choosing from a laundry list of best logistics practices and applying them at random. The initial targets of opportunity described in Table 4-1 represent areas identified by world-class organizations for their SCM implementation efforts. The SCM team should develop its supply chain

---

[2] David L. Anderson, Frank E. Britt, and Donavon J. Favre, "The Seven Principles of Supply Chain Management," *Supply Chain Management Review,* Spring 1997.

[3] Logistics Management Institute, *Survey of Senior DoD Logistics Managers,* Report, Jeffery P. Bennett, Donna McMurry, Stephanie Ellis, May 2000.

strategic vision, high-level objectives, and customer support perspective before embarking on any significant development path.

*Table 4-1. SCM Implementation Team—Initial Focus Areas*

| Focus area | Purpose |
|---|---|
| SCM training | Identification of applicable SCM training resources |
| Customer relationships | Development of concept for establishing integrated relationships with customers, including capturing requirements at point of need |
| Supply chain information sharing | Development of concepts for providing management and operational information to all supply chain participants and customers |
| Supply chain functional/ organizational integration | Development of concept for process integration/ communications across functional and organizational boundaries (e.g., logistics acquisition) |
| Supplier relationships | Development of concept for supply chain integration with and management of full range of material/service suppliers |
| Supply chain metrics | Identification of initial group of supply chain-oriented performance and cost metrics for DoD application |

# Select Initial Tools to Support SCM Implementation Process

Managing the supply chain implementation process will require the capability to effectively structure and document strategies, processes, information, organizational relationships, resources, and actions associated with the initiative. Very early in the organizational phase, the SCM implementation team should select several basic tools that will be used throughout the long-term implementation process. These tools will be used to communicate information to management and project participants, to assist in process analysis (including simulations), to document progress against established milestones, and to record narrative and quantitative reference information. Some of these tools are as basic as standard office word processing, spreadsheet, graphics, and database program suites. Almost any available suite of products will suffice, providing the programs are standard among the majority of project participants. Team access to e-mail and file transfer capability over a local area network (LAN) or the Internet also is a fundamental required capability. Automated programs that permit group sharing of work in process also are very desirable.

In addition to office management basics, the team should use an automated project management tool to assist in managing and tracking the progress of the SCM initiative and to ensure early detection and resolution of deviations from the plan. There are dozens of such tools on the market. In certain cases, contractor support may be used to install and maintain the project management system. The particular tool selected, like the basic office products, must be used and shared among all team participants.

The importance of effective project management to successful SCM implementation cannot be overemphasized. SCM team members are leaders and catalysts for SCM implementation throughout the organization. Failure to effectively orchestrate and coordinate team activities invariably will result in missed deadlines, unacceptable products, and ultimately the demise of the total effort. Michael Greer details 14 key principles for project management success.[4] (These principles are documented in Appendix A.) Team leaders and members should be thoroughly versed on these basic tenets of project management. Keeping the team focused on attaining broad SCM program objectives may be the most critical element of success. A usable, easily updated project management and scheduling program is a key ingredient for effective management of the SCM initiative.

Once the team has obtained and mastered the basic support tools that are common to any project management effort, they should ensure the availability of several capabilities that are required specifically to support SCM implementation. One of the most important of these capabilities is software for creating process flow diagrams (PFDs). The PFD is one of the simplest yet most powerful tools for understanding and analyzing business activities.[5] The PFD is a graphic description technique that was developed from the disciplines of process and systems engineering; it is based on the idea of describing or analyzing complex structured activities by flow charting. One or more PFDs can describe any human or automated activity. The level of detail described for a given activity can be as general or detailed as needed for the intended use. Each PFD connects functions in the chain along a timeline, including manual operations performed by users and operations performed by

---

[4] Michael Greer, "Planning and Managing Human Performance Technology Projects," *Handbook of Human Performance Technology*, San Francisco: Jossey-Bass, 1999.

[5] Formerly, DoD activities were encouraged to use the integrated definition (IDEF) method for documenting business processes. Although IDEF is a useful tool for certain applications, we do not recommend it for describing and documenting supply chain processes, particularly at the higher level. It is especially important that the SCM implementation team not become bogged down with in-depth, detailed, functional process modeling efforts.

external entities. The capability to create PFDs is required early in the SCM implementation effort because these diagrams concentrate on the total process—and its users and interfaces—rather than on the specific functionality of each node in the overall supply chain. The team's high-level PFD will provide a consistent framework for adding organizational, procedural, and systems details as the design effort progresses. PFDs are useful for (but not limited to) the following purposes:

◆ Documentation of the overall, end-to-end supply chain process

◆ Preparation of operational node connectivity diagrams

◆ Task visualization for business activity troubleshooting and problem solving

◆ Definition of standard methods and procedures

◆ Planning and deployment of any new business system, activity, function, or organization

◆ Analysis of cross-function customer/supplier relationships within an organization

◆ Employee job training

◆ Development of product maintenance processes

◆ Preparation of procedural manuals.

The selection of specific PFD software is at the discretion of the team. Dozens of good packages are commercially available. Certain selection criteria are applicable, however:

◆ The PFD software should be easy for non-computer-oriented personnel to learn and include online or classroom training.

◆ Diagram structure and conventions should be easily understandable.

◆ Output products should be producible in "hard" and electronic copy.

◆ Diagrams should be viewable, exchangeable, and updatable on a LAN.

◆ Software costs should be commensurate with the size of the overall project.

Early selection and installation of flowchart software will enable the implementation team to visually document the planned supply chain design. Creation of a basic outline of the organization's major high-level activities that will provide an initial structure for accomplishing the design phase of SCM implementation is highly desirable. By using the PFD capability from the beginning, team members will gain proficiency in using the automated tool, and the transition to the more detailed to-be and as-is documentation will be facilitated. Often, the first application of the PFD tool will be the operational node connectivity diagrams discussed in Chapter 3. Using the same process documentation tools throughout the design phase will help to ensure consistency in content and presentation.

DoD organizations charged with implementing business process improvements have long been hampered by the lack of sufficient information on the cost of processes or activities. Conversely, having access to valid cost data adds significantly to the credibility and acceptability of process improvement efforts. The traditional DoD budgeting structure simply does not capture costs in a manner that is amenable to relating expenditures to activities. Likewise, DoD accounting systems are woefully inadequate for capturing and analyzing activity cost factors. Functional managers who are contemplating policy and process changes cannot establish a valid baseline of as-is costs, estimate the cost that would be incurred if the planned to-be change is implemented, or determine actual costs after the change is made. Investment decisions frequently are based on notional concepts that attempt to estimate costs by making unverifiable or unrealistic assumptions and allocations or ignore cost factors altogether.

As part of the initiative to implement SCM, the implementation team should begin to address this deficiency of activity cost information. Early on, the team should adopt an activity costing mechanism and associated software tools to begin the accumulation of process cost data related to the supply chain process. Although the effort may be modest at first, the credibility of the SCM initiative will be significantly enhanced by including even high-level cost information as part of the implementation process. The basic concept for acquiring required cost information in a structured way is called activity-based costing (ABC). ABC is a methodology that measures cost and performance of activities, resources, and cost objects; assigns resources to activities and activities to cost objects, based on their use; and recognizes causal relationships of cost drivers to activities. An ABC system maintains and processes financial and operating data on a firm's resources, activities, cost objects, cost drivers, and activity performance measures.[6] For DoD activities, an ABC tool will help break down general budgetary groupings (i.e., personnel, operations, procurement) into homogeneous resource categories and assign costs to specific activities performed, such as item identification, material ordering, receiving, transportation, and warehousing.

A wide range of ABC software tools is available for use by the implementation team. Early development of a capability to capture and measure activity costs will be valuable in identifying the largest cost components or cost drivers across the supply chain. This information will be needed as the team attempts to identify and prioritize targets of opportunity for process improvement and measurement of major performance assessment factors.

Another tool that will assist the SCM team in quantification of information required for more effective SCM is benchmarking. Benchmarking is a methodology for establishing rational performance goals through the search for best practices that will lead to superior performance. Benchmarking can be divided into two categories: strategic and operational. At the strategic level, managers should be asking what their organization could do to provide desired overall performance at the best cost. Operational benchmarking involves comparative analysis of the performance of an organization with similar activities for specific functions such as warehousing, inventory control, and order processing.

Another important tool that should be adopted early by the SCM team relates to building a benchmarking capability. As organizations come under increasing pressure to improve customer service, they want to know how others manage to meet ever-higher customer expectations without sacrificing service or raising costs. Benchmarking provides a tool for managers to measure their supply chain operations against those of organizations that stand out from the crowd for their mastery of SCM. For the SCM implementation team, benchmarking is a way to assist in developing and quantifying measures that are meaningful to supporting performance goals and objectives and in identifying enabling best practices. Benchmarking can be done internally

---

[6] Definition from *CAM-I Glossary of Activity-Based Management,* edited by Norm Raffish and Peter B. B. Turney, Arlington, Virginia, 1991.

and externally to the DoD logistics process. The SCM team may wish to determine the best performers within DoD or other government agencies first before looking at world class private-sector organizations.

To get started in benchmarking, the SCM team should adopt a benchmarking software tool to assist in structuring its benchmarking activities and effectively capture, display, and analyze benchmarking data. Again, selection of benchmarking software is at the discretion of the SCM team. Dozens of useful and effective commercial software packages are available. The team may wish to engage the services of a consultant who is well versed in benchmarking activities to assist in establishing and executing the benchmarking effort.

Another tool recommended for SCM is a business process simulation capability. A simulation capability will provide a cost-effective, nondisruptive means of testing and experimenting with SCM policy, processes, and technology insertion in a virtual, nondestructive environment. A properly developed simulation will permit a "fly before buy" approach for logistics information systems and other technology enablers that support implementation of the best strategies for managing the supply chain. Because the ultimate metrics for DoD SCM are weapon system, equipment, and personnel readiness; customer satisfaction; and cost, the best simulations monitor the end-to-end logistics process and can quantify, in terms of enterprise metrics, the benefits of alternative logistics business processes.

In many cases, the SCM team will not have sufficient expertise (or time) to develop and exercise the required simulation capability. In this case, numerous support contractors can provide this service. The team should clearly define the simulation requirement, however, and closely monitor the results of any simulation effort. In many cases, simulation results can be used effectively as part of management reviews to reinforce the anticipated results of the improvement initiative.

## Prepare a Plan of Action and Milestones

Most people resist change. They generally change for one of two reasons: they fear the consequences of not changing, or they are excited by the potential benefit that making a change will bring. In today's world of dramatic change, team members need a direction-setting tool that provides access to the organizational vision, motivation, and purpose, and is flexible enough to enable the team—collectively and individually—to adjust the program and action plans to changes that inevitably occur.

The team needs a tool that will help provide a "helicopter" overview and document significant objectives and required implementing actions. With such an effective planning and change management tool, the team will be in the best possible position to embrace change, accomplish its mission, and meet target deadlines. Effective documentation of the steps required to implement SCM can be accomplished with a tool as simple as a standard plan of action and milestones (POA&M). Creation of a POA&M for the SCM team should be accomplished very early in the process. This effort is much more, however, than just another item for management's routine checklist. The POA&M serves as the coordinating vehicle to ensure that the individual activities of team members are fully integrated and are focused on common objectives.

Creating a POA&M should be a joint effort of all team members. Although a key team member or manager may draft the initial POA&M, finalization of the action document should be the topic of full team brainstorming sessions before it receives management approval. This process helps to ensure that each team member fully understands the overall project objectives and actions and can more easily see his or her part in the total effort. The initial POA&M may be developed at a relatively high level. At a minimum, it should include the areas included in the list of initial targets of opportunity developed by the team. Later, separate POA&Ms should be developed for each significant SCM implementation task. As the implementation plan evolves, the POA&M should be kept updated to reflect current activity status and as a record of the progress and accomplishments of the SCM team.

Although there are many acceptable POA&M formats, basic entries for each identified task should include those listed in Table 4-2.

*Table 4-2. Supply Chain Management Implementation—POA&M*

| Task number[a] | Description |
|---|---|
| Supply chain subarea | Identifier of significant supply chain program task area |
| SCM objective | List SCM implementation objective being supported |
| Task name(s) | Name of specific action |
| Deliverable | Description of results of task or activity |
| Start date | Calendar date |

61

*Table 4-2. Supply Chain Management Implementation—POA&M*
*(Continued)*

| Task number[a] | Description |
|---|---|
| Planned completion date | Calendar date |
| Required resources | Personnel, funding, technology, and infrastructure required to complete task |
| Critical inhibitors or obstacles | Describe issues/items |
| Milestones | Sequential listing and description of task milestones |
| Team leader | Name, phone, e-mail, and location |
| Comments | Document other relevant information |

[a] Each discrete task should be identified with a sequential task number for easy reference.

For ease of use, updating, and communications, we suggest that POA&Ms be created and updated electronically on the team's LAN.

## Open Issues List for Team Management

We suggest one additional tool to help manage SCM team activity. The open issues list (OIL) is the best lubricant the program manager can use to speed up and increase the effectiveness of periodic project meetings (typically held every week to discuss why the project is behind schedule and over budget). The OIL also is useful for tracking progress on individual issues and actions.

The OIL should be prepared on a standard form that is designed for the purpose. Besides spaces for meeting purpose, date, and attendees, columns should be provided for the following items:

◆ Issue number (assign numbers in serial order)

◆ Issue (necessary task or concern, whether in the original plan or not)—add new issues as they come up in the course of the meeting

◆ Date opened

◆ Person responsible for resolving the issue

◆ Action to be taken to resolve the issue

◆ Completion due date

◆ Status (current state of completion, roadblocks, etc.).

Each open (not completed) issue should be reviewed in each meeting. (If you run out of time, schedule a follow-up meeting as soon as possible to complete the review.) Update the issue's status and discuss roadblocks, assign help, add issues, and so forth, as appropriate.

As each issue is completed, leave it on the list, but mark it completed. That way, all team members can see progress as it is made. Update and distribute copies of the OIL the following day. Better yet, keep the list as a database on the project "scribe's" laptop computer and print updated copies for everyone at the end of each meeting, as well as periodically between meetings.

In Chapter 5, we begin in earnest to describe specific actions required to accomplish the six-step approach to successfully implementing SCM in DoD logistics activities. After the formation of the SCM team, the key next step is to develop a comprehensive, credible, and feasible implementation strategy.

# Chapter 5
# Developing Your Implementation Strategy

Implementing an integrated supply chain can be very difficult. Problems arise in establishing objectives, setting performance targets, crossing organizational barriers, overcoming cultural resistance, and implementing supporting information systems, especially regarding the need to share information among the many participating organizations in a supply chain environment as complex and extensive as DoD. In the preceding chapters, we discuss some of the obstacles to SCM implementation, as well as basic principles and initial actions needed to accomplish the transition to SCM in DoD. In this chapter, we discuss the fundamental components of an SCM implementation strategy for DoD activities. In subsequent chapters we present an approach for using these elements in an integrated way to design the future supply chain.

Prior to the creation of extensive process models or the acquisition of elaborate and technologically advanced computer software, the implementation team must document its strategic plan for accomplishing the transition to an SCM-oriented logistics process. By putting the plan in writing, the path to the future becomes tangible and more understandable for personnel who must execute the plan, managers who must approve the plan's actions, and customers who will be affected by the plan's changes. Although each strategic plan must be tailored to the specific needs of the particular DoD organization, every successful SCM implementation effort must address some fundamental, common issues. In Chapter 4, we identify some initial targets of opportunity for the SCM team to begin its efforts. As the team formulates the more detailed, long-range strategy described in this chapter, the initial focus areas will be expanded and further developed to create a comprehensive strategy for implementing SCM across the enterprise. Including fundamental goals in the SCM strategic plan will help responsible managers and customers of the supply chain to start with a reasonable understanding of what the initiative is trying to achieve.

Organizations are striving to get a better handle on their supply chains for many reasons. Several years ago, to better understand the role of SCM,

Peter T. Funke, director of marketing for Chemical Lehman Tank Lines, (quoted by Tim Minihan) identified the following process change drivers:[1]

- *Improve service.* Develop tighter cycle schedules and more accurate delivery forecasts and execution between suppliers, shippers, distribution facilities, carriers, and customers.

- *Reduce total costs.* Eliminate redundant and inefficient processes from the supply chain.

- *Increase asset utilization.* Eliminate assets that aren't essential to the organization's core function, and devise more efficient methods of using remaining assets.

- *Increase scope.* Use information technology to expand the amount and type of information shared with suppliers, customers, and internal groups. Increase the speed and accuracy of decisions and processes.

Today more than ever, these objectives remain relevant for all supply chain managers and for DoD activities in particular. In Chapter 2, we convert the universal objectives outlined above into 12 SCM principles that are more aligned to DoD terminology and circumstances. An SCM strategic plan document should include references to basic objectives or principles. Once the basic objectives are determined, the next step is to lay out strategies to effect SCM implementation. Figure 5-1 describes these basic courses of action in graphical form. This pictorial view will aid us as we identify specific actions required to satisfy SCM objectives.

---

[1] Tim Minihan, "What Drives the Supply Chain?" *Purchasing,* July 11, 1996.

*Figure 5-1. Supply Chain Management Implementation Strategy Diagram*

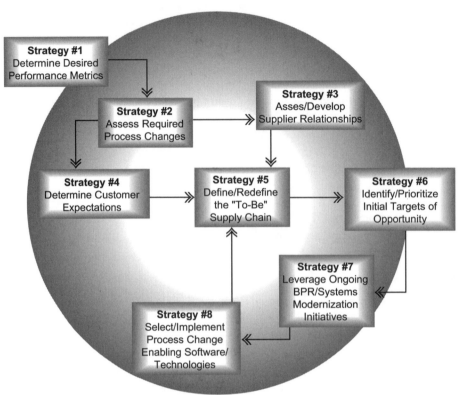

Note: BPR = business process reengineering.

## Paradigm for Supply Chain Management Strategy

As we begin to develop the strategy for SCM implementation, we must distinguish actions that target strategic change from other important, but less critical activity. In a white paper written for Andersen Consulting's ASCET initiative, Donald Hicks describes three levels of decisions: operational, tactical, and strategic.[2] Operational and tactical decisions generally involve choices or decisions about current business processes. Although strategic decisions may relate to the current business process, they often focus on significant changes that are required to alter the direction of the enterprise, its basic objectives, its organizational structure, or its way of doing business.

[2] Donald Hicks, "Next Generation Supply Chain Strategic Planning Technology and Applications," Achieving Supply Chain Excellence through Technology (ASCET) Project, Andersen Consulting Corporation, February 2000.

SCM implementation in DoD is a strategic decision. It is a fundamental change in the way the Department accomplishes its materiel support to the warfighting customer. The SCM implementation team must approach its task from a strategic perspective. SCM implementation does not involve merely acquiring new software, shortening processing cycles, and dealing with suppliers and customers in a new way. The key to successful implementation of SCM in DoD is identification and, ultimately, integration of key elements of the supply chain into an effective end-to-end process. This integration factor is the single most essential characteristic of SCM.

## Strategy 1. Determine Desired Performance Metrics

In documenting the strategy for SCM implementation, the team must identify and stay focused on strategic changes required to accomplish the transition to the desired supply chain environment. As Figure 5-1 shows, the implementation strategy begins with the determination of supply chain performance metrics.

> Leading organizations today are rigorously assessing their supply chain performance by establishing a baseline profile, identifying strengths and weaknesses, and targeting opportunities for improving service while reducing costs. Doing that requires a structured program that evaluates current performance and sets a future path.[3]

In their efforts to develop meaningful supply chain measures in the private sector, world-class companies have recognized factors that help quantify significant process improvements that directly benefit customer service levels and reduce operational costs.

To assess the performance of the supply chain and its component processes completely and accurately, the implementation team should adopt objective

---

[3] John M. Hill, "Grading Your Supply Chain," *Modern Materials Handling*, November 1, 1999.

performance measurement information. Examples of such areas include the following:

- Sales volume
- On-time delivery
- Product/service cost
- Cycle times
- Quality
- Asset utilization
- Customer service
- Responsiveness
- Accurate identification of products and services offered

The SCM implementation team must advocate the strategic decision to transition the organization's supply chain from existing functionally oriented performance metrics to customer support metrics and total process cost measures. The team also must lead the effort to obtain management approval of the proposed supply chain metrics. Ultimately, metrics will be required for the full spectrum of supply chain segments. As the implementation effort progresses, high-level performance and cost metrics will be developed and supporting or diagnostic metrics determined. Diagnostic metrics are measures that relate to specific segments of the supply chain that must be quantified, managed, and improved to ensure achievement of overall performance and cost goals. Initially, however, the team should identify higher-level metrics required to monitor the overall performance of the supply chain. After implementation, those metrics will become barometers of success for future supply chain operations. To select appropriate metrics, the team should assess the applicability of potential performance measures in light of the following criteria:[4]

- Use customer-focused measures to assess how well customer needs are being met.

- Link functional performance measures and goals to overall DoD business and mission objectives; promote mutual execution of functional responsibilities and discourage functional conflict.

- Establish process measures that monitor use of DoD resources.

---

[4] U.S. Department of Defense, Deputy Under Secretary of Defense (Logistics), *Logistics Functional Requirements Guide*, August 1998, pp. 5–8.

- Establish baselines to provide a context of historical performance for evaluating improvement initiatives.

- Establish comparison benchmarks to provide clear performance targets and feedback; facilitate progressive improvement.

- Establish measures to prevent the cost of information collection and analysis from exceeding the benefits derived.

- Assist managers in managing current operations and facilitating future planning by providing tools that evaluate program performance, cost, and management; provide a basis for changing the program; support planning, programming, and budgeting.

Management information that currently is available to DoD logistics managers usually falls into one of three categories: workload, current resource expenditure and outputs, and performance compared to standards and goals. Current metrics often focus on performance or resources used by individual segments of the supply chain. As its first action, the SCM implementation team must identify and support measures that will give DoD logistics managers, suppliers, and customers a consistent and quantified picture of total supply chain performance and related costs. Although no single set of performance measures is universally appropriate for every organization or every process level, significant strides have been made toward identifying basic enterprise-level supply chain metrics for DoD activities. Once metrics are identified and a baseline of credible data is accumulated, the team will use these metrics to help design the process that will deliver the required level of performance in future logistics operations. We propose that the SCM implementation team begin with metrics that have been developed through recent research that uses the "balanced scorecard" approach[5] and industry experience as documented by the Supply Chain Council in its SCOR model. The balanced scorecard approach requires measures in the following areas:

- Meeting the strategic needs of the enterprise

- Meeting the needs of individual customers

---

[5] Robert S. Kaplan and David P. Norton, "The Balanced Scorecard—Measures that Drive Performance," *Harvard Business Review* 70, no. 2 (January–February 1992).

◆ Addressing internal business performance

◆ Addressing process improvement initiative results.

A more detailed listing of performance metrics suggested by the Supply Chain Council is included in Appendix D. These metrics will be useful as the SCM team explores the supply chain design in greater detail. Initially, however, the team should focus on developing and obtaining approval for a concise set of enterprise metrics that are oriented to total supply chain performance.

A study by the Logistics Management Institute (LMI) applied the balanced scorecard concept to basic industry-oriented performance and cost measures as documented in the SCOR model.[6] LMI's study assessed numerous factors that are applicable to the military supply chain and recommended a set of performance measures developed for DoD use:

◆ *Perfect order fulfillment.* A perfect order meets the following standards:

> ➤ Delivered complete: all items delivered in the quantities requested

> ➤ Delivered on time, using the customer's definition of on-time delivery

> ➤ Complete and accurate documentation (including packing slips, bills of lading, and invoices) to support the order

> ➤ Delivered in serviceable condition and in the correct configuration to be used by the customer; correctly installed (as applicable).

◆ *Supply chain response time.* The total average length (measured in days) of the supply chain. This metric is derived from the average plan, source, maintain (repair), and deliver cycle times. Generally speaking, the "best" supply chains are the "shortest" supply chains. DoD managers recently have focused on a variation of supply chain response time: "customer wait time" (CWT). The CWT measure also

---

[6] Logistics Management Institute, *DoD Supply Chain Management: A Recommended Performance Measurement Scorecard,* Report LG803R1, Larry S. Klapper et al., March 1999.

captures the time from input of the customer requirement to delivery of the required material.

◆ *Percentage change in customer price, compared to inflation.* This customer-focused cost metric measures the combined impact of material costs (getting the best price) and SCM costs. The metric would be computed by using a "market basket" approach similar to that used to compute the consumer price index.

◆ *SCM costs as a percentage of sales* (at standard price). This metric is a measure of overhead to operate the logistics system with respect to the amount of material that moves through it. SCM costs include costs for the supply chain-related management information system, finance and planning, inventory carrying, materiel acquisition, and order management.

◆ *Weapon system logistics costs as a percentage of the acquisition price* (adjusted for inflation). This metric represents the cost of ownership of individual weapon systems as a function of their acquisition price.

◆ *Inventory turns.* This metric is total sales at acquisition price divided by the value of inventory at acquisition price; it measures how effectively assets are managed. Excluded from the computation are assets held in war reserve accounts (because they are not for peacetime consumption).

◆ *Upside production flexibility.* This metric is the number of days required to achieve an unplanned sustainable increase in production, including repair to support most-demanding current operational scenarios.

◆ *Weapon system not-mission-capable (NMC) rates.* This metric represents the percentage of time a weapon system fleet is not mission capable because of problems relating to supply (lack of parts), maintenance (lack of maintenance resources), or both. NMC rates should be produced for key weapon systems and used with other performance metrics that can be filtered by weapon system (e.g., perfect order fulfillment and supply chain response time).

◆ *War reserve ratio.* This metric is the ratio of war reserve assets on hand to the war reserve requirement. This measure is an indication of

71

readiness to sustain most-demanding current operational scenarios until the industrial base is mobilized (as measured by upside production flexibility).

The LMI report also describes a series of more detailed functional performance metrics that could be used as analytical diagnostics of the enterprise measures outlined above. The SCM implementation team should review the detailed analysis contained in the LMI report and assess the applicability of the proposed measures to its particular supply chain development effort. There are ongoing initiatives within each DoD component to determine the valid family of performance metrics for modernized logistics processes. The SCM team should review and build on these efforts and seek to influence management's ultimate selection of logistics metrics toward measures that will have meaning in the future supply chain environment.

In addition to influencing the selection of enterprise-level SCM metrics, the implementation team should include in its strategic planning an initiative to determine the availability of data required to compute and track trends for these measures. Ultimately, a new or modified corporate data repository should be put in place to act as the authoritative source of the enterprise and supporting functional process measurement history. The SCM team should not necessarily prejudge the technical solution for the metrics data repository. Recent innovations in data warehousing and virtual data storage concepts may lead to significantly different solutions regarding the requirement to provide online, real-time, universally accessible sharing of metrics and other supply chain information. In accomplishing the implementation strategy, the SCM team should concentrate primarily on identifying essential enterprise metrics and assuring that this information is readily available for all appropriate supply chain suppliers, participants, and customers.

## Strategy 1 Actions

*Action 1*—Select and define enterprise supply chain metrics and supporting functional measures. Obtain management approval.

*Action 2*—Determine sources and updating methodology of actual metrics data.

# Strategy 2. Assess Required Process Changes

Once the SCM implementation team has made a preliminary selection of enterprise-level performance measures, it should proceed to documenting fundamental changes required to implement SCM. In keeping with the six-step approach outlined in Chapter 3, the team should take actions needed to drive the design of the future supply chain process. This design will be influenced by three principal factors:

◆ Existing organizations, procedures, and infrastructure assets

◆ Desired future performance objectives

◆ Required process changes identified by the SCM team.

Obviously, the first factor is least controlled by the team's efforts. A practical consideration in any change initiative is the recognition that existing organizations are made up of people and will resist change. Bringing change to government organizations never starts with a blank page. Implementing SCM in DoD organizations will require the SCM team to sell the changes to management and to rank-and-file employees as being in their best interest. The team also should leverage ongoing change initiatives, particularly in automated data processing (ADP) systems modernization that may be heading in the same general direction as the SCM effort. Finally, the team should clearly document future performance objectives and required process changes and utilize them to help drive the organization's overall future direction. Thus, by concentrating on the second and third design factors, the team can minimize and ultimately overcome the natural inertia inherent in the first factor. In other words, the SCM team must bring change to the table and be persistent in advocating supply chain-oriented actions.

In Chapter 7 we identify a series of specific process changes needed to implement SCM in DoD. In building the strategic plan, however, the team should document fundamental change requirements at a relatively high level. Just what are these changes? To bring about transformation to a true supply chain environment, we must first understand the nature of the current process. Let's start with a perspective of that process. Although this system has served the nation well for many years, the changing world situation implies that DoD must make fundamental alterations to the way it accomplishes its logistics business. The current system evolved from the organizational structure that developed during World War II and processes implemented through the first generation of computer systems of the 1950s and 1960s.

Organizations and ADP systems were constructed along functional lines such as supply, maintenance, and transportation. To a large degree, they still operate this way. Logistics processes and the people who operate them work in functional compartments (stovepipes). Each area attempts to optimize its part of the logistics structure, with little regard for the cause-and-effect impacts between organizations and systems. Figure 5-2 portrays an overview of the current DoD logistics process.

*Figure 5-2. Current DoD Supply Process*

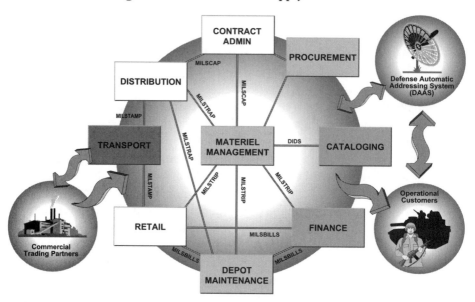

As Figure 5-2 shows, current DoD logistics functions are essentially stand-alone entities that are connected primarily by communication networks that permit information transfer by standard transactional interfaces or "handoffs." In fact, there is little sharing of common data or real-time exchange of information. Therefore, each functional area is concerned primarily with its own internal operation or, perhaps, its immediate interface with its closest neighbors in the process. Interaction with commercial suppliers of goods and services generally involves an "arms length" relationship that is based on formal contractual arrangements. To successfully implement SCM in DoD, the SCM team must promote significant changes in the existing, fragmented process. The SCM principles outlined in Chapter 2 provide the basis for identifying required changes. The SCM strategic plan should include a series of requirements statements that focus on implementing SCM principles in the team's organization. Table 5-1 restates the SCM principles and suggests some basic implementation approaches as a point of departure. The SCM team will want to build its own high-level list of implementation requirements.

*Table 5-1. DoD Logistics SCM Potential Implementation Actions*

| SCM guiding principle | High-level actions |
|---|---|
| 1. Structure logistics procedures and systems to provide agile response during crises and joint operations | • Identify applicable metrics and data sources<br>• Develop supply chain process flow diagram<br>• Identify and eliminate redundant process steps<br>• Document decision support system functional requirements |
| 2. Focus on satisfying warfighter requirements at the point of need | • Identify applicable metrics<br>• Develop an approach for timely and accurate identification and segmenting of customer requirements (e.g., priority, commodity, location, scenarios.) |
| 3. Link customers directly to source of material and services support | • Identify applicable metrics<br>• Document required end-use customer-level information for planning and sourcing material and services support |
| 4. Balance use of all available logistics resource elements to deliver customer requirements at lowest cost | • Identify applicable metrics<br>• Develop requirements for ABC capability across supply chain |
| 5. Measure total supply chain performance based on effective delivery of products and services to customers | • Identify applicable metrics<br>• Document required information and asset tracking capabilities<br>• Develop time-definite delivery capability |
| 6. Make maximum, effective use of competitive, global commercial capabilities | • Identify applicable metrics<br>• Develop sourcing strategy that routinely identifies and evaluates all possible sources of material and services |
| 7. Accomplish common requirements cooperatively | • Identify applicable metrics<br>• Develop an approach to routinely search out and evaluate alternative government or commercial activities to provide needed supply chain support |

*Table 5-1. DoD Logistics SCM Potential Implementation Actions (Continued)*

| SCM guiding principle | High-level actions |
|---|---|
| 8. Provide a consistent structure, content, and presentation of logistics information, particularly when supporting common interfaces among military services, Defense agencies, and international partners | • Identify applicable metrics<br><br>• Identify significant groupings of functional information required by multiple supply chain participants, suppliers, and customers<br><br>• Quantify information exchange volume and locations |
| 9. Address logistics requirements and related costs early in the acquisition cycle | • Identify applicable metrics<br><br>• Identify information acquired during equipment initial acquisition phase that should be maintained throughout sustainment life cycle |
| 10. Include all logistics requirements and costs in program baseline and develop them initially without any internally or externally imposed financial constraints | • Identify applicable metrics<br><br>• Define planning, programming, and budgeting data required to support supply chain future design<br><br>• Initiate ABC |
| 11. Replace the practice of information ownership with a concept of information stewardship (e.g., shared data) | • Identify applicable metrics<br><br>• Identify all logical groupings of information required to implement end-to-end supply chain design |
| 12. Provide effective training and supporting technology to logistics personnel | • Identify applicable metrics<br><br>• Document basic training requirements for all supply chain participants, based on future supply chain design |

After completing the documentation of high-level logistics process changes needed to implement SCM, the team should begin to "drill down" in selected areas to identify specific best practices and technology solutions to accomplish comprehensive SCM implementation. Chapter 6 discusses an approach for constructing the more detailed design of the future supply chain. Chapter 7 documents a substantial number of potential process improvements. The team may use these suggested changes as a starting template for initiating the long-term SCM implementation.

## Strategy 2 Actions

*Action 1*—Build the high-level list of required process changes in support of SCM principles. Obtain management approval.

*Action 2*—Begin long-term effort to document-specific process changes to accomplish implementation of the future SCM design.

# Strategy 3. Assess/Develop Supplier Relationships

Supply chains come in two forms. An internal supply chain links all of an organization's functions together to fill a customer's order. An external supply chain is defined as a group of independent organizations working together in a specific channel to deliver a product or service. For example, a confectionery manufacturer, grocery wholesaler, and supermarket chain might join forces to deliver candy into the consumer's hands. The SCM implementation team must recognize both forms of supply chains in DoD. In assessing supplier relationships, the team focuses primarily on the external part of the supply chain.

In the case of materiel support, virtually all of DoD's requirements for spare parts, repair material, and commodities—such as fuel, clothing, medical, subsistence, and construction materials—initially derive from private-sector suppliers. Contractors provide about 40 percent of all depot maintenance services and much of DoD's transportation requirements. In recent years, DoD has begun significant efforts to minimize the portion of military inventories maintained in DoD-owned warehouses by obtaining materiel support directly from private-sector suppliers to end-use customers. At the same time, the Department has promoted significant reform of the acquisition process to streamline regulations and procedures for acquiring material and services.

The implementation team must recognize that successful SCM depends to a large degree on establishing different and sometimes longer-term relationships with commercial vendors and suppliers of materials and logistics services. Achieving these relationships also requires a different internal partnership among supply chain managers and acquisition managers within DoD. Interactions among external supply chain partners are highly dependent on the terms of purchasing contracts. In building these new relationships with commercial providers, logistics and acquisition members of the SCM team must first establish their own partnership to pursue needed changes on the government side of the contracting process. Despite some progress in acquisition reform, at the organizational levels where actual contracts with suppliers are executed, many of the traditional arms-length procedures remain in place between government procurement authorities and private-sector contractors. In fact, government activities will never be able to achieve the fully integrated relationships that world-class private-sector supply chain partners achieve. Having DoD partner with its suppliers in the same way that Procter and Gamble partners with Wal-Mart is an unrealistic expectation. There are opportunities, however, to substantially improve current supplier relationships.

First, the SCM team must understand that no single approach to creating and managing supplier relationships fits every circumstance. All types of contract agreements that currently are in use remain viable for DoD supply chains. The trick is to determine which arrangement to use for various commodities, end items, customers, and suppliers. The SCM team should develop a supplier relationship strategy for the organization's supply chain process by segmenting (dividing) items for which they have support responsibility by supplier categories and by types of item characteristics. As Figure 5-3 demonstrates, segmentation of suppliers is a formidable task. For all of DoD there are more than 100,000 suppliers at the national level, as well as many thousands more serving local activities in CONUS and overseas. Building supply chain alliances ordinarily begins with a selected group of key suppliers, including those providing important components or commodities and those providing high volumes of items.

> Forging partnerships does not come easy to most organizations. The traditional business model is to look out for your own best interests and let the other guy do the same. But being a partner means sharing…sharing information about upcoming production plans, forecasts, new-product introductions, and even certain financial data. That need to share is particularly important in the relationship between an organization and its logistics-services providers. James P. Fields, Vice-President of Business Development at Menlo Logistics, explains: "For the partnership between the customer and the logistics-services provider to reach its full potential, customers must openly share accurate information on their business, their customers, their suppliers, and any other relevant information about the operating environment. This helps the service provider build a supply-chain strategy that supports the business strategy." Partnershipping also means sharing the risks and rewards. Now, sharing the risks doesn't pose much of a problem for most organizations. But sharing the rewards demands a leap of faith that many activities still find difficult to make.[7]

---

[7] Francis J. Quinn, "Building a World Class Supply Chain," *Logistics Management and Distribution Report* (quoting James Fields of Menlo Logistics), June 1998.

*Figure 5-3. National-Level Suppliers and Distributors*

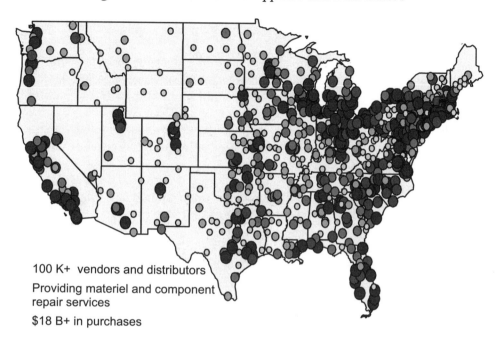

100 K+ vendors and distributors

Providing materiel and component repair services

$18 B+ in purchases

Although the SCM team should devise its own approach to segmenting suppliers, we provide an initial template of criteria for accomplishing this task. Step one is to develop business rules for selection of sources. These rules should incorporate the following factors:[8]

♦   *Responsiveness*—the ability to deliver the right quantities of the right item to surge or respond quickly to new workload and surge requirements

♦   *Cost*—the monetary price or resource demands

♦   *Cycle time*—the time from a request to the delivery of a product or service

♦   *Quality*—the likelihood that a product will satisfy performance standards.

---

[8] *Logistics Functional Requirements Guide*, pp. 8–13.

The team also should adopt criteria for segmenting support items into logical profile categories that ultimately will help to determine groupings of suppliers. The following list is a starting point for item categorization:[9]

- Items in a broad commodity group with substantial private-sector use and sources (e.g., medical supplies, food, batteries, photographic film, bulk metal, lumber, and transistors)

- Items used principally by DoD with limited or no commercial applications or commercial markets (e.g., military munitions, uniforms, and airframe parts)

- Items with unique design or performance requirements (e.g., fighter aircraft canopies and nuclear propulsion components)

- Items with shelf-life, pilferable, or hazardous material controls (e.g., tires, drugs, solvents, and precious metals)

- Items that use new or untested technologies, unstable design, unique material, or high-security or dangerous items (e.g., laser technology items, cryogenic applications, and radioactive material)

- Items that are subject to limited or no stockage when the support alternative includes maintaining castings and forgings or the appropriate source is manufacture-on-demand

- Items with a surge or substantially increased wartime usage or items that are needed only in wartime or contingency situations.

Although no category should be summarily included or excluded initially in considering the source of support, each group has characteristics that should be fully considered in selecting sources.

In most cases, the categorization of items will help the SCM team determine logical groupings for suppliers and ultimately for segmenting supplier relationships. No single supplier strategy will fit all circumstances. Supply chain expert William Copacino has devised an approach he calls the "Segmented Purchasing Strategy" (SPS).[10] Under this strategy, items or item families are segmented into one of four groupings. In DoD, this segmentation

---

[9] Ibid.

[10] Copacino, *Supply Chain Management, The Basics and Beyond*, p. 122.

is particularly important. Many logistics managers have taken a one-dimensional view of future logistics sourcing arrangements. Often, this view proposes to outsource *all* materiel support through contractor logistics support or direct vendor delivery strategies. This one-size-fits-all approach is as inappropriate in today's environment as the old stock, store, and issue approach would be. By adopting the segmented purchasing strategy, supply chain managers can assess the most appropriate materiel acquisition approach on the basis of meaningful criteria. Figure 5-4 illustrates this approach.

*Figure 5-4. Segmented Purchasing Strategies Framework*

| | |
|---|---|
| Mission-related repair parts<br>• Lower-volume items<br>• Corporate contracts lock in long-term support<br>• Maintain minimum inventories as required | Essential system weapon items—reparables and essential consumables<br>• Develop strategic partnerships with suppliers |
| Low dollar/noncritical items<br>• Nonmission essential<br>• Mechanized purchasing<br>• E-malls<br>• Direct vendor delivery<br>• Outsource support | Consumable commodities<br>• High volume/low market risk<br>• Government leverage volume buys/corporate contracts<br>• Prime vendor/contractor logistics support (CLS) |

Risk (High / Low) — Economic impact (High / Low)

SPS provides a framework for the SCM team to segment and focus materiel purchasing procedures in a strategic way to maximize use of procurement methods and resources and select the optimum approach to improve customer support for the highest risk/greatest economic impact item categories.

In conjunction with segmentation of items and suppliers, the SCM team should identify approaches to build appropriate strategic alliances with key logistics suppliers and service providers. As the SPS framework suggests, strategic, long-term alliances are not functionally or economically viable for all supplier relationships. For the foreseeable future, DoD activities will continue to use all modes of interface with suppliers (from buy, stock, store, and issue to full CLS). With many small and medium-sized suppliers, current contract relationships will remain the most practical for technical and economic reasons. The future supply chain design must take this fact into consideration by providing the mechanism to select the right sourcing approach for the right item segments and supplier types.

For cases in which more sophisticated, longer-term supplier relationships are appropriate, several relationship strategies that have evolved in the commercial sector have significant potential for DoD supply chains. In 1995, J. M. Schmitz, R. Frankel, and D. J. Frayer published a report for the Grocery Manufacturers Association that may provide a basic roadmap for the SCM team to explore its supplier relationship strategy.[11] Their general model has several levels. Within each level, managers must consider strategic and operational issues that coincide with each step of development.

- ◆ *Level One—Alliance conceptualization* begins when an organization determines that a collaborative arrangement has appeal and provides a potential alternative to the current arrangement. This level involves significant joint planning to determine what the "ideal strategic alliance" would be in an "ideal world" and then project what a more "realistic" alliance might be.

- ◆ *Level Two—Alliance pursuance* occurs when the decision to form an alliance is finalized, and the organization establishes strategic and operational considerations that will be used to select the alliance partner.

- ◆ *Level Three—Alliance confirmation* focuses on partner selection and confirmation. Managers determine strategic and operational expectations for the arrangement through joint meetings with the alliance partner, and the relationship is solidified.

- ◆ *Level Four—Alliance implementation/continuity* creates a feedback mechanism to administer and assess performance continually to determine whether the alliance will be sustained, modified, or terminated. If a conflict occurs, the firm may need to explore different types of conflict-resolution mechanisms.

---

[11] J. M. Schmitz, R. Frankel, and D. J. Frayer, *Efficient Customer Response Alliances: A Best Practice Model*, Washington, D.C.: Grocery Manufacturers Association, 1995.

Alliances between DoD activities and private-sector logistics providers generally take one of the following three forms:

◆ *Exchange*. Relationships that involve notifying a trading partner of a business event (e.g., purchase orders/contracts, invoices, or payments).

◆ *Collaboration*. Relationships that involve working with several business partners to jointly solve business problems. These relationships include collaborative planning for supply, maintenance, transportation, and related services.

◆ *Integration*. Relationships that link the organization's business processes into an extended enterprise.

Today, the vast majority of DoD—private-sector sourcing relationships fall into the first category. The SCM team should use the conceptual alliance development approach as a general roadmap to develop the organization's strategy for selectively building and managing long-term supplier relationships. As the discussion of SPS suggests, for selected categories of items the supply chain-oriented organization may wish to transition from the traditional exchange relationship to the collaborative or even integrated type of partnerships. In the private sector, a more structured process—collaborative planning, forecasting, and replenishment (CPFR)—has been developed to provide guidelines and methods to build these more mutually productive partnership arrangements. The SCM implementation team should adapt the CPFR process as a principal strategy tool for improving supplier and service provider relationships. Use of the CPFR approach will assist the organization in building alliances required to transition these relationships from the current exchange level to appropriate collaborative and integrated status. CPFR also provides a framework for identifying and executing requirements for information-sharing among supply chain partners.

The CPFR process consists of five basic steps:

◆ *Developing a front-end agreement*—Establishing measures that will be used to track progress toward success criteria

◆ *Concluding a joint business plan*—Documenting actions to be accomplished by DoD and each trading partner

◆ *Demanding forecast collaboration*—Establishing processes to share customer demand forecast information and supplier production/ delivery projections

◆ *Ordering forecast collaboration*—Sharing plans and related information on planned future orders

◆ *Ordering generation and delivery execution*—Building the most effective capability to process orders, track deliveries, and resolve forecast accuracy and inventory stockage issues.

These steps are only a high-level perspective of CPFR. As a point of departure, the SCM team should obtain more detailed information regarding implementation of CPFR. A good starting place is the Web site of the Collaborative Planning, Forecasting and Replenishment Committee of the Voluntary Interindustry Commerce Standards Association, http://www.cpfr.org/. This site provides substantial information resources for implementing the CPFR approach.

By using the CPFR methodology, the SCM team should be able to determine categories of information and, ultimately, specific data elements required to establish effective supply chain partnerships with material and service providers. Some basic types of information to be shared include the following:

◆ Historical, actual, and forecast customer demands

◆ Supplier production and delivery capabilities

◆ Pricing information

◆ Technical data

◆ Forecast accuracy and support issues

◆ Government and commercial inventories

- Repair capacity and schedules

- Planned future orders

- Production/delivery lead-times

- Transportation capacity and channels

- Tracking of orders and material deliveries.

As part of the CPFR strategy, the SCM team should develop an information-sharing template to be included in alliance agreements with private-sector suppliers and with government supply chain providers, such as maintenance activities and military transportation carriers. By preparing a basic set of information requirements for data exchange with supply chain partners, the team will be better able to assess and obtain the most effective technologies to implement required information sharing among supply chain participants.

## Strategy 3 Actions

*Action 1*—Develop an internal strategy between the logistics and procurement organizations to identify opportunities and ground rules for long-term supplier relationships. Use CPFR as a baseline concept for this strategy.

*Action 2*—Assess and segment items managed by the organization, and develop logical groupings on the basis of item characteristics.

*Action 3*—Document the range of capabilities of current material and service providers and assess the feasibility of establishing partnership alliances, especially with key providers.

*Action 4*—Develop an information-sharing template that includes criteria, data elements, and mechanisms for information-sharing with supply chain partners.

*Action 5*—Develop several pilot partnerships with key commercial suppliers to formulate operating procedures.

# Strategy 4. Determine Customer Expectations

So much has been written about customer-focused supply chains that the idea that a successful supply chain is one that satisfies the collective and individual needs of its customers has become a cliché. The SCM implementation team must go deeper and address several corollary issues that derive from the obvious basic requirement to satisfy the customer. The team strategy should provide the means to answer the following questions:

◆ Who are the DoD supply chain customers?

◆ What are their requirements?

◆ How will overall customer satisfaction be measured in future DoD supply chains?

Let's begin with identifying our supply chain customers. Because DoD is a hierarchical organization with numerous layers, defining the DoD "customer" sometimes is confusing. In the private sector, customers are nearly always organizationally separate from the logistics providers. Therefore, customers are relatively easy to identify. Moreover, private-sector customers generally operate independently from their sources of logistics support. Conversely, in DoD, the operational customers of the military logistics process are part of the same overall organization with the same national security objectives. Furthermore, DoD operational customers, in practice, have limited choices in selecting logistics support providers. The DoD supply chain is a relatively "closed-loop" system in which customers rely on pre-selected sources of support, whether these are government or commercial organizations. At the same time, the DoD supply chain *must* support *all* military customers. Therefore, from the military customer perspective, market forces such as competition have little near-term impact. Despite being "captive" customers, however, operational military forces are becoming more knowledgeable in their perspective of the value added and cost of the supply chain and more demanding regarding the accuracy, timeliness, and quality of service they expect.

Because the DoD supply chain ultimately must satisfy 100 percent of all valid customer orders, the SCM team should have a comprehensive and specific definition of the term *customer*. Let's start with the following definition:

> A DoD supply chain customer is any activity (organization) that is authorized to order material or related logistics services from/through the supply chain.

This definition takes into account organizations that are end-use customers (e.g., actual military operational units) *and* organizations that may order material to be consumed as part of a supply chain function that ultimately is a provider of material or services to military operational units (e.g., depot maintenance, motor pools, repair ships). Once the SCM team has accepted this definition of a supply chain customer, the next step is to identify factors that differentiate customers so that supply chain delivery requirements can be differentiated. In the private sector, this categorization of customers is called segmentation. For the purposes of the future DoD supply chain design, required delivery time is the most important customer segmentation factor.

In an annual online survey of SCM benchmarks, the Performance Measurement Group (a subsidiary of Pittiglio Rabin Todd & McGrath) found that

> companies operating at the level of best-in-class delivery performance are meeting the customer request date at least 94 percent of the time. In some industries, best-in-class delivery performance to request (DPTR) approaches 100 percent compared with the median, ranging between 69 percent and 81 percent. DPTR levels for best-in-class performance have remained essentially unchanged since 1995. Surprisingly, a large number of companies do not track performance against customer request date, and many track performance against their contractual commitment to customers, rather than the customer's actual request. Yet the most fundamental measure of customer satisfaction is the frequency with which companies can meet request dates. This measure shows how well a supply chain is configured to meet customer expectations.[12]

Other corollary factors are priority of need, geographic location, material cost, quantities needed, item technical characteristics, organizational relationships, and types of weapons/equipment supported. In building the DoD supply chain design, however, the delivery time factor generally is built on these related elements. Obviously, short delivery times may require priority or expedited processing. Longer delivery times allow supply chain participants to make more optimum inventory, repair, transportation, and

---

[12] Performance Measurement Group, "Survey: Top Performers Cut SCM Costs to 4% of Sales," *Modern Distribution Management*, August 25, 1999.

sourcing trade-offs. With customer delivery time as the primary segmentation factor, all elements of the supply chain process can be made aware of and focus on meeting customer requirements. Of course, satisfying a customer-driven delivery schedule is not the only component of customer satisfaction.

In Chapter 3 we briefly discuss the seven R's of customer satisfaction:[13]

- ◆ The Right product

- ◆ Delivered to the Right place

- ◆ In the Right condition and packaging

- ◆ In the Right quantity

- ◆ At the Right cost

- ◆ To the Right customer

- ◆ At the Right time.

To achieve customer satisfaction, the integrated supply chain must consistently provide all seven factors close to 100 percent of the time. The design of the future supply chain must clearly delineate each supply chain participant's actions and responsibilities for achieving target performance in each of the seven areas. We suggest using factor 7, however, to differentiate effective use of supply chain resources on an order-by-order basis. Thus, the supply chain must be designed to meet factors 1 through 6 *every* time for *every* customer order. By using factor 7—"Right time"—as the principal segmentation factor, supply chain participants have an element of flexibility that permits them to "trade off" the use of scarce resources. For example, supply chain participants can achieve maximum customer satisfaction by delivering orders requested in 5 days in *that* period of time or by delivering orders requested in 30 days in *that* period of time. By matching actual supply chain delivery performance to specific customer-driven requirements, the foundation of customer confidence in the streamlined process can be improved.

As the SCM team works to build the integrated supply chain design to enable customer satisfaction, it should give equal attention to satisfying the

---

[13] Kuglin, *Customer-Centered Supply Chain Management*, p. 72.

customer's supply chain information requirements. A decade ago, the events of the Persian Gulf War highlighted the critical place of logistics support in achieving military victory. One of the deficiencies clearly identified in that conflict was the need for dramatically improved material asset visibility. In the early 1990s, the term *total asset visibility* (TAV) was coined to refer to the availability of information regarding quantity, location, condition, and other factors for material inventories. Efforts to achieve TAV in DoD are continuing—with mixed results.

In the context of SCM, however, the military customers' requirement for information goes significantly beyond the scope originally envisioned under the TAV initiative. Under SCM, the traditional role of the customer—as a passive participant in the logistics process—should be transitioned into a more partner-like role. Under the current logistics process, information exchange between logistics providers and customers follows the "I order, I receive, I pay" model. Under SCM, customers are increasingly vocal and sophisticated in their demands. More and more, issues such as requirements validation, delivery times, inventory stockage rules, material returns, and prices are subject to negotiation among customers and providers. Furthermore, in addition to visibility of assets, customers desire information that will permit optimal use of logistics resources, greater mobility of logistics deployment and sustainment capability, and coordination of common-user and cross-organization logistics support.

Recently, as part of the development of the focused logistics concept, the Joint Staff has developed a series of desired operational capabilities (DOCs). A DOC is a concept-based statement of the operational capabilities required to satisfy a Joint Force Commander's needs in 2010 and beyond to meet 21st century challenges. Table 5-2 lists current SCM logistics-related DOCs that have been developed and validated by the Joint Staff, military services, DoD agencies, and CINCs.

*Table 5-2. Focused Logistics Desired Operational Capabilities*

| No. | DOC | Description |
|---|---|---|
| FL-01 | Provide unimpeded access to operational and logistics information for all who need it. | Provides an operating architecture that allows any user access to operational and logistics data worldwide. |
| FL-04 | Provide timely and accurate enhanced asset visibility, control, and management. | Provides a fully synchronized means to collect and access continuous real-time information on the location, movement, status, and identity of units, personnel, equipment, and supplies; includes the ability to act on that information. |
| FL-05 | Provide fully enabled mobility system to optimize rapid joint force projection, delivery, and hand-off of forces and sustainment assets worldwide. | Provides a fully integrated process to deploy forces and sustainment worldwide. |
| FL-06 | Deploy and distribute required forces and sustainment at the place and time required. | Provides assets to deploy and distribute forces and sustainment worldwide. Includes airlift and sealift assets, afloat pre-positioning assets, and enroute support. |
| FL-07 | Support rapid force maneuver within the joint operations area. | Provides a fully integrated capability to sustain and support maneuver in the battlespace. |
| FL-17 | Provide effective, efficient, and responsive infrastructure and logistics support to meet CINC/warfighter operational requirements. | Provides, maintains, and coordinates optimum levels of logistics forces, materials, and consumables to sustain forces in the execution of theater strategy and joint operations. |
| FL-20 | Provide capability to synchronize, prioritize, direct, integrate, and coordinate common user and cross-Service logistics functions. | Coordinates logistics support to sustain the force in the execution of theater strategy, campaigns, and joint operations. |
| FL-35 | Optimize logistical operations across and between all echelons, coalitions, and host nations. | Provides sustainment support from sources other than the U.S. military. |

In developing its strategy for implementation, the SCM team should fully take into account the operational customer's logistics information requirements. A customer-driven supply chain must consistently satisfy the customer's information needs as well as material and service needs. A more detailed description of these requirements is included at Appendix B. More updated information on focused logistics is available at the Joint Chiefs of Staff Web site: http://www.dtic.mil/jcs/j4/index.html.

In designing the supply chain, the SCM team must take into account the delivery requirements (the seven R's) and customer information needs (focused logistics DOCs). Additional functional design requirements that are peculiar to the organization should be added to these general needs. Together with internal process information exchange needs, these requirements become a substantial basis for satisfying the customer service performance and information-sharing capabilities of the supply chain.

In the private sector, logistics managers have found that customers may be viewed as a monolithic entity (i.e., "all customers are alike"), or customers may be divided into groupings, based on distinctions such as geographic location, type of weapon system/equipment supported, organizational priority, or other factors. An effective DoD supply chain mandates customer segmentation. Through creative segmentation, supply chain organizations can find new ways to identify the right mix of capabilities to consistently assure customer satisfaction. Customer segmentation by group characteristics enables the DoD supply chain to deliver tailored support on the basis of immediate customer needs, using the right combination of capabilities that already are built into the overall supply chain process. The SCM team should take the lead in defining segmentation categories and placing customers into meaningful groups.

For the foreseeable future, DoD supply chain activities will continue to use a variety of support strategies to support military customers. Customer segmentation also helps to identify and manage an effective range of these strategies. Support strategies range from traditional methods to recent innovations, including stocking inventories at government facilities, prepositioning inventory at or near operating sites, choosing alternative transportation modes, using direct vendor deliveries, employing contractor logistics support, and using vendor-managed inventories. In the future supply chain, material delivery strategies will combine with sourcing strategies to provide optimal customer support. Success is measured by using supply chain-oriented management performance and cost measures.

Finally, satisfying customer expectations goes well beyond processing and delivery of material orders and services. In the supply chain concept, customer satisfaction must incorporate the concept of *customer value*.[14] Customer value refers to the way the logistics provider is perceived by the customer. It goes further than concentration on satisfying current customer orders. Today's DoD logistics process is characterized by significant redundancies of inventory, systems, and facilities. Most of these redundancies were put in place because of a wide-ranging lack of confidence in the ability of the DoD system to meet customer needs. Even the logistics providers themselves often do not have full confidence in their own process. The three principal elements of customer value are

◆ consistently meeting customer needs as expressed in the seven R's,

◆ providing responsive customer support when demand for material or services exceeds supply, and

◆ maintaining a two-way exchange of accurate and current status information between providers and customers.

Managing large numbers of high-demand variability items—typical of DoD—suggests a particular requirement to focus the supply chain on building and maintaining a customer value perspective. World-class private-sector supply chain managers have determined that the customer value approach permits significant reduction of process, inventory, service, and facilities across the total supply chain. In Chapter 6 we discuss in greater detail the implementation of specific performance metrics that enable the total supply chain to consistently attain the customer's required delivery times and contribute to an increased perception of customer value.

## Strategy 4 Actions

*Action 1*—Define and identify actual supply chain customers by individual organizations or logical, homogeneous groupings.

*Action 2*—Develop and document elements of customer satisfaction to be incorporated into the supply chain design process.

---

[14] David Simchi-Levi, et al., *Designing and Managing the Supply Chain,* Boston, MA: Irwin, Magraw, Hill, , 2000, p. 200.

*Action 3*—Document provider/customer information exchange requirements.

*Action 4*—Develop criteria for customer segmentation and apply to organizational customers or customer groupings.

## Strategy 5. Define/Redefine the To-Be Supply Chain

In recent years, the approach DoD has followed to accomplish process engineering and reengineering has involved starting with the development of a model of the current process (way of doing business), with the idea of formulating a plan to "migrate" to the future to-be process. In many cases, this approach resulted in the expenditure of significant time and resources to document the current process. To accelerate the transition to the future SCM environment, we suggest that the SCM team focus on building the to-be process model first. An operational node connectivity diagram is a good convention for this model. Later, this model of the future end state may be selectively validated and redefined against current processes and desired performance goals. The SCM team should remember that the objective of the supply chain design is to attain customer satisfaction, not preserve current functions. This premise will help guide the design effort and minimize the natural tendency to duplicate current process steps and activities. Consistency in documentation at this stage of the design process will pay dividends later, in the approval and redesign stages. The team should use the process flow diagram tool we suggest in Chapter 4 to produce the operational node connectivity diagram and subsequent, more detailed, graphic descriptions as needed.

The design of the future supply chain process model is not a freeform exercise. Even the most cutting-edge, world-class private-sector logistics providers include certain basic capabilities in their processes. The fundamental functions of logistics will continue to be important elements of the future supply chain process. DoD supply chains will continue to accomplish functions such as cataloging, technical data management, requirements determination, asset management, warehousing, maintenance, order processing and delivery, material returns, and disposal. The way these processes are performed, how they are integrated, and, in some cases, who performs them will change. In addition, the measures of success will be significantly different.

Documentation of the future supply chain design is extremely important. In Chapter 3, we outline a six-step SCM implementation approach. Step four is the supply chain design. The implementation team should prepare the high-level concept graphic as quickly as possible and begin work on the operational node connectivity description. By spending sufficient time and resources on these graphical representations of the supply chain, the SCM team will build the foundation for documenting the transformation of the current DoD logistics process into a true supply chain. In Chapter 6 we go into greater detail on procedures and tools that are available to construct supply chain descriptive documents. We also discuss the concept of creating customer value through innovation. Innovative thinking is a critical ingredient of the successful future supply chain design. This process involves devising new ways of accomplishing the functions of logistics in a supply chain environment. The SCM implementation team will derive these new approaches primarily from their assessments of how supply chain metrics and best business practices can be applied in DoD. Figure 5-5 summarizes the steps for completing the initial supply chain to-be design products.

*Figure 5-5. Supply Chain To-Be Design*

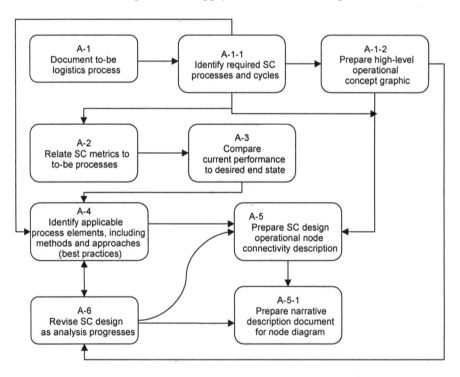

The SCM implementation team should prepare graphic representations of the future supply chain design by completing the steps in Figure 5-5. Although some concurrent action may be possible, we recommend the following general approach:

- ◆ At a relatively high level, document functional activities to be included in the supply chain design. These activities generally are referred to as process elements.

- ◆ Using the documentation of basic process elements of the supply chain, create the high-level operational concept graphic.

- ◆ Complete the identification and descriptions of supply chain performance and cost metrics. Using the process element documentation, cross-reference these metrics to specific elements or element groupings.

- ◆ Document a baseline of actual data to quantify the selected supply chain metrics.

- ◆ Perform "gap" analysis to document differences between the performance of the current process and desired performance goals.

- ◆ Using the documentation of basic supply chain process elements, identify potentially applicable business practice improvements.

- ◆ Prepare the overall initial operational node connectivity diagram to document the end-to-end future supply chain process. Include narrative descriptions.

- ◆ On a continuing basis, revise the operational node connectivity diagram to reflect further refinement of process relationships and application of additional business process improvements.

The operational node connectivity diagram represents the heart of the SCM implementation strategy. It provides the means for documenting the supply chain design and presenting supply chain requirements for approval and implementation. In Chapter 6, we provide more detail regarding the use of the operational node connectivity diagram and selection of implementing processes and enabling technologies.

## Strategy 5 Actions

*Action 1*—Complete the future supply chain functional process element list.

*Action 2*—Prepare the high-level concept graphic.

*Action 3*—Document performance metrics relationships with supply chain functions. Quantify metrics for current process and desired end-state.

*Action 4*—Document/assess applicable initial process improvements (best practices).

*Action 5*—Prepare initial operational node connectivity diagram with narrative descriptions.

*Action 6*—Continually revise connectivity diagram and supporting documentation as process develops.

## Strategy 6. Identify and Prioritize Initial Targets of Opportunity

In Chapter 4 we outline several initial areas of opportunity for the SCM implementation team to begin the transformation to the future SCM environment. The topics we suggest focus on actions that would be part of the building blocks for SCM implementation. As the team begins the future supply chain design process, it should identify any potential opportunities for early realization of improved customer satisfaction, more effective sourcing, shortened cycle times, reduced inventories, or operational savings. In most organizations—including DoD—in the long term, implementation of efficiencies should fund the change process. Furthermore, because implementation of all desired changes may take several years, transformation initiatives need early successes to help maintain management's interest and support. The SCM team is most likely to identify opportunities for early payback during supply chain training sessions, supply chain metric development, and review efforts to identify applicable best practices. During these actions, the team should make a concerted effort to identify specific process improvements or cost benefits that might be implemented in the near term. It is especially important that such initial target areas

♦   are consistent with long-range SCM implementation objectives;

◆ have quantifiable costs and benefits and are cost-effective;

◆ have support from management, supply chain participants, and customers;

◆ are technically and practically feasible;

◆ are measurable in terms of performance improvement or cost savings; and

◆ can be implemented in the near term (i.e., within 6–12 months).

Generally, no more than four to five major near-term SCM initiatives should be active at any one time. Furthermore, these initiatives should be prioritized in terms of initial cost, length of payback period, and degree of difficulty. Obviously, the quicker the near-term initiative benefits can be achieved, the greater the quantitative value and the impact on continued management commitment. Successful supply chain managers often use viable near-term initiatives for leverage to influence and focus ongoing business process reengineering programs or systems modernization efforts on SCM requirements.

A final word on near-term initiatives—the SCM team should pursue such initiatives only in the context of overall SCM program objectives. In some instances, the inherent appeal of "fads" and new technology can be intoxicating. Do not let a near-term initiative become a program in and of itself. By definition, these efforts must fit clearly into the longer-term, comprehensive implementation process. To avoid such pitfalls, a sunset date for "stand-alone" near-term initiatives may be set to terminate the separate activity or integrate the action into the larger process.

## Strategy 6 Actions

*Action 1*—Conduct research to identify and select initial near-term initiatives.

*Action 2*—Prepare a high-level cost-benefit assessment of potential actions.

*Action 3*—Take action to obtain management approval of individual initiatives. Obtain implementation resources.

*Action 4*—Initiate implementation of approved near-term initiatives.

*Action 5*—Ensure integration of near-term initiatives into overall SCM program.

*Action 6*—Ensure documentation of initiative results and lessons learned.

## Strategy 7. Leverage Ongoing Business Process Reengineering and Systems Modernization Initiatives

> The only way that integrated supply chain strategies will be made to work is through the use of the correct people and correct investment, and risk taking. These cost dearly.[15]

The first six elements of the SCM implementation strategy can be accomplished unilaterally to a large degree by the SCM team. These elements focus on defining and obtaining support for SCM implementation from management, supply chain partners, and customers. Strategy 7 includes development of the leadership role of the SCM team as the proponent of implementation of supply chain concepts and practices as part of organizational business process improvement and ADP systems modernization. In the private sector, high-level management officials often have direct authority (and corresponding funding approval) over functional and systems change programs. In DoD organizations, policy, functional proponents, and technical systems managers are more likely to be in separate organizations, reporting through different channels. Often, advocates of functional process modernization have ambiguous and tentative working relationships with those responsible for systems modernization. This situation makes the transition from development of functional improvements to their ultimate implementation in application systems a difficult process. The problem is made worse when the technical strategy is heavily dependent on the acquisition of commercial-off-the-shelf (COTS) software. In the worst-case scenario, COTS software sometimes is acquired even though the functional requirements of the DoD organization have not been clearly determined. In this case, the benefits of using COTS software may be overcome by the gap between the desired to-be functionality and the actual capabilities of the COTS product. The problem is exacerbated by lack of interoperability between COTS and government-unique applications and by incompatibilities between the products of different commercial vendors.

---

[15] Robert M. Monczka and James P. Morgan, "Competitive Supply Strategies for the 21st Century," *Purchasing*, January 13, 2000.

The SCM team must face these issues head-on in building relationships with other organizational players in the functional and systems modernization processes. In taking the leadership role in SCM implementation, the team must become the proponent of SCM-related changes and the de facto government integrator of SCM-related ongoing business process reengineering initiatives and organic/contractor-supported systems modernization projects. Often the SCM team can turn the lack or inadequacy of clearly defined functional requirements in large-scale ADP systems modernization projects to an advantage. The team should look for opportunities to partner (formally or informally) with government systems modernization offices and their supporting contractors, allowing the team to serve as the source of SCM functional expertise and future business requirements. The actions outlined in strategies 1–6 in this chapter are designed to facilitate this critical SCM team responsibility.

To execute this strategy, the SCM team should accomplish several management actions:

- Develop a compendium of current and planned business process and technical systems initiatives that have recognized or potential SCM-related implications (including significant commercial or other military service/Defense agency initiatives).

- Present a strategy proposal to high-level management to obtain approval and support of the SCM team's liaison role. Emphasize that the SCM team will represent management as the principal advocate of SCM implementation.

- Establish lines of communications with key participants in related initiatives.

- Ensure that potential functional and technical process improvement partners are informed of the goals, objectives, and plans of the SCM team. Develop formal or informal cooperative agreements, as appropriate.

The purpose of the foregoing actions is to enable the SCM team to leverage the resources and capabilities of ongoing efforts to promote implementation of SCM-related improvements. The SCM team is unlikely to receive authority, personnel, or funding resources—especially early in the team's life—to accomplish the full range of initiatives needed for SCM implementation on a broad scale. Therefore, the team must develop working relationships with activities that have sufficient resources to execute required supply chain implementation actions.

An important aspect of the SCM team's success in working with other process and systems change organizations is the quality and content of SCM requirements documentation. The team must spend sufficient time and resources on the high-level process description graphic and operational node connectivity diagram to ensure that implementation partners have a full understanding of future SCM design requirements. Furthermore, initial targets of opportunity identified by the SCM team may provide a starting point for interaction with other business process improvements and systems modernization initiatives. The SCM team also may participate in joint efforts with the business process or systems modernization organization to prepare high-level activity models of specific supply chain process segments. Activity model development is manpower intensive, however, so the SCM team should participate in such efforts only to the extent that these tools are needed to define and implement requirements for segments of the organization's supply chain. As part of strategy 8, we discuss several approaches to transitioning from SCM design requirements to actual implementation.

DoD prescribes activity models as part of the creation of an operational perspective view of a process architecture.[16] An activity model describes data and information exchanges within a process or between multiple processes. Models are hierarchical in nature; that is, they begin with a single box that represents the overall activity and proceed successively to decompose the activity to the level required by the purpose of the architecture. The activity model captures activities performed in a business process or mission and associated inputs, controls, outputs, and mechanisms. Mechanisms are resources that are involved in performance of an activity. In addition, the activity model identifies the mission domain and viewpoint reflected in the model. Activity definitions and business flows should be provided in additional text as needed. Annotations to the model may identify nodes where activities take place or costs (actual or estimated) associated with performing each activity. The activity model can capture valuable information about an architecture and promote the necessary common understanding of the subject area under examination. Care must be taken, however, to ensure that the modeling process is performed efficiently and usefully and that needed

---

[16] Assistant Secretary of Defense (Command, Control, Communications, and Intelligence [C3I]), *C4ISR Architectural Framework Version 2.0*, December 18, 1997. Additional information on DoD architectures and activity models is available at http://www.c3i.osd.mil/org/cio/i3/AWG_Digital_Library/index.htm.

information is captured without excessive layers of decomposition and without inclusion of extraneous information.

The SCM team should work closely with other activities that are responsible for business process improvements and systems modernization. In addition to these efforts, however, the team should explore the development of a small number of prototype initiatives to help demonstrate practical application of supply chain concepts and capabilities in a DoD working environment. Prototypes represent live, but controlled, pilots for future implementation. An organizational activity selected for running a prototype should be a key activity, with high visibility and motivated people. Remember that the purpose of a prototype is not to demonstrate new technologies but to help ensure the applicability of supply chain methods in a DoD context. Therefore, the SCM team should carefully select prototype functional areas to demonstrate how SCM can help attain target process improvements or cost reductions. In building a prototype strategy, the team should first identify segments of the supply chain design as demonstration areas. Examples could include the following:

- ◆ Source selection methodology

- ◆ Demand planning

- ◆ Maintenance planning and execution

- ◆ Order management

- ◆ Delivery execution and tracking

- ◆ Warehouse management

- ◆ Activity-based costing.

Smaller subsets of these areas often will be targeted for initial prototype efforts. In some cases, the team can construct prototype initiatives on the basis of further development of targets of opportunity identified as part of strategy 6. Adopting a continuous improvement approach to SCM helps to ensure constant refreshment of the supply chain process in support of customer requirements.

## Strategy 7 Actions

*Action 1*—Develop a compendium of ongoing business process improvement and systems modernization initiatives.

*Action 2*—Obtain management support and build partnerships with business process improvement and systems development organizations.

*Action 3*—Promote SCM implementation by participating in other organizations' efforts.

*Action 4*—Develop SCM prototype initiatives.

## Strategy 8. Select/Implement Process Change, Enabling Software and Technologies

Strategy 8 is where everything must come together. Selecting and putting in place required SCM elements is the most difficult, costly, and time-consuming aspect of SCM implementation. The SCM implementation process often tends to focus attention on computers, software, communications capabilities, and other technologies. In fact it is an exercise in change management, aimed squarely at the people involved in (and affected by) the implementation effort. Implementation of SCM in DoD requires no new technologies or radical breakthroughs in logistics procedures. Virtually all required process changes and supporting technologies are known and readily available in the commercial marketplace to accomplish a large-scale supply chain start-up.

The SCM implementation team must follow a structured approach to implement changes required for supply chain process improvement. In strategies 1–7, the team will develop tools to permit identification of required changes, focus change initiatives on key segments of and participants in the supply chain, design the future supply chain structure, identify initial and long-term targets of opportunity, and develop allies to facilitate implementation.

In strategy 8, the SCM team should complete the following actions:

◆ Use the supply chain performance/cost metric goals to select key supply chain target segments in the to-be connectivity node diagram for process improvement. Initially, segments should be selected on the basis of quantifiable, high-payback opportunities to improve performance or reduce costs. In the private sector, this approach is referred to as "establishing the basis of competition." Normally, customer-centered performance metrics are principal candidates for improvement efforts.

◆ Use gap analysis to set process improvement priorities and determine specific functions requiring change. Gap analysis involves evaluating opportunities for improvement in each significant target business segment on the operational connectivity node diagram by relating current performance to desired performance goals.

◆ For each target business segment, build a cross-reference matrix of required business practice improvements that can be expected to improve performance metrics. Some practices may involve multiple process segments.

◆ As the gap analysis is progressing, update the operational connectivity node diagram to reflect proposed changes to business practices.

◆ For each significant segment, prepare a requirements document that describes the updated supply-chain configuration, updated processes, and enabling practices.

The last stage of strategy 8 is for the SCM team to participate in selection of applications software and supporting technology capabilities required for SCM implementation. As we note in our discussion of strategy 7, this action may not necessarily be accomplished directly by the SCM team. Unfortunately, DoD has a tradition of separating functional organizations from technically oriented organizations. This schism developed during the days of mainframe computers, when physical isolation of ADP systems was required (primarily for reasons of cleanliness and environmental control). This separation also helped to perpetuate the mystique of computer analysts and programmers. Today, with personal computers, networks, and high-powered workstations, this partition is no longer actually required, but lives on, especially in the acquisition of applications software. In many DoD activities, the technical community has allied itself with the procurement office to retain control of the assessment and acquisition of functional applications software. In many cases, this approach—which tends to minimize or even eliminate the functional requirements development process—has contributed to numerous failed systems modernization efforts, involving billions of dollars.

The SCM implementation team must work diligently to overcome the burden of past modernization failures and organizational resistance to change. Effective and comprehensive documentation of SCM requirements is an essential element of success. The team also should take responsibility for reviewing the myriad commercially available software applications and cataloging these packages with regard to functional capabilities. By attaining a working knowledge of available software and supporting technologies, team members can be in a position to assist systems modernization personnel in matching the organization's requirements to commercially available software/technology.

In recent years, the dramatic reduction of government personnel in DoD has substantially reduced the organic capability for ADP systems design and implementation. In DoD logistics, there is virtually no significant organic workforce capable of taking on a large systems development and implementation initiative. At the same time, the proliferation of commercially available software and support technology has all but eliminated in-house development of proprietary software in major corporations. For the DoD logistics community, future logistics systems modernization probably will involve adaptation of commercial software packages and related technologies to satisfy logistics functional requirements. Fortunately, the quality of such software is increasing dramatically in functionality and effectiveness.

The task of SCM implementation in DoD logistics processes has become an effort to match the Department's wide range of support requirements to commercially available software and enabling technologies. The SCM implementation team should play a key role in this effort.

To date, no single software package or commercial suite of applications from a single provider comprehends the full range of supply chain functional requirements. Several providers are working on such packages and have made some progress. For the foreseeable future, the SCM team should expect that a comprehensive supply chain solution would require an integration of several software packages. A high-level discussion of supply chain management tools is included in Chapter 9.

In working with systems modernization organizations and personnel, the SCM team should be proactive in presenting and advocating required functional improvements that must be included in selected technical solutions. By completing the documentation products included in this strategy, the team will be in a position to help ensure that proposed software/technologies will substantially satisfy the functional needs of the organization and its customers.

As supply chain-oriented software developers have proliferated, a large cadre of consulting companies has developed, with varied capabilities to assist SCM teams in assessing requirements, devising business process solutions, and selecting implementation capabilities. The team usually will desire to augment its in-house staff with experienced consulting or integrating contract support, particularly to help accomplish functional requirements development, business practices review, and software package selection.

## Strategy 8 Actions

*Action 1*—Perform gap analysis to develop future supply chain design through a synergy of performance metrics, best business practices, and process analysis.

*Action 2*—Document a structured compilation of future supply chain business process improvement requirements.

*Action 3*—Participate in continuing assessment and selection of supply chain software and technical enablers.

The eight strategies outlined in this chapter are designed to guide the SCM team toward successful implementation of the SCM concept in a DoD environment. As the initiative moves forward, the team undoubtedly will find new and innovative approaches to pursue the objective and accelerate progress. In Chapter 6 we focus in greater detail on actions required to design a DoD-oriented supply chain process.

# Chapter 6
# Designing and Evaluating
# the DoD Supply Chain

To be successful, the SCM implementation team must create and document the future supply chain structure to capture the essential concepts of SCM in an integrated, end-to-end way. In preceding chapters we discuss several concepts, principles, and strategies to accomplish the design task. The SCM team should use these basic building blocks to construct more detailed descriptions of the future integrated supply chain process.

In creating the to-be supply chain design, the SCM implementation team's efforts will be constrained to some degree by existing organizational relationships, current practices and procedures, regulatory constraints, and cultural mores. Ignoring these constraints completely and still expecting "buy in" from management, supply chain participants, and customers is not practical. The challenge for the team is to recognize things that simply will not change and work around these impediments. Fortunately, very little of the DoD logistics process design is directly grounded in law. The current DoD logistics process was put in place to provide logistics support for operational forces during the Cold War period. The process was developed in an evolutionary and fragmented manner. Current rules and procedures were adopted principally to meet specific problems or to facilitate operation of specific functions.

The SCM team can take advantage of the fact that customer support remains the primary objective of the logistics process, as it always has been. Furthermore, modern SCM does not eliminate fundamental functions such as cataloging, supply, maintenance, warehousing, transportation, or distribution; it accomplishes these basic logistics processes in more streamlined, integrated, faster, and less costly ways. Therefore, implementing SCM in DoD does not involve elimination of the current process in its entirety. The SCM team must ensure that management, supply chain participants, and customers understand that the "radical reengineering" or "start over" philosophy[1] that was popular in the early 1990s is not applicable to the supply chain implementation initiative in DoD. Nevertheless, significant changes in the way DoD activities do their business are required. In fact, substantial changes must occur

---

[1] Michael Hammer and James Champy, *Reengineering the Corporation,* New York: Harper Business, 1993), p. 49.

rapidly. The good news is that tools to assess and document supply chain requirements and mechanisms to accomplish implementation of required changes have proliferated and improved dramatically in the past decade.

To a large degree, implementation of SCM in DoD is a matter of determining basic performance and process requirements and matching them to enabling procedural and technological solutions. As always, "The devil is in the details."

The challenge for the SCM team is to adapt supply chain concepts developed by the private sector to meet DoD requirements. Once supply chain requirements are adequately documented, the team should participate in the selection of the range of specific solutions required to effect the transition to modern SCM.

## Document Supply Chain Design Requirements

As we outline in Chapter 3, the SCM team should prepare graphical representations of the future supply chain in the form of high-level operational concept graphics and operational node connectivity diagrams. These documents are essential to illustrate the end-to-end scope and key functional components of the DoD supply chain process. The SCM team also must be highly focused on the supply chain principles described in Chapter 2, as well as characteristics identified during the team's assessment of desired performance/cost metrics and customer/supplier segmentation. Once the high-level process description documents are completed, the SCM team should begin the analytical "drill-down" effort that will lead to the selection and implementation of the elements of the supply chain solution.

Many analytical tools are available to assist the SCM team in physically constructing the supply chain design. Several companies in the private sector have begun to migrate toward the SCOR model developed and advocated by the Supply Chain Council. The SCOR model is characterized as a process reference model in Supply Chain Council literature. A process reference model integrates the concepts of business process reengineering, benchmarking, and process measurement into a structured approach. The analytical process recommended by the SCOR model consists of three basic steps:[2]

1.  Capture the as-is state and derive the desired to-be future state.

2.  Quantify the operational performance of similar organizations and establish internal targets on the basis of "best-of-class" results.

3.  Characterize and implement management practices and software solutions that result in best-of-class performance.

An important value of the SCOR approach is the building of cause-and-effect relationships between desired performance metrics, process activities, and applicable best practices/technologies. The SCOR methodology prescribes an analysis process that entails identification of quantifiable improvement goals, selection of specific functional elements where problems occur or improvement is required, and application of known business process improvements that can effect the required impact on supply chain measures of success. Using the SCOR model and its corresponding analytical methodology as part of the implementation approach would enable the SCM team to[3]

♦   communicate with current and potential vendors, using common terminology and standard descriptions;

♦   use the model as a planning and forecasting tool;

♦   leverage metrics and benchmarking to determine performance goals, set priorities, and quantify the benefits of a process change;

♦   link functional and process metrics to enterprise performance in a structured way;

♦   understand and select the best practices to obtain the best performance;

---

[2] The SCOR model has been developed and endorsed by the Supply-Chain Council (SCC), an independent not-for-profit corporation, as the cross-industry standard for SCM.

[3] Klapper et. al., *DoD Supply Chain Management: A Recommended Performance Measurement Scorecard,* March 1999, pp. 3–4.

◆　understand SCM and performance evaluation; and

◆　help to identify software tools that are best suited for DoD processes.

Appendix D contains more detailed information regarding the SCOR methodology.

We strongly recommend that all members of the SCM team receive training on the SCOR model and methodology as provided by the Supply Chain Council or affiliated organizations. This training provides an excellent basis for understanding supply chain concepts, and would provide the team with experience in performing analysis of their supply chains.

Although the SCOR methodology is not the only approach to supply chain implementation, it is increasingly becoming an industry standard. SCOR also is a good example of a structured and disciplined approach to supply chain implementation. Because the SCOR model has evolved into a de facto industry standard for development of supply chain process models, the SCM team may wish to explore the use of automated tools to assist in constructing a SCOR-type process model as a complementary supplement to the operational node connectivity diagram. These two documents, used together, help to construct a picture of the future supply chain process that captures the streamlined private-sector perspective of a supply chain as well as DoD-oriented supply chain process elements.

New products have emerged recently that can be useful in preparing an automated version of the SCOR model. One of these new products, E-SCOR, is a good example of a personal computer (PC)-based tool for designing and continuously updating the organization's SCOR process model.[4] Other products for facilitating the SCOR development also are commercially available. Although we recommend SCOR as a tool for use by DoD SCM teams, it has several characteristics that may limit its application as the primary analytical tool. The SCOR model does not encompass all process elements that normally are included in DoD logistics models. For example, SCOR does not cover configuration management or the material repair activity, although the Supply Chain Council is working to incorporate material repair in the model. In addition, SCOR uses generic process elements in describing supply chain activities (e.g., "Establish sourcing plans" or "Identify delivery resources") to

---

[4] E-SCOR is a software product of Gensym Corporation. This reference is not a DoD endorsement of this specific product.

describe supply chain activities. Although these terms are applicable to DoD, the team may wish to describe DoD supply chain process elements in greater detail by using DoD terminology, particularly in developing the operational connectivity node diagrams. The SCM team should determine early in its analysis when and where to use the structured SCOR methodology as part of its assessment of future supply chain requirements. In Chapter 9, we discuss some technology enablers that are available for analyzing and managing supply chains.

Development of the future supply chain design is an iterative process that requires the team to decompose the total supply chain perspective into workable segments for purposes of assessment of performance metrics, process element improvement targets, and best practices application. DoD supply chains are much too complex to be analyzed in their totality. Successful supply chain analysis will capture the overall perspective of the supply chain, then move to progressively lower levels of detail. To begin, team members should focus on key desired metrics and selective process elements as initial targets for improvement. The supply chain design effort should incorporate the following basic steps:

1.  At a relatively high level, the SCM team should identify and document functional activities to be included in the supply chain design. These activities generally are referred to as process elements. A good method is to begin with delivery of materiel and services to the supply chain customer(s) and build the chain backward to the sourcing process. To assist in identifying all applicable process elements, the team may wish to start with available as-is documentation, in the form of existing process models developed as part of previous process improvement initiatives. Appendix C contains an example of a high-level hierarchical process element list. Using available documentation of basic process elements of the organization's supply chain(s), the team should first create the high-level operational concept graphic. Figure 6-1 depicts an example of an overall operational concept graphic for DoD supply chains.

    The concept graphic should portray an integrated, end-to-end perspective of the supply chain. This view helps the SCM team, management, and supply chain customers to focus change efforts on the critical requirement to improve customer support, as well as the role of individual functions and organizations as part of the total enterprise. SCM team members should create their own view of the organization's supply chain at a similar level of detail. This document will provide the framework for building more detailed descriptions of the future supply chain. It also provides a useful tool to explain and promote the supply chain concept to management, suppliers, and customers. The SCOR process suggests using a geographic representation of each supply chain (as shown in Appendix D).

2.  Except for a highly specialized DoD organization, the SCM team will need to identify and document the organization's separate supply chain designs, based on differences in performance requirements and support processes for different weapon systems, commodity groups, categories of suppliers, product technical characteristics, customer performance requirements, or other logical groupings. The results of the team's effort to segment suppliers and customers should be used to separate and document organizational supply chains into groups with similar characteristics. This process will help the team identify supply chains with different processing and performance characteristics. As a general rule, no more than four to six different supply chains are required.

3.  The SCM team should prepare the overall initial operational node connectivity diagram to document the process elements of the end-to-end future supply chain process. To the extent possible, this initial diagram should be constructed to take into account known business process improvements and attainment of improved performance metrics (e.g., elimination of redundant or unneeded steps to help minimize cycle times.) Figure 6-2 is a simplified example of a supply chain-oriented connectivity node diagram.

## Figure 6-1. DoD Supply Chain High-Level Operational View Graphic (OV-1)

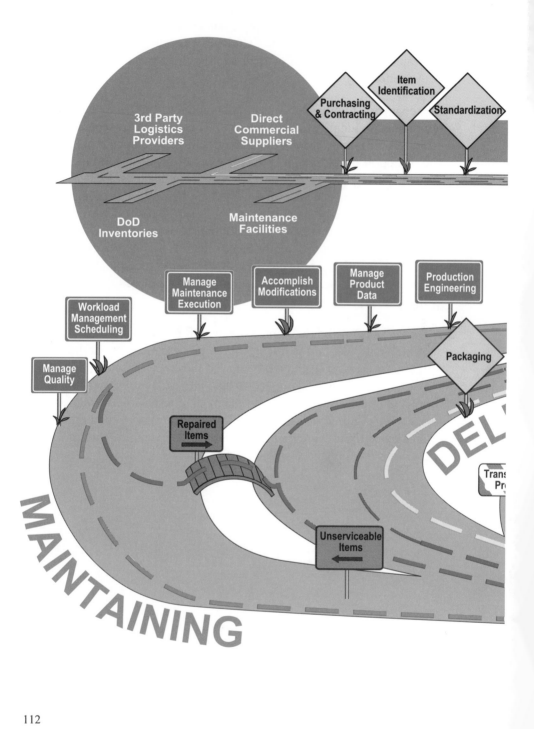

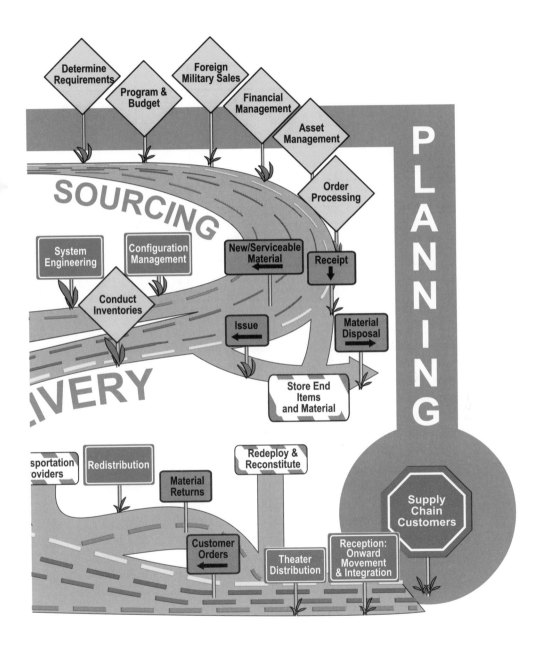

*Figure 6-2. DoD Supply Chain Operational Connectivity Node Diagram
(Example)*

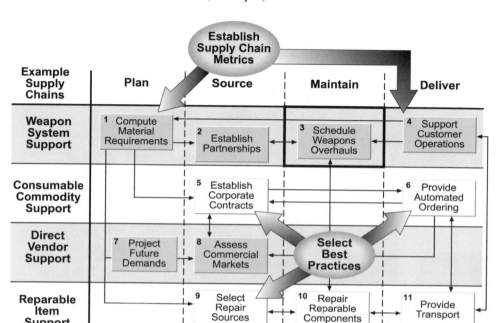

Operational node connectivity diagrams are used to document the end-to-end supply chain for each group segmented in step 2. This graphic approach helps to scope the total supply chain and to decompose each chain into logical segments for selection of applicable performance metrics and enabling best practices. Figure 6-2 also shows how metric selection and process improvement applications are related to nodes of the supply chain process. The team may wish to prepare a consolidated diagram that shows all supply chains and then prepare individual chain diagrams as required to capture lower levels of detail. This action will help the team identify and construct each of the organization's separate, distinct supply chain paths. It is also a useful convention for developing a numbering scheme to identify and reference specific nodes on the diagram. This diagram should include all process elements required to execute each chain. Node diagrams should be updated as improved business practices are adopted to modify or re-sequence node relationships and to eliminate redundant or unneeded process elements.

4.  A narrative description should accompany each significant process element of the connectivity diagram to document activities, process metric relationships, and potential applications of business practice improvements as they are identified.

5.  The team should complete the identification and description of supply chain performance and cost metrics for each major segment in the operational node connectivity diagram. The team should cross-reference these metrics to specific elements or element groupings (nodes), as shown in the operational node connectivity diagram. For example, a "perfect order fulfillment" metric relates to processing of orders and delivery cycles. In some cases, supporting metrics should be developed at lower levels of process detail.

6.  The SCM team should document a baseline of current actual data that quantifies the supply chain metrics it selects. The team should establish initial future performance targets for each metric. The team should conduct gap analysis and benchmarking to document differences between the performance of the current process and desired performance goals.

7.  Using the operational connectivity node diagram, for each major supply chain segment the SCM team should identify and assess selected business practices that will result in improved process performance/cost metrics. For each process metric, the team should develop an entry in the initial cross-reference matrix (step 5) for selected business improvements against each process element or logical grouping of elements. The SCM team should prioritize its analysis efforts to focus initially on key performance metrics and related process elements or groupings. (An analytical process for selecting applicable business practice improvements is discussed later in this chapter.) Table 6-1 is an example of a cross-reference matrix.

*Table 6-1. Metrics, Process Element, Process Improvements Matrix*

| Metric | Process element | Process improvement |
|---|---|---|
| Supply chain response time | Perform buy decision | Use online catalogs |
| | Perform buy decision | Share demand information with vendors |
| Perfect order fulfillment | Prepare shipping documents | Produce advance shipping notices automatically |

Documentation of change requirements inherent in SCM is absolutely essential to successful implementation in any large organization. Based on steps 1–7, the SCM team should begin to prepare a comprehensive reference document that describes the organization's future SCM design requirements. Ultimately, all supply chain metrics and related process elements in the future supply chain design should be covered in this reference document. This product becomes a "living" document that helps assess progress against milestones and acts as a roadmap for future action. At a minimum this document will include the following items:

◆ The organization's SCM principles of operation

◆ A high-level operational concept graphic

◆ Operational node connectivity diagram(s) with explanatory narratives

◆ Performance/cost metrics descriptions with actual/desired quantification

◆ Documentation of applicable business process improvements

◆ A matrix of process elements/metrics/business practice improvements.

The actions outlined above are intended to suggest a basic plan of action for the SCM implementation team to develop and document the future supply chain design. However, the SCM team will want to tailor its action plan to the specific needs, resource availability, and timetable of its own organization. Redesign of complex supply chains such as those in DoD is a long-term effort. The SCM team cannot possibly address all elements of the supply chain process or large numbers of business process improvements simultane-ously. Once the initial principles, high-level graphics, and initial operational node connectivity diagrams are completed and approved by management, the team must carefully assess and prioritize its focus for future actions on high-visibility or high-pay-back areas. The key is a carefully throughout and documented plan of action and milestones.

## Applying Best Practices and Technologies

The SCM implementation team's primary responsibility is to identify changes that must be accomplished to effect SCM in the DoD logistics proc-ess. This responsibility, however, cannot be executed successfully in isola-tion. Organizations outside the control of the SCM team often have direct authority and resources for implementation of business process improve-ments and associated technology enablers. Therefore, the SCM team must participate with these organizations to help accomplish the transition to a supply chain process. Unfortunately, many senior managers in DoD equate business process improvement directly with acquisition of new computer systems, software, and related technologies. Managers should recognize, however, that replacing or upgrading ADP systems is the most costly and time-consuming business process improvement. The SCM team should iden-tify and advocate alternatives to purchases of new hardware and software whenever possible. Many of the most successful private-sector business practices involve changes in policies or people-centered procedures rather than automated systems modifications. In analyzing each supply chain proc-ess element, the SCM team should examine potential process changes in the following sequence:

1. Manual or automated processes or subprocesses that can be eliminated.

2. Changes that improve manual processes or procedures.

3. Changes that require modified or new software.

4. Hardware replacement.

By completing the analytical processes and products suggested in this *Guide*, the SCM team will be in a position to influence and effect business process changes in policies, procedures, and systems.

# Validating the Supply Chain Design

The SCM team must remain focused on the principal objective of the SCM initiative: to fully satisfy customer logistics requirements and to meet those requirements at the least possible cost. One of the primary strategies for achieving the supply chain objective is establishment and management of appropriate performance and cost metrics. These metrics are quantifiable expressions of success for the supply chain process. Ordinarily, an organization uses metrics to measure the effectiveness and efficiency of an existing process. Our approach to implementation of SCM in DoD activities relies on metrics to guide and validate the desired to-be supply chain design as well.

In Chapter 5 we outline the strategy for selecting supply chain-oriented performance and cost measures. Selection of metrics must be one of the earliest steps toward developing the supply chain design. To a large extent, the characteristics of the future supply chain design should be driven by implementation of improved business practices that directly contribute to improvements in performance and cost metrics.

In the supply chain environment, selected high-level metrics must relate directly to customer satisfaction and best value cost objectives. Although other internal or subprocess-focused measures are important, they are secondary to enterprise-wide metrics. Once enterprise metrics are selected, they should be quantified on the basis of the current baseline and desired future levels of performance and cost. In many DoD organizations, considerable effort may be necessary to build the current metrics baseline because of the fragmented nature of legacy DoD logistics systems and an unfortunate deemphasis of collection and analysis of management information in recent years. In any case, development of a quantified performance and cost baseline is an important element of the SCM implementation effort.

Quantification of target levels of performance and cost also can be a challenging task. In the private sector, this action often is accomplished through a process called benchmarking. Benchmarking is defined as "a basis of establishing rational performance goals through the search for industry best practices that will lead to superior performance." In a 1996 article that discusses the popularity of benchmarking, James Cooke writes,

> Benchmarking provides a tool for managers to measure their logistics operations against those of companies that stand out from the crowd for their mastery of supply-chain management. A lot of organizations—no matter what industry—want to understand how they stand vis à vis competitors or other functional areas, says Steven Y. Gold, a partner in consulting firm

KPMG's National Manufacturing, Retailing, and Distribution practice in Chicago. The only way to get that information is to benchmark and try to compare where you are to [where] other industry players stand. Most important of all, benchmarking provides an excellent way to learn from others. It allows logistics managers to get fresh ideas on how to improve an operation, boost productivity, and pick up a few tips from the best. No wonder so many companies have turned to benchmarking as part of an on-going effort toward continuous improvement.[5]

A good approach to using benchmarking effectively is to find benchmarking partners, when practical, or utilize a benchmarking service. This strategy will allow you to see whether your performance for each key performance indicator is best in class, average, or below average. A good improvement strategy might be to set goals to move your performance from average to world class in one or more key performance indicators for areas in which you want to distinguish your organization from that of your peers.

Commercial consultants can provide the SCM team with the knowledge they have gained through hundreds of engagements with commercial clients. They have the advantage of having seen what has worked and what has failed in the real world. DoD product support teams may want to retain the services of private consultants, especially when dedicated in-house human resources and expertise are limited. DoD SCM teams may want to learn more about the efforts of the Performance Measurement Group and KPMG—two examples of commercial supply chain management benchmarking and best practices projects.

## The Performance Measurement Group, LLC

The Supply Chain Council sponsors (at reduced rates) a benchmarking program offered by the Performance Measurement Group (PMG), a subsidiary of Pittiglio Rabin Todd & McGrath (PRTM). PMG's purpose is twofold: to conduct rigorous benchmarking studies of core business process performance—primarily in high-technology industries—and to provide study participants with custom benchmarking analysis, online, 24 hours a day, 7 days a week. This program is a great way for organizations that are interested in improving supply chain performance to get involved in benchmarking activities. More information is available at PMG's Web site: http://www.pmgbenchmarking.com/.

---

[5] James Cooke, "Benchmarking 101," *Logistics Management*, October 10, 1996.

# KPMG Global Benchmarking Studies

KPMG has conducted several global supply chain studies that address metrics, benchmarking, and best business practices. For more information about the *Global Supply Chain Study,* call KPMG at its supply chain information hotline at (312) 938-5033. Additional information also is available at KPMG's Web site: http://usserve.us.kpmg.com/cm/article-archives/actual-articles/global.html.

According to research by the University of Cambridge's Institute for Manufacturing, there are four types of benchmarking:[6]

◆ *Internal*—Comparison among similar operations within one's own organization

◆ *Competitive*—Comparison to the best of one's direct competitors

◆ *Functional*—Comparison to companies with similar processes in the same function outside one's industry

◆ *Generic process*—Comparison to others who have innovative, exemplary work processes.

The SCM team may wish to use a combination of these methods to help determine the quantification of target performance and cost objectives for the future supply chain. Although the performance and cost metrics of the DoD logistics system often are considered inferior to those of world-class companies in the private sector, the comparison is not equitable. The DoD supply chain is not a mirror image of commercial chains in terms of size, customer needs, regulatory constraints, or even basic objectives. The SCM team may wish to examine supply chain performance in selected private-sector companies, however, to gain perspective on quantification of world-class performance. Figure 6-3 illustrates a basic approach to benchmarking analysis.[7]

---

[6] See details at http://www-mmd.eng.cam.ac.uk/people/ahr/dstools/proces/benchm.htm.
[7] Ibid.

*Figure 6-3. A 10-Step Approach to Benchmarking*

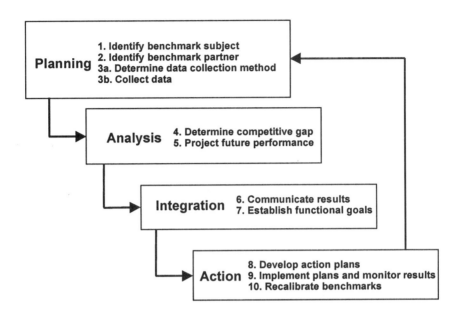

In Chapter 4, we discuss adoption of a benchmarking software tool to assist the team in accomplishing comparative analysis of performance and cost factors in other organizations. Automated benchmarking tools may be useful as part of the team's analysis of applicable performance metrics and quantification of performance and cost targets. Effective application of benchmarking requires a significant level of expertise. The SCM team should acquire such a level of knowledge and experience through training of team personnel or through support from a consulting contractor.

## Assessing and Selecting Business Practices

Selection of applicable business practices for process improvement is a critical element of the eight-step analytical approach described in Chapter 5. The SCM team must maintain a continuous focus on the objective to achieve implementation of SCM principles as the mechanism for attaining the organization's quantitative performance and cost goals. In the selection of enabling business practices, the team should pursue the actions as depicted in Figure 6-4.

*Figure 6-4. Selection and Assessment of Improved Business Practices*

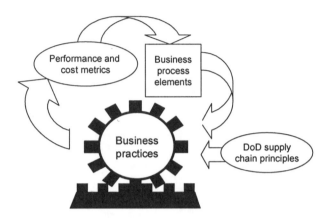

This process involves determination of applicable target metrics for selected business process elements or element groupings, and application of SCM principles to select specific business practice improvements that are expected to result in achievement of target levels of performance or cost reduction.

Assessment of improved business practices for SCM requires substantial knowledge of functional process elements included in the end-to-end supply chain. The team's operational node connectivity diagram provides functional reference points for selecting target process elements for the analysis. This evaluation also requires the analytical capability to select specific process changes (business practices) that can be expected to result in desired levels of improvement in performance metrics. In Chapter 7 we present a representative group of business practices from multiple sources in the private sector and government that have potential application for improving DoD supply chains. Although matching of business practice solutions to desired results must be accomplished on a case-by-case basis, several evaluation factors and conditions are consistently apparent in DoD (and other) business processes. By recognizing these problems and applying the correct combination of best business practices, process analysts have a useful mechanism to assist in determining appropriate solutions. Robert Handfield and Ernest Nichols have developed an excellent compendium of common process deficiencies. Their findings are summarized in the Table 6-2.

## *Table 6-2. Common Supply Chain Process Deficiencies*[8]

| | |
|---|---|
| • Waiting—Inordinate wait time in multi-step processes | • Non–value-added activities— Activities that should be eliminated |
| • Serial vs. parallel operations— Activities that could be accomplished simultaneously | • Repeating process activities— Nonrequired duplication of activities |
| • Batching—Unnecessary combining of activities, causing delay | • Excessive controls—Unneeded approvals or reviews |
| • Lack of synchronization in materials movement—Inefficient movement or poor timing of required movement | • Ambiguous goals and objectives— Organizational objectives not understandable and clear to employees, suppliers, or customers |
| • Poorly designed procedures and forms—Inefficient design or use of tools that delays or disrupts supply chain | • Poor communication—Ineffective flow of information between personnel or systems |
| • Lack of information—Information not available or non-existent | • Outdated technology—Failure to modernize equipment |
| • Limited coordination—Failure to obtain required input or action from employees or managers | • Lack of/ineffective training—Training not available or not properly focused on correct subject matter |
| • Limited cooperation—Lack of commitment or understanding from supply chain participants; poor motivation or lack of common objectives | |

Ultimately, the SCM team should accomplish the analysis steps suggested in Figure 6-4 by using potential process deficiencies (or others, as appropriate), individually or collectively, to relate target performance objectives, business process elements, and selected business practice improvements.

As part of its analysis process for selecting applicable business process improvements, the SCM team should employ a business process simulation capability. This simulation capability will help the SCM team quantitatively validate selected business process improvements relative to their impact on attaining performance/cost objectives. As additional business practices are recommended for inclusion in the simulation model, their impact can be assessed against the baseline model. Numerous commercial simulation packages are readily available for this purpose. The simulation probably will

---

[8] Robert B. Handfield and Ernest Nichols Jr., *Introduction to Supply Chain Management,* Upper Saddle River, NJ: Prentice Hall, 1999, pp. 54–56.

require tailoring to a DoD supply chain configuration, however. Like bench-marking, running business process simulations requires expertise that may be obtained most easily through experienced consulting contractors. The most difficult aspect of the simulation process often is obtaining and evaluating the correct input data. The simulation capability should be put in place early in the SCM implementation process. This early implementation will enable the simulation managers to determine data availability and make provisions to populate required databases. Furthermore, the simulators must be able to participate in the supply chain design effort to ensure full understanding of business processes being simulated and relationships to required process performance metrics.

An effective simulation capability is essential to the progress of supply chain implementation. This capability may be the team's principal quantitative determinant of the potential effectiveness of the new business practices in attaining desired target performance and cost metrics prior to actual implementation of revised procedures and new software. Unfortunately, there are practical limitations to simulation capabilities. The SCM team must work to mitigate these shortcomings.

There is no doubt that the SCM team must import specialized expertise to develop and operate the simulation process. Simulation of supply chain operations is a complex and difficult process. In a white paper on future supply chain planning, Donald Hicks discusses the difficulty of supply chain operations planning and strategic design decision making in particular.[9] He writes, "There are four phases or steps in deciding on the basic structure of the supply network. These are:

♦ *Network optimization*—where optimization models are used to select a network configuration that minimizes total cost of satisfying customer demands.

♦ *Network simulation*—where complex simulation models are used to determine how a particular supply chain design will run–but not necessarily how to make it better.

---

[9] Donald A. Hicks, *Next Generation Supply Chain Strategic Planning Technology and Applications*, Llama-Soft Inc., 2000, available at http://www.ascet.com/ascet2/pdf/hicks.pdf.

◆ *Policy optimization*—where goal-seeking methods are used to evaluate business rules.

◆ *Design for robustness*—where an attempt is made to evaluate supply chain performance if the unexpected happens."

Hicks indicates that there are limited automated assessment tools for accomplishing steps 1 and 2 and virtually no software support for steps 3 or 4—which, of course, would be of particular value to the SCM team. In any case, the team should attempt to obtain simulation capabilities that may be available to help quantify the impact of selected business practices on the desired performance or cost reduction metrics.

In the ever-expanding world of SCM, there is no shortage of gurus offering business process reengineering and associated software solutions for improving supply chain operations—for a price. Often the problem is not a lack of answers but an overabundance of them. In Chapter 7 we review potential business practice improvements documented from a broad range of sources in the private sector and government activities. The challenge for the SCM team is to use its collective and individual wisdom to select a few roses from among the many available thorns.

# Chapter 7
# Supply Chain Best Practices for DoD

In the private sector, the 20-year evolution of the SCM concept has resulted in the development and adoption of many innovative changes in the operation of the logistics process. As companies searched for increasingly effective ways of operating their supply chain business, many forward-looking logistics managers realized that attempting to modernize their own activities individually, without capitalizing on industry-wide or even global advancements, was exceedingly time-consuming and costly. Today, many supply chain managers recognize that sharing innovative ideas and best practices is significantly more advantageous (and profitable) than cloaking their business processes in proprietary shielding. In fact, many leading companies actively participate in associations that provide permanent vehicles to exchange information—not only on new ways they're doing business but how the changes have improved their performance results. In some major companies, informal sharing of new methods and technologies has evolved into a consulting business profit center.

There are many business organizations today whose objective is the exchange of best practice and other process improvement information among member organizations. In preceding chapters, we discussed two of the most prominent: the Supply Chain Council and the Council of Logistics Managers (CLM). Each of these organizations is an excellent source of information on the latest innovations in implementing SCM. As we outline in Chapter 4, there are many sources of formal education on SCM, as well as dozens of authoritative books and innumerable periodical articles for persons who wish to keep current on this rapidly developing area.

The purpose of this chapter is to provide the DoD SCM team with an initial baseline of supply chain best practices that have been proven in the private sector and have high potential and applicability for DoD's logistics processes. This listing is categorized on the basis of the SCOR model's grouping of individual practices: Plan, Source, Maintain, and Deliver. An additional category, "All," is provided for cross-functional practices. Although individual practices are organized into logical categories for structure and context, they often affect a range of functions throughout the supply chain.

Section 347 of the Strom Thurmond National Defense Authorization Act of 1999 required each of the military departments to submit to Congress a schedule for implementing best commercial inventory practices. In response to this requirement, each military service submitted its required report in the summer of 1999. Subsequently, Congress directed the General Accounting Office (GAO) to review the Service reports. Although the reports and the GAO review were developed independently, GAO's findings were nearly identical in each case. GAO's overall perspective was as follows:

> The (Service's) schedule is generally responsive to the act. However, the schedule provides a management framework that lacks specific elements such as an overall strategy and outcome-oriented goals and performance measures.... There is no comprehensive strategy or plan that guides the efforts. Consequently, no detailed framework exists to increase the likelihood that the initiatives are coordinated and do conflict or duplicate efforts. Also, there are no specific performance goals established to measure the overall results of the initiatives.[1]

GAO had similar findings for each of the three Services. GAO's assessment provides a good "lesson learned" for our approach to SCM implementation. That is, merely adopting industry's best practices individually is unlikely to result in an integrated program across the logistics process. We must devote particular attention to ensuring that the practices and technologies we select for application to DoD are assessed fully regarding the probability that they will contribute significantly to meeting the objectives of the SCM process and that these results are measurable quantitatively.

In addition to providing a reference list of best practices, the tables in this chapter are intended as a working tool for the SCM team to build a cross-reference with the process elements in the operational node connectivity diagram. A separate column is provided for use as a checklist to identify best business practices that may be applicable to one or more process element nodes. By using this tool as an assessment of the relevance and value of available process improvement opportunities, the SCM team can help focus people and financial resources on attaining the maximum performance improvement and the most efficient return on investment. Furthermore, such an analytical approach helps to counter future GAO criticism.

---

[1] General Accounting Office, *Improved Management Framework Needed to Guide Army Best Practice Initiatives*, GAO/NSIAD-99-217, September 1999, p. 2.

The listings in Tables 7-1 through 7-5 originally were published in 1998 in the *DoD Logistics Functional Requirements Guide;*[2] they have been substantially updated for this document, however. SCM is a rapidly changing concept. Nearly every day, new approaches, procedures, and technologies are introduced. We suggest that the SCM team use this list as an initial baseline, updating it frequently as the team discerns additional capabilities that may benefit the organization's process.

*Table 7-1. Best Practices—SCOR Plan*

| SCOR category[3] | Requirement | Operational connectivity node reference |
|---|---|---|
| Plan | Provide an automated capability to publish and update DoD and component strategic plans and related guidance in electronic form, with online access and notification to all users worldwide. Maintain a historical reference database of published plans. | |
| | Provide online access for authorized users to all logistics planning and execution documents within the Planning, Programming, and Budgeting System and logistics planning processes. Develop an analytical and query capability. | |
| | Provide an automated, online capability to document logistics plans of action and track actual accomplishments compared to approved objectives and strategies in a logical database that is accessible by all authorized users and managers. | |
| | Provide the capability to automatically update applicable planning documents to the desktop of all authorized logistics managers. | |
| | Provide automated tools, online, to facilitate program and project planning for managing design, schedule, and resources of logistics initiatives, projects, and programs. | |
| | Provide capability to implement the CWT metric, DoD-wide. | |

---

[2] U.S. Department of Defense, Deputy Under Secretary of Defense (Logistics), *DoD Logistics Functional Requirements Guide*, p. B-1.

[3] The best practices included in these tables incorporate a portion of the commercial practices included in the SCOR model, but they are tailored to DoD requirements and include material that is not contained in SCOR documentation.

*Table 7-1. Best Practices—SCOR Plan (Continued)*

| SCOR category | Requirement | Operational connectivity node reference |
|---|---|---|
| Plan | Use the three-tiered approach (enterprise, functional, and program/project levels) to develop a performance measurement capability that includes, at a minimum, proposed performance measures or equivalents approved by management. | |
| | Provide the capability to project readiness trends for each weapon system on the basis of current readiness posture, projected failures, and losses, based on commanders' operational intent and the impact of projected maintenance returns on overall readiness. | |
| | Provide the capability to automatically update applicable performance information to the desktop of all authorized logistics managers. Maintain an automated history database of actual and projected performance measures. | |
| | Accumulate performance data generated as a normal process of daily operations and provide for retrieval of the data in the form of user-designed formats. Provide for standard reports as required by users and management. | |
| | Provide a flexible, real-time, online interrogation capability for performance management reports as required by authorized users. Primary performance measures are updated at least daily and are available online to all logistics pipeline managers. | |
| | Provide capability in the automated performance measurement system to set phased performance targets, online, for each individual measurement. Implement the balanced scorecard concept. The CWT metric is the first priority. | |
| | Give managers an automated capability to set performance levels to make cost-service tradeoffs that optimize the logistics process as a whole through the establishment of targets that collectively encompass the total process. | |
| | Establish accessible databases or other channels of communication to ensure sharing of performance information between cross-functional activities and organizations. | |
| | Ensure that managers receive an easily recognizable indication of the latest trends of the most important performance measurements through an automated "red light" system. | |

*Table 7-1. Best Practices—SCOR Plan (Continued)*

| SCOR category | Requirement | Operational connectivity node reference |
|---|---|---|
| Plan | Employ expert systems and artificial intelligence techniques to tailor performance information to the specific management need, and perform rudimentary analysis. | |
| | Ensure that automated systems summarize key trends, identify out-of-tolerance conditions, or highlight other anomalies associated with basic performance or process sizing data. | |
| | The collaborative planning, forecasting, and replenishment (CPFR) strategy is required to provide guidelines and methods to build more mutually productive partnership arrangements. | |
| | Develop an automated, online system designed to assist in developing, documenting, and comparing the relative performance and costs of operating commercial-type activities in-house and by contract. | |
| | Ensure that fully integrated logistics systems are online to support force deployment, sustainment, and redeployment worldwide. Access to these systems should be available simultaneously to the JTF logistics manager and all logistics support organizations. | |
| | Ensure that online applications have the capability and data access to provide real-time force tracking and project or validate force closure, based on unit equipment and personnel scheduled to arrive or actually arrived in theater. | |
| | Ensure that an automated decision support tool is in place to produce or revise a support force structure and deployment flow (time-phased force and deployment data) within 72 hours, including modal load planning and scheduling. | |
| | Provide visibility and availability of commercial transportation assets available for employment into an area of operation or in support of a mission. | |
| | Provide visibility, status, disposition, and location (in process, in transit, or in storage) of airlift (CONUS, inter-theater and intra-theater), sealift, and rail assets. | |
| | Provide visibility, status, location, and time tables for departure and arrival of assets (personnel, cargo, etc.) moving into, through, or out of the theater of operation. | |

*Table 7-1. Best Practices—SCOR Plan (Continued)*

| SCOR category | Requirement | Operational connectivity node reference |
|---|---|---|
| Plan | Ensure that the automated logistics process provides fully sourced and time-phased logistics course-of-action (COA) evaluation products, with alternatives. Ensure that vulnerability assessments, sensitivity analyses, and draft execution documents are provided. | |
| | Ensure that commanders and logistics managers have full visibility of current requirements for personnel, equipment, and sustainment support movement, as well as the means to make changes throughout the logistics pipeline. | |
| | Provide capability to project asset shortfalls within each class of supply, based on commanders' operational intent and projected consumption factors. | |
| | Provide visibility and availability of commercial supplies available for employment in an area of operation or in support of a mission. | |
| | Provide visibility, status, and location of all prepositioned deployment/war reserve material within a theater of operation. | |
| | Ensure that automated tools provide end-to-end movement planning from theater reception, staging, onward movement, and force integration capacity and constraints and working backward toward force departure from home station and mob station. | |
| | Provide automated planeload and shipload planning capabilities. Develop an integrated database capability for all air and sea port information. | |
| | Ensure that full real-time visibility of assets in transportation pipeline is available to all logistics users and customers. Include flow analysis and transportation closure status. | |
| | Determine en route support requirements, including strategic refueling, automatically by using all available resources. | |
| | Ensure that deployment managers have end-to-end, real-time force-tracking capabilities from home station to the point where the deployed force is integrated with the supported CINC's theater force structure. | |

## *Table 7-1. Best Practices—SCOR Plan (Continued)*

| SCOR category | Requirement | Operational connectivity node reference |
|---|---|---|
| Plan | Ensure that maximum tailoring, equipping, and loading of asset packages occur before actual deployment, based on CINC-defined requirements for the operative scenario. | |
| | Provide visibility, status, location, and capabilities of maintenance repair units/assets within a theater of operation or those scheduled to deploy into a theater of operation. | |
| | Provide visibility of all potential host nation or commercial repair facilities/infrastructure available in a theater of operation. | |
| | Provide capabilities to perform follow-on COA evaluation in terms of logistics sustainability and problem areas, including capability to project shortfalls and excesses. | |
| | Provide an automated capability to estimate gross resupply requirements, based on planning factors, CINC critical item lists, and time-phased requirements. | |
| | Provide automated online planning tools and decision aids for rapid, accurate logistics assessments, analysis, and forecasting, including joint service and multinational requirements. | |
| | Provide a capability to simulate logistics operations (planning, deployment, operations, sustainment, and redeployment) online in real time. Logistics processes should interface with Joint Force Requirements Generator. | |
| | Provide an automated historical database of logistics transactions, consumption, activity, and related information to support redeployment and future deployments. | |
| | Provide the capability to identify, share, and exchange logistics information with allies and coalition partners to enhance international interoperability within disclosure policies. | |
| | Maintain an online historical database of all cost and pricing information (initial costs and changes) for an item of inventory managed by DoD. Similar histories are required for logistics services (e.g., transportation and maintenance costs). | |
| | Use automated online technology to communicate organizational objectives and track actual process performance directly to employee and manager desktops. | |

*Table 7-1. Best Practices—SCOR Plan (Continued)*

| SCOR category | Requirement | Operational connectivity node reference |
|---|---|---|
| Plan | Provide the capability to collect, index, and array design, configuration, and technical data so actions applicable to a logistics process can be directly related to the readiness objective and operating costs of the weapon system. | |
| | Provide decision support and simulation tools that project weapon system availability against predicted scenarios and facilitate evaluation of alternative support policies, structures, and procedures to improve availability. | |
| | Provide the capability to acquire timely and accurate access to weapon system information, including planned or actual force composition, planned and actual operational availability, and related factors. | |
| | Ensure that logistics managers have a robust data model and repository that includes the full set of logistics support data acquired during acquisition process and will retain life-cycle consequence. | |

## Table 7-2. Best Practices—SCOR Source

| SCOR category | Requirement | Operational connectivity node reference |
|---|---|---|
| Source | Provide the capability to store and maintain initial weapon system "as built" configuration records and related data, as well as specifications to access and maintain performance and maintenance data from organic and commercial sources. | |
| | Ensure that weapon system managers have online, real-time access to corporate third-party and original equipment manufacturer ordering vehicles to arrange parts supply, commercial technical support, and competitive repair and remanufacture. | |
| | Ensure that logistics managers have the capability to assess design stability during the acquisition development phase and determine financial risks that are applicable to life-cycle support. | |
| | Ensure that services and agencies have a repository of potential commercial sources to support and repair weapon system assemblies and components. Establish corporate contracts to leverage DoD market share. | |
| | Modify logistics requirements systems to enable a diversified support package, including specific provisions for contractor support of design unstable assembles and components. | |
| | Provide the capability to create interactive support management plans that enable incremental scheduling and implementation of support, based on configuration indenture and delivery of weapon systems and equipment. | |
| | Ensure that logistics managers have decision support tools that assist program managers in generating contract requirements for built-in monitoring, single electronic component fault isolation, redundant performance to offset logistics support costs. | |
| | Ensure that weapon system managers have a capability to generate technical manual contract requirements based on design characteristics, mission requirements, and projected life of existing systems. | |
| | Ensure that logistics managers have a repository of reusable technical manual objects to promote an interchange of information and interoperability for all weapon systems and military services. | |

*Table 7-2. Best Practices—SCOR Source (Continued)*

| SCOR category | Requirement | Operational connectivity node reference |
|---|---|---|
| Source | Life-cycle requirements determination systems should interface directly with product data repositories, including configuration status, program data that include all fielding schedules, and technical directives that schedule modifications. | |
| | Ensure that logistics managers have access to online databases containing applicable past and projected operating programs, including densities, locations, and operating tempos for DoD weapon systems, equipment, and major reparable assemblies. | |
| | Ensure that the automated logistics process includes prepared, coordinated, and online planning and implementation documentation for mobilization to expedite National Command Authority approval in the event of mobilization. | |
| | Ensure that the process provides visibility of critical mobilization resources, organic and commercial, including raw material, technical weapon system components, long-lead-time items, and selected logistics maintenance and distribution capabilities. | |
| | Ensure that actual customer demands and usage are captured at point of sale and used to update future requirements for each supply chain segment. Variances outside established parameters should be flagged for management analysis and action. | |
| | Ensure that logistics pipeline resources information (e.g., inventory, repair capacity, and delivery capability), organic and commercial is assessed, aggregated, and made available online to all logistics managers in a virtual logical database environment. | |
| | Ensure that the logistics process supports joint service agreements among suppliers, logistics managers, and customers to obtain maximum supply flexibility in lead time and repair production and delivery strategies to offset near-term demand volatility. | |

*Table 7-2. Best Practices—SCOR Source (Continued)*

| SCOR category | Requirement | Operational connectivity node reference |
|---|---|---|
| Source | Ensure that information about quantities, condition, and location of all in-storage, in-process, on-order, and in-transit material assets, including organic and commercial providers, is made available online, concurrently to all appropriate logistics managers and customers. | |
| | Provide a unique item tracking capability for visibility of specific units of assets or asset groups for inventory control, safety, security, or engineering analysis. Use AIT and serial number control technology to support tracking requirements. | |
| | Use sparing algorithms and capabilities to enable real-time computations that optimize support across multiple support echelons and account for the indenture of potential maintenance actions and logistics design redundancies. | |
| | Ensure that algorithms for developing future procurement, repair, or transportation requirements encompass the logistics process from suppliers to customers and incorporate all reasonably available options for satisfying customer requirements. | |
| | Ensure that logistics managers have the automated capability to develop requirements through tradeoffs among procurement, repair, transportation, and redistribution alternatives, including organic and commercial sources, based on optimum customer support. | |
| | Ensure that product and service requirements for each segment of the logistics process are prioritized and aggregated on the basis of near-term customer need, scheduled backlogs, and projected future product requirements. | |
| | Provide to all appropriate logistics managers the ability to recompute quantitative procurement and repair requirements rapidly as changes occur in demand, configuration, price, or asset availability. | |
| | Ensure that all managers can run simulated "what if" scenarios, based on changes in demand, product supply, price, cycle times, or other factors that affect product delivery to the customer. | |

*Table 7-2. Best Practices—SCOR Source (Continued)*

| SCOR category | Requirement | Operational connectivity node reference |
|---|---|---|
| Source | Provide a visualization decision support tool and On-Line Assessment Programs to assist logistics managers in collecting, organizing, and displaying logistics activity and status rapidly and accurately in a readily understandable format. | |
| | Ensure that online databases provide managers with historical and current cycle time information (e.g., procurement, repair, and delivery cycles), broken down by logical item, commodity, organization, weapon system, or other required groupings. | |
| | Provide an automated consumption-planning tool to perform sustainment planning, monitor actual consumption, and estimate and source requirements to the item (National Stock Number and Part Number) level. | |
| | Provide the capability to make procurement decisions on the basis of projected consumption and losses in support of an operation. | |
| | Ensure that logistics managers and customers have full visibility of the status of products in the logistics pipeline, including notification of potential service disruptions (e.g., long-lead-time items, back orders, and production problems). | |
| | Provide an online capability to source all combat support requirements, including end items, fuel, subsistence, munitions, clothing, medical equipment and supplies, construction material, spares, and repair parts in response to CINC requirements. | |
| | Ensure that customer orders for logistics services are transmitted directly to the selected source of support without manual or automated intervention and provided concurrently to other requiring activities through access to online databases. | |
| | Establish innovative lot-sizing methods, techniques, and models for determining procurement and repair quantities that minimize the quantity of material placed on order in the logistics pipeline. | |
| | Ensure that all sources of supply (e.g., multiple producers, vendors, production lines, on-demand manufacturing, accelerated repair, and product redistribution) are checked and evaluated automatically to satisfy customer demands. | |

*Table 7-2. Best Practices—SCOR Source (Continued)*

| SCOR category | Requirement | Operational connectivity node reference |
|---|---|---|
| Source | Ensure that an automated evaluation system is in place to make a source selection and tradeoff delivery of less-critical customer requirements when expediting delivery of more important customer requirements. | |
| | Ensure that all inventory, regardless of location, is properly categorized (e.g., active, useable, excess, and obsolete) and that mechanisms are in place to take proper retention, redistribution, and disposal action against these inventories. | |
| | Ensure that Electronic Data Interchange (EDI) ordering and status reporting is used throughout the process to minimize ordering times and streamline the business processes of organic and commercial sources for high-volume product ordering and data exchange. | |
| | Provide automated sharing of demand, asset, and other management information with vendors to enable just-in-time links between customers and vendors. | |
| | Provide a capability to identify cost tradeoffs by assessing various item sourcing or disposition alternatives and the affect each alternative has on transportation, inventory, and repair costs. | |
| | Ensure that the process supports sourcing buys and repairs prior to the actual requirement, consolidating repetitive buy and repair actions and using indefinite delivery contracts, forward pricing agreements, and mobilization-based contracts. | |
| | Ensure that the process makes quantity discount and holding cost tradeoff decisions automatically. | |
| | Ensure that buy or repair quantities may be adjusted, based on the latest requirements information, before the material order is actually submitted. | |
| | Ensure that component maintenance support capabilities—including depot, intermediate, and contract sources—are assessed online and real time to determine the best value source of repair for each logical grouping of repair actions. | |

*Table 7-2. Best Practices—SCOR Source (Continued)*

| SCOR category | Requirement | Operational connectivity node reference |
|---|---|---|
| Source | Use an anticipatory maintenance/parts ordering concept to collect and analyze true mission maintenance data, reductions in force structure, and revised authorized stockage lists. Support a consumption-based system vice the current demand-based system. | |
| | Prebuild subassemblies at the highest generic level to minimize cycle times by allowing assemble to order lead-time capability. Prekit accessories into modular packages. | |
| | Provide a capability to rapidly produce products to meet unique customer requirements. Support engineer-to-order concept. | |
| | Ensure that vendor-managed inventory is used whenever economically justified to reduce inventory costs and delivery times. | |
| | Ensure that private-sector vendors are linked to their DoD customers through direct access to DoD databases or through commercial EDI capabilities. | |
| | Provide an automatic process to replenish stocks when a customer's usage of an item or group of items is steady and a responsive production base exists. | |
| | Ensure that customers have online capability to obtain price quotes for item acquisition and distribution costs that can be converted into orders electronically. | |
| | Ensure that material ordering and financial management processes are fully integrated and electronically accessible. Ensure that invoices are validated electronically and automatically and bills are paid using electronic funds transfer. Ensure that the system fully supports credit card ordering and billing. | |
| | Ensure that customers have remote, worldwide ordering capability, using a simplified priority system, including adequate electronic communications access directly to the source of supply and to the shipment tracking system of the transportation provider. | |
| | Provide an integrated order management process that treats each order as a separate transaction, but integrates customer orders by activity, commodity, equipment, source, and status as required to provide required delivery time at best price. | |

*Table 7-2. Best Practices—SCOR Source (Continued)*

| SCOR category | Requirement | Operational connectivity node reference |
|---|---|---|
| Source | Provide a simplified, priority-based ordering process online to all authorized providers, logistics managers, and customers worldwide. | |
| | Provide an automated analysis capability to ship from commercial sources to the DoD geographic storage location that provides best value, whether that location is closest to customer or closest to vendor. | |
| | During crises and contingencies, provide a capability to allocate scarce material and distribution resources among competing demands. An automated allocation system is required to facilitate this process. | |
| | Establish more effective identification, management, storage, and procurement processing of hazardous material and hazardous waste. Use commercial, direct vendor sources to provide and manage hazardous material when possible. | |
| | Adopt commercial-off-the-shelf software to exchange product data and adopt commercial product data exchange standards as they develop. | |
| | Provide an analytical capability to categorize and source DoD-used items according to an item characteristic profile. Include characteristic coding in a virtual item description database for use in source selection. | |
| | Ensure that an automated product source and services selection tool to facilitate competitive sourcing is available online for all appropriate logistics managers to permit visibility of and selection of sourcing alternatives, using an online logical database. | |
| | Provide logistics managers and customers with online access to comprehensive and product-specific commercial databases (including original equipment manufacturers' repositories) to accomplish market analysis and identify potential product sources. | |
| | Provide an automated, online capability to identify, compute, and source war reserve and contingency requirements, using a strategy that minimizes or eliminates most government stockage of these items. | |

*Table 7-2. Best Practices—SCOR Source (Continued)*

| SCOR category | Requirement | Operational connectivity node reference |
|---|---|---|
| Source | Ensure that product configuration and technical data (e.g., performance and design specifications, packaging, security, test equipment, handling, and environmental) are online to providers and customers. | |
| | Ensure that the process supports viable, long-term contracting vehicles to support direct vendor programs. Ensure that the contracting process is largely automated and transparent to logistics customers. | |
| | Ensure that warranty and quality deficiency processing programs are automated and online to service logistics customers. | |
| | Ensure that logistics providers (organic and contractor) and customers worldwide have automated, online access to a virtual product catalog for all DoD-used items. | |
| | Ensure that the DoD-maintained catalog is online as an integral component of the virtual catalog and a back-up system for direct electronic ordering processes and for products that are not covered by direct ordering from commercial providers. | |
| | Provide contractor-related information—such as pricing, quantities, and value of orders; order status; projected in-process production; billing; shipment status; government furnished material in contractor possession; and related logistics data—is provided online to government users. | |
| | Provide a capability to track and provide visibility of vendor support performance in an automated management information system. | |
| | Develop the capability to separately identify costs of direct vendor support programs in DoD working capital, procurement, and operations and maintenance (O&M) budgets for appropriate categories (e.g., by weapon and equipment, commodity, or organization). | |
| | Adopt and automate an arithmetic modeling approach to support depot maintenance sourcing deliberations. Use of arithmetic modeling in lieu of decision trees will provide a decision support mechanism equal to the complexity of the repair sourcing decision. | |
| | Provide the ability for contracting officers down to the JTF level to track contracts and potential commercial contract sources. | |

## Table 7-2. Best Practices—SCOR Source (Continued)

| SCOR category | Requirement | Operational connectivity node reference |
|---|---|---|
| Source | Provide a capability for online processing (e.g., EDI, networking) of requests from customers for logistics material and services to support deployment and sustainment. | |
| | Provide online visibility of theater logistics support requirements across military service or appropriate multinational organizational lines. | |
| | Provide online visibility of all in-theater assets that are not in the control of tactical commanders, including unit equipment, personnel, and sustainment supplies. | |
| | Automate contract sourcing information by material category, function, and location and make information available online to theater logistics managers. | |
| | Manage common theater base support and services requirements and capabilities as common user services through an automated management and asset repository system. | |
| | Capture user consumption requirements by the customer and provide real-time availability of these requirements directly to applicable logistics providers and online to all authorized logistics managers. | |
| | Provide an ability to select sources of logistics support on the basis of projections of availability and timeliness of delivery, with cost and priorities as secondary decision elements. | |
| | Provide an automated, online system to develop support alternatives (e.g., direct delivery via best transportation mode, offshore or prepositioned inventories afloat, and rapid delivery via short take-off and landing, ship or helicopter). | |
| | Ensure that the logistics process supports management and integration of third-party logistics support and contingency contracting. | |
| | Provide a capability for redistribution of working capital fund assets regardless of physical location or organizational ownership. Develop governing business rules. | |
| | Develop a capability to prepare consolidated working capital fund budgets encompassing the entire logistics pipeline to the point of sale, including maintenance and transportation elements, regardless of organizational boundaries. | |

## *Table 7-2. Best Practices—SCOR Source (Continued)*

| SCOR category | Requirement | Operational connectivity node reference |
|---|---|---|
| Source | Provide an automated analytical tool for logistics managers to assist in assessment of cost input factors, historic trends, computational algorithms, and related elements to support cost recovery factors (e.g., prices and surcharges). | |
| | Provide analytical tools online to assist managers in reviewing available financial data for analysis of customer resources and other purposes. | |
| | Ensure that the Fiscal Year Defense Program (FYDP) database is online for all authorized users in a secure environment and that logistics portions of component Program Objective Memorandums are online and accessible by all authorized users. | |
| | Ensure that working capital, procurement, military personnel, and O&M logistics budget databases are online for authorized users in a secure environment. The scope of access will depend on need and organizational level. | |
| | Ensure that logistics managers have analytical tools to link and assess different portions of budget databases. | |
| | Ensure that logistics costs (material requirements, maintenance, transportation, logistics personnel, and related elements) are identifiable separately to the lowest organizational level shown in the FYDP. | |
| | Provide a unit cost capability within the annual operating budgets of all logistics activities. Automate budget preparation from source databases to the maximum possible extent. | |
| | Automate budget preparation from source databases to the maximum possible extent. | |
| | Provide logistics budget execution data online to authorized users at appropriate detail and summary level. Ensure that automated, online analytical tools are available to compare planned, budgeted, and actual budget execution. | |
| | Provide DoD inventory requirements and assets stratification procedures as an automated capability at all DoD activities and support contractors responsible for inventory management of Defense material. | |

*Table 7-2. Best Practices—SCOR Source (Continued)*

| SCOR category | Requirement | Operational connectivity node reference |
|---|---|---|
| Source | Ensure that logistics operating cost elements are defined and their data sources are accessible in a virtual budget database for all working capital, O&M, military personnel, and procurement budgets at all organizational levels. | |
| | Provide an online, automated budget database, including actual execution data updated as close to real time as practical. Facilitate updates by providing system access to actual source data records regardless of organizational ownership. | |
| | Ensure that DoD inventory management and accounting systems use the same automated virtual database for individual item accountability regardless of the physical inventory location or the IT application. | |
| | Provide the capability to maintain and prepare the DoD Supply System Inventory Report updated online and as near real time as possible, using source data from appropriate logistics and financial accounting systems at all echelons. | |

*Table 7-3. Best Practices—SCOR Maintain*

| SCOR category | Requirement | Operational connectivity node reference |
|---|---|---|
| Maintain | Provide a capability to locate, maintain, archive, and download (provide access to) engineering drawings, maintenance procedures, maintenance planning data, maintenance resources, provisioning, and field feedback data. | |
| | Provide a logical, corporate technical data repository and global communication capabilities to access required technical data throughout the services and agencies to support the full array of engineering and logistics functions. | |

*Table 7-3. Best Practices—SCOR Maintain (Continued)*

| SCOR category | Requirement | Operational connectivity node reference |
|---|---|---|
| Maintain | Provide an automated capability to concurrently review engineering change proposals for logistics impact and coordinate implementation of technical directives. | |
| | Provide the military services with the capability to consolidate weapon system and end-item performance and maintenance data collection into logical repositories for systemic analysis and evaluation. | |
| | Design weapon systems to support automated performance and maintenance data collection, using built-in prognostics. Capabilities should include decision support tools for data mining, root cause analysis, and simulation. | |
| | Modify maintenance management and data collection systems to support performance-based support concepts and extended warranty programs. | |
| | Provide the capability to identify areas of potential design instability and isolate areas for intensive interim support. | |
| | Provide a standard interface and performance specification for acquisition of portable maintenance devices. Specifications should incorporate an open-systems approach. | |
| | Provide logistics managers with the capability to eliminate manual recording of maintenance and configuration status accounting events and the corresponding capability to automatically generate any periodic or ad hoc reports. | |
| | Provide logistics managers with an interface to automatically cross-reference spare and repair part requirements to maintenance events and automatically generate all required documentation and transactions to order spare and repair parts. | |
| | Design all repairable assemblies and components with AIT to minimize manual recordkeeping. | |
| | Ensure that weapon system product data repositories include technical manuals and test program sets. An active data dictionary will enable cross-referencing of common test program sets and common elements of technical manuals and support multiple formats. | |

*Table 7-3. Best Practices—SCOR Maintain (Continued)*

| SCOR category | Requirement | Operational connectivity node reference |
|---|---|---|
| Maintain | Provide logistics managers with the capability to upload maintenance, test, and evaluation data directly to weapon system product data repositories from organic and commercial sources. | |
| | Provide logistics managers worldwide with a real-time link to information that is not available at maintenance job sites, including interactive maintenance aids, diagnostics, and interactive training sessions. | |
| | Provide a capability to automatically receive field support requests and deficiency reports, store and process (e.g., categorize, sort, and access related deficiencies), assign responsible organizations, and automatically route and track disposition. | |
| | Provide analytical tools for performance of proactive and reactive supportability analyses against incoming deficiencies (e.g., failure analyses; readiness analyses; maintenance analysis; parts utilization; and support costs). | |
| | Provide a global infrastructure and addressing capability to facilitate electronic distribution of computer support products, including technical manuals, test program sets, and appropriate operational software. | |
| | Provide logistics managers with decision support tools to evaluate manning levels based on readiness requirements and projected maintenance workload. | |
| | Provide the capability to identify obsolete equipment and assemblies that can be cost-effectively replaced with modern equipment and assemblies that significantly reduce the need for technicians and operators. | |
| | Ensure that the process supports a transition from time-based maintenance activity to condition-based, reliability-centered maintenance when possible. | |
| | Provide a capability to project estimated time in commission for non–mission-capable equipment return to mission-capable status, based on availability of repair parts, personnel, and support equipment. Establish "should-take" time standards for each repair cycle segment and provide standards to logistics managers and customers. | |

*Table 7-3. Best Practices—SCOR Maintain (Continued)*

| SCOR category | Requirement | Operational connectivity node reference |
|---|---|---|
| Maintain | Implement more direct and continual information exchange between maintenance and materiel managers, production lines designed for fast setup, quick turnaround and faster through-put, and integration of commercial supplier techniques. | |
| | Ensure that the maintenance function exploits the rapid pace of change in technology that supports maintenance operations, such as networking, robotics, artificial intelligence, and flexible computer-integrated manufacturing. | |
| | Use an enterprise resource planning strategy (e.g., Manufacturing Resources Planning II [MRPII]) to increase maintenance productivity, reduce material defects, and improve production line efficiency through expanded use of maintenance industrial engineering automated technologies. | |
| | Implement a standard information exchange network that can process and convert technical data, help develop manufacturing plans, support shop floor control, and support coordination of maintenance, supply, and procurement functions. | |
| | Implement an automated process to collect and analyze actual versus standard repair cycle times. | |
| | Prioritize induction quantities and schedule primarily on the basis of customer-driven requirements and item criticality. | |
| | Update and execute repair authorization and funding on a bi-weekly cycle. | |
| | Track and measure actual repair cycle delays by incident and duration by line item. | |
| | Implement a total logistics process diagnostic strategy that fully takes advantage of available technologies, such as embedded test equipment, advanced fault isolation and verification technology, and online access to technical manuals. | |
| | Use electronic document management for technical manuals, drawings, and related information to improve maintenance process planning accuracy and currency. | |
| | Ensure that the process supports integration of maintenance management and information exchange among all organizational levels and reduced number of maintenance levels. | |

## Table 7-3. Best Practices—SCOR Maintain (Continued)

| SCOR category | Requirement | Operational connectivity node reference |
|---|---|---|
| Maintain | Ensure that the process supports individual accountability for maintenance tools. | |
| | Ensure that the process supports embedded maintenance diagnostics integrated with built-in test and built-in test equipment capabilities to map an entire system in which to isolate and identify failures. Embedded diagnostics provide cause-of-failure data to formulate troubleshooting procedures. | |
| | Ensure that the process supports maintenance health monitoring systems, which provide onboard monitoring of critical mechanical systems such as controls, engines, drive train, and/or life-limited components. | |
| | Ensure that the future process will use a portable network interface device to provide single-point data entry for full integration with the end item and all logistical and maintenance support networks. | |
| | Ensure that the future process will maximize dependence on organic and commercial maintenance sources in CONUS, with a corresponding use of accelerated transportation times. | |
| | Base repair and production schedules on actual customer orders rather than forecast demands. Ensure that the scheduling process uses shared resources, such as production equipment and that cellular manufacturing is used when applicable to facilitate small-lot, continuous-flow production. | |
| | Embed preventative maintenance in production schedules. | |
| | Ensure that bill of material (BOM) configuration, inventory requirements, and scheduling are supported by automated tools to enhance data integrity and system accuracy. | |
| | Ensure that the scheduling process considers product characteristics to optimize product changeover times and costs. Use finite capacity scheduling that is based on the actual capacity of individual process segments. | |
| | Use modern, flexible production equipment with a focus on continual reduction in setup times and lot sizes to reduce cycle times. | |

*Table 7-3. Best Practices—SCOR Maintain (Continued)*

| SCOR category | Requirement | Operational connectivity node reference |
|---|---|---|
| Maintain | Use applicable just-in-time techniques to deliver support material to repair and production lines. Use two-bin floor stock process when warranted. | |
| | Use automated process control and data collection technologies to support repair and production processes. Apply statistical process control techniques. Make access to quality feedback available at each point of production and repair. | |
| | Insert packaging as an integral part of the repair and production process. Use automatic label and seal verification processes. | |
| | Provide online production operations status for equipment, jobs, and other resources with the scheduling process in a continuous feedback loop between planning and execution activities. | |
| | Use demand-pull mechanisms to manage provision of raw and support material for repair and production. Establish safety stocks of selected critical items when significant variations in demand or certain quality issues exist. | |
| | Automate and design setup and production parameters with fail-safe capabilities to minimize operator errors. Provide electronic work instructions. | |
| | For virtual prime vendor and integrated supplier programs, provide an automated capability to assess the accuracy of maintenance bill of material (BOM). Provide BOM analysis online for review of factors such as replacement rates and units per assembly. | |

## Table 7-4. Best Practices—SCOR Deliver

| SCOR category | Requirement | Operational connectivity node reference |
|---|---|---|
| Deliver | Provide the capability to track actual resource use by weapon system at all management levels and to reallocate available resources by weapon system on the basis of changes in priorities and conditions. | |
| | Provide a capability that enables visibility and analysis of the multi-echelon interaction of supply, maintenance, and transportation functions. | |
| | Provide current information on all orders and shipment status to all appropriate logistics managers and customers, using applicable commercial industry standards and information exchange conventions (e.g., electronic data interchange). | |
| | Ensure that order processing software automatically assigns a promised delivery date on order entry and provides this date to the customer. | |
| | Use Internet ordering, electronic malls, and online catalogues, when applicable, to reduce cycle times and provide support alternative sources directly to customers. | |
| | Ensure that electronic linkages exist between all product sources, repair elements, and delivery providers to attain smooth, integrated operation of the pipeline and to ensure that disruptions in product delivery to the customer are quickly communicated and responded to. | |
| | Ensure that delivery quantity requirements can be adjusted by customers until time of delivery. | |
| | Use supplier certification programs to reduce or eliminate receiving inspections. Ensure that certification information is automated and accessible online. | |
| | Ensure that suppliers—including repair activities—deliver products directly to appropriate stockage points or point of use. Customer time frames should drive delivery times. | |
| | Accomplish asset balancing at DoD distribution centers and storage points by using timely and accurate knowledge of on-hand assets, impending receipts at each distribution center and storage location, and customer usage patterns. | |

*Table 7-4. Best Practices—SCOR Deliver (Continued)*

| SCOR category | Requirement | Operational connectivity node reference |
|---|---|---|
| Deliver | Implement distribution resource planning techniques and related computational tools to allow logistics managers to anticipate and react to customer stock replenishment requirements. | |
| | Ensure that movement planning and execution status information is online and updated in real-time. Portray deployment status in an automated system, with integrated information from origin to destination. | |
| | Implement an automated capability to diagnose delivery problems and test theories of causes, using data-based analyses. Implement automated tools to track problems to the cause and implement corrective actions. | |
| | Use an efficient consumer response strategy to share information across organizational lines, including commercial partners. | |
| | Support the total package concept to ensure that weapon systems and equipment are fully supportable when fielded. | |
| | Develop logistics pipeline strategies to meet the needs of each customer segment, stratified by variable support requirements and customer characteristics. | |
| | Provide a support and pricing segmentation scheme that is based on required logistics support that different customer segments expect to receive and associated costs of different support levels and customer delivery requirements. | |
| | Establish a fully integrated distribution center structure composed of closely grouped depots by networking DoD and commercial distribution centers and other storage locations to operate as a single organizational and operational entity. | |
| | Apply increased leverage with the smaller set of core carriers to simplify transportation rate structures. Eliminate the practice of tacking on accessorial charges to the single rate quote. | |
| | Streamline the level of scrutiny applied to the transportation auditing and payment process in accordance with the value of the bill being paid and the costs of the business to accomplish the auditing. | |

## *Table 7-4. Best Practices—SCOR Deliver (Continued)*

| SCOR category | Requirement | Operational connectivity node reference |
|---|---|---|
| Deliver | Implement a time-definite-delivery strategy for all shipments to customers from organic or contractor sources. Place orders through a DoD simplified priority system, based on customer requirements. | |
| | Require DoD core transportation carriers to provide near–real-time shipment tracking services and support customer access to their shipment tracking system by using a common user interface mechanism (e.g., global transportation network). | |
| | Ensure that customer orders are received and tracked electronically through direct connection to the applicable order processing host, credit card, World Wide Web applications or through industry and DoD standard electronic transactions. | |
| | Provide customers and logistics managers with electronic visibility of stock availability, backlogs, order status, shipments, scheduled receipts, repair production, and current inventory positions. | |
| | Ensure that retrograde material is fully visible to applicable managers at all echelons on initial shipment. Categorize retrograde shipments automatically (e.g., excess, unserviceable, redistribution stocks). | |
| | Provide a flexible and integrated distribution center inventory process to ensure that peripheral functions, such as inventories and quality inspections, can be conducted in the normal course of accomplishing other primary functions, such as picking and stowing. | |
| | Increase the use of automated and integrated statistical sampling techniques to reduce resource requirements and improve effectiveness in conducting location audits and physical inventories. | |
| | Establish a streamlined and integrated receipt and issue process at storage locations to enable distribution centers to issue material to customers directly from receiving (cross-docking) as required. | |
| | Electronically link item shelf-life information to item locations worldwide through a logistics database and AIT interface. | |

## Table 7-4. Best Practices—SCOR Deliver (Continued)

| SCOR category | Requirement | Operational connectivity node reference |
|---|---|---|
| Deliver | Ensure that distribution channel selection balances the needs of customers and the characteristics of items involved. Consolidate orders by customer, product, commodity, weapon and equipment, source, or carrier. | |
| | Select transportation modes to optimize customer priority, required delivery times, and transportation costs. Ensure that logistics managers have online access to transportation alternatives. | |
| | Provide an online transportation modeling and analysis capability to analyze transportation routing and scheduling and perform rate analysis and carrier and route selection. Prepare advance shipping notices automatically. | |
| | Provide electronic shipment tracking and tracing capability through networks and satellite communications. Track selected high-visibility shipments on a real-time basis using AIT and global positioning system. | |
| | Ensure that material receiving uses integrated AIT with online cross-reference to purchasing, shipping, and related documentation to facilitate automated receiving and storage. | |
| | Ensure that storage location assignments use lot control, zoned locations, frequency of access criteria, special handling, and security requirements to optimize physical storage. | |
| | Ensure that material issuance uses rules-based picking strategies that are optimized for labor, cost, and timing requirements. Base cost on the total enterprise cost. | |
| | Provide online, accurate, and timely knowledge of packaging requirements from and to vendors, item managers, storage activities, transporters, and customers. Use commercial packaging standards and methods whenever possible. | |
| | Enhance automatic material handling capabilities at all storage locations to ensure timely, safe, and secure movement and storage of material. | |
| | Use electronic downloading and production of shipping documentation to process and expedite shipments. | |

*Table 7-4. Best Practices—SCOR Deliver (Continued)*

| SCOR category | Requirement | Operational connectivity node reference |
|---|---|---|
| Deliver | Provide logistics managers and customers with near-continuous exchange of order data/shipping information (for customers) and requisitions and inventory data (for suppliers). | |
| | Provide visibility to private-sector providers in support of direct vendor delivery, prime vendor, and integrated supplier arrangements; have in-storage, in-process, and in-transit information from DoD logistics processes and customer assets. | |
| | Conversely, that the asset visibility capability permits contractor visibility of DoD-held inventories, customer requirements, organic in-process production quantities, BOM requirements, organic in-transit visibility, payments, and related government data. | |
| | Develop an automated contract billing and payment process to ensure verification of government receipt of products and services from all sources and prompt payment, using EDI and Electronic Funds Transfer (EFT) capabilities. | |
| | Provide automated, timely determination of transportation infrastructure and lift requirements, based on preplanned scenarios and actual customer requirements. | |
| | Determine movement modes to port-of-entry on the basis of minimizing total logistics pipeline times. | |
| | Provide the capability to identify and automatically track delivery, in-transit status, and location of CINC-specified critical items. | |
| | Provide capabilities for intra-theater logistics support for deployed forces. Ensure that in-theater storage capacity is highly automated and tailored for asset characteristics and is moveable and temporary when possible. | |
| | Provide automated information exchange and data access capabilities to minimize the need to dedicate theater logistics force structure to asset and in-transit visibility functions. | |
| | Integrate applicable AIT into theater asset management systems with appropriate interfaces with logistics providers, including contractors, outside theater boundaries. | |

*Table 7-4. Best Practices—SCOR Deliver (Continued)*

| SCOR category | Requirement | Operational connectivity node reference |
|---|---|---|
| Deliver | Implement an automated transportation coordination system to provide visibility of theater-level transportation resources and movement status, online and accessible by all authorized logistics managers and customers. | |
| | Provide a capability to track forces and related assets during reception, staging, onward movement, and integration phases of theater deployment and redeployment. | |
| | Provide a capability for automated information interfaces among national command, theater support commanders, operational, and tactical commanders during actual execution of logistics support to operations. | |
| | Provide automated development and support to deliver tailored logistics support packages (e.g., logistics organizations, supplies, and maintenance capacity) directly to users. | |
| | Provide support for mobilization or war reserve stocks that are positioned primarily in CONUS or afloat and are configured in tailored packages for rapid delivery. | |
| | Provide a capability for real-time, online, in-transit visibility of all DoD shipments, using AIT and worldwide communications to update virtual item records (e.g., United Parcel Service and Federal Express item tracking). | |

## Table 7-5. Best Practices—SCOR All

| SCOR category | Requirement | Operational connectivity node reference |
|---|---|---|
| All | Make accumulation, collection, and dissemination of management information an integral (imbedded) part of operational logistics processes. Ensure that the process effectively gathers, stores, and assesses logistics intelligence at all organizational levels. | |
| | Ensure that logistics cost accounting and Planning, Programming Budgeting System processes interface automatically, at appropriate management levels, with the information management process to permit cross-referencing of resource requirements. | |
| | Ensure that automated systems comply with appropriate access restrictions and security protocols, including encryption needs. The detail level of management information should appear to the user as a single logical database of meaningful functional groupings. | |
| | Satisfy logistics information assurance requirements (e.g., security, timeliness, content accuracy, and aggregation), including systems certification, information storage redundancy, recovery, and acceptable protection from intrusion, worldwide. | |
| | Provide an automated capability to prepare integrated planning and budget submissions by weapon system, covering all appropriate logistics resource factors (e.g., material and transportation). | |
| | Develop an automated repository of performance-based benchmarks to assess weapon system support and cost. This repository should include government as well as commercial benchmarks. | |
| | Implement an enterprise resource planning approach, managing requirements and resources across the logistics process by appropriate weapon system, equipment, commodity, supplier, customer, or other logical grouping. | |
| | Ensure that corporate and component plans; policy, procedural, and related management guidance; references; and regulations are available online to every DoD and authorized contractor support logistics manager and kept current through electronic updates. | |

*Table 7-5. Best Practices—SCOR All (Continued)*

| SCOR category | Requirement | Operational connectivity node reference |
|---|---|---|
| All | Use single logical records within distributed logistics databases to record and access materiel management, repair, physical inventory, vendor, transportation, customer, and financial inventory data to eliminate duplicate record reconciliation. | |
| | Use paperless production control when environmental conditions permit. Apply electronic data collection to improve management information and identify non–value-added activities. | |
| | Provide logistics functional users with a single, automated interface protocol regardless of the enabling technical data accessing method (i.e., EDI, Web-based, terminal). | |
| | Provide logistics managers with full online access to financial and accounting databases for programming, budget, and cost data. | |
| | Use ABC (built on a certified cost accounting process) for all logistics processes throughout DoD. Ensure that logistics ABC databases are logically linked to permit detailed analysis of source data and management report summarization. | |
| | Use an automated analytical tool to help identify, catalog, and quantify common process requirements. | |
| | Use a logical database to capture logistics capital and personnel resources and process capacity (e.g., maintenance capacity, warehouse space, transportation lift capacity, data storage and retrieval capability, and logistics skills). | |
| | Use an expert system analytical tool to facilitate management review of opportunities to share resources to satisfy common requirements. | |
| | Use an online repository of existing inter-service logistics support agreements. Provide an online logistics support agreement publishing capability, including standard clauses and provisions. | |
| | Provide logistics managers with an online logical database of planned and implemented logistics process improvement initiatives, technical innovations, and major ADP system changes across all components. | |

## Table 7-5. Best Practices—SCOR All (Continued)

| SCOR category | Requirement | Operational connectivity node reference |
|---|---|---|
| All | Provide the capability to use commercial data exchange standards (e.g., EDI, extended markup language) in all transaction-oriented logistics applications to enable electronic interface among DoD processes, industry, and vendors. | |
| | Provide an analytical tool to document and analyze commercial performance measures (e.g., cycle times, quality elements, and costs) as the basis for benchmarking private-sector product delivery and functional process accomplishment. | |
| | Ensure that deployment systems are fully integrated with online access by all users, from customer to national levels, and access to virtual databases by all authorized process applications. | |
| | Provide a capability for real-time, secure communications and data exchange interoperability for logistics support entities and command and control functions worldwide, using virtual networking concepts. | |
| | Implement an integrated system to provide real-time information on the location, condition, and status of forces and sustaining assets, including assets in process, in storage, and in transit regardless of location, including applicable contractors. | |
| | Provide a global logistics information network with the capability to tailor information requirements from operational and support perspectives and link all applicable source data systems, in real time, in a secure and survivable Common Operating Environment (COE). | |
| | Provide a joint theater logistics command and control capability (policies, business rules, and procedures) for seamless logistics operations among joint force components. | |
| | Implement an automated, real-time support system to identify, synchronize, prioritize, direct, integrate and coordinate common user and cross-service logistics requirements and functions in-theater. | |
| | Provide a capability to coordinate joint and common logistics support requirements and interfaces with logistics support structure outside theater boundaries—national, intermediate, and inter-theater, including contractor and allied logistics providers. | |

## Table 7-5. Best Practices—SCOR All (Continued)

| SCOR category | Requirement | Operational connectivity node reference |
|---|---|---|
| All | Provide an automated management system capability to identify, track, and assess service and multinational logistics requirements, capabilities, and assets in a theater. | |
| | Ensure that theater logistics managers have online, real-time communications with the systems of all logistics material and services providers throughout the logistics pipeline for coordinating JTF logistics requirements. | |
| | Ensure that logistics, procurement, and financial databases are separate from processing applications but that appropriate applications share common data. Ensure that data elements, formats, and definitions required by functional users are standardized or cross-referenced. | |
| | Provide the capability for services and agencies to freely execute financial transactions across the DoD enterprise nonintrusively for logistics business processes that directly support the warfighter. | |
| | Ensure that financial data are updated online and accessible by all authorized users. Ensure that logistics-related accounting and budgeting systems are compliant with federal or commercial standards. | |
| | Provide logistics managers with full online access to financial databases. Ensure that modern analytical tools and modeling capabilities are readily available and usable by functional managers. | |
| | Provide immediate, real-time availability and status of logistics-related funds (expenditures, obligations, and remaining amount) at each level of command. | |
| | Provide visibility of all financial obligations, commitments, and transactions, from the national strategic level to the tactical level. | |
| | Ensure that logistics performance management systems have automated access to financial databases to support construction of logistics performance indicators that have financial subsets (e.g., ratio of logistics material sales to costs of logistics operations). | |

## Table 7-5. Best Practices—SCOR All (Continued)

| SCOR category | Requirement | Operational connectivity node reference |
|---|---|---|
| All | Provide logistics managers with online visibility of logistics-related (material, maintenance, transportation, logistics personnel, and related elements) budget information from O&M, military personnel, and procurement budgets. | |
| | Replace paper-based planning, programming, budgeting, and execution data forms and repositories by an integrated automated virtual database, using a single updater, multiple reader, accessing concept. | |
| | Maintain and update a single logical record for individual item quantities—by location, condition, or other characteristics—for each individual item of supply, using AIT with minimal human intervention. | |
| | At every DoD activity with a logistics mission, develop the automated capability to identify discrete logistics processes and determine separately identifiable costs to accomplish each process. | |
| | Provide automated analytical tools to enable authorized logistics managers to access the activity and cost database by using ABC and activity-based management (ABM) methodologies. | |
| | Provide a uniform logistics business case analysis process methodology, supported by automated analysis tools, and provide online access for all appropriate logistics managers. Provide automated access to required source data. | |
| | Provide comprehensive and automated access to computer-based training for all logistics managers covering the full scope of logistics knowledge and skills applicable to all levels of the workforce. | |
| | Provide standard online training courses for logistics managers to accomplish functional oversight of commercial material and service providers. | |
| | Provide standard training and state-of-the-art tools to support logistics corporate cultural, organizational, and functional process improvements. Standardize training material and reference documentation DoD-wide. | |

*Table 7-5. Best Practices—SCOR All (Continued)*

| SCOR category | Requirement | Operational connectivity node reference |
|---|---|---|
| All | Implement distance-learning capabilities throughout the logistics workforce. Use electronic network capability to transfer briefing and training slides automatically, using communications links throughout the logistics community.<br><br>Have logistics activities use cross-functional teams and multiple skill training to maximize workforce effectiveness.<br><br>Provide commercial informational and training material and training courses for the logistics workforce—at their desktop location whenever possible.<br><br>Provide desktop, laptop, or PC networking capability at the physical location of each DoD logistics worker, worldwide, linked to required applications and databases. Develop an on-line database register of all members of the DoD logistics workforce. | |

# Chapter 8
# Applying Technologies
# for Managing DoD Supply Chains

DoD has a long history of "improvement" initiatives that follow the path of acquiring new technology for its own sake, as opposed to buying technology to enhance performance or reduce costs. Of course, every new technology acquisition is touted as a solution for ineffective or inefficient operations; only in rare cases, however, has the business case for acquiring the technology been made prior to acquisition. Dependence on technology solutions has become an American tradition. We all enjoy the benefits of helpful technologies in our daily lives. Unfortunately, the "technology solution in search of a problem" is a common phenomenon in the DoD logistics community. In fact, most of the requirements to improve logistics processes and reduce the cost of logistics operations ultimately will require some technical enablers. Throughout the Department, there are literally hundreds of technology-driven initiatives in various stages of development or implementation. Most of these initiatives have not been properly evaluated against desired operational performance objectives or potential cost reductions.

The most difficult task that the SCM implementation team faces may be to match available software and supporting technology solutions to the functional requirements of the future supply chain process. This task must begin with documentation of functional requirements. Once these requirements are known and approved, a comparative analysis can be made to ensure that the operational performance or cost benefits of adopting the technology can be effectively assessed. Cost and difficulty of implementation are additional considerations in selecting solutions. Of course, no combination of technology applications is likely to provide the "perfect" solution. The team will face numerous compromises, trading off required capabilities against cost, time, and degree of implementation difficulty. In preceding chapters we discuss several actions that are designed to help the SCM team document future supply chain implementation requirements.

We cannot overemphasize the importance of assessing the contribution of planned technical solutions to desired functional performance or cost reduction objectives. The SCM implementation team must take a leadership role in this effort if desired process improvements are to be achieved.

In Chapter 5 we outline an overall strategy for assessing and evaluating technological solutions for future supply chain development. The application of technologies must support redesigned activities and processes. Making this assessment is particularly difficult today because of the increasing popularity of "integrated" supply chain suites of application software. These "off-the-shelf" packages offer a significant range of capabilities for many segments of the supply chain. To the extent that specific packages do not fully comprehend the organization's future functional needs, integrating contractors usually propose additional software—called "bolt-ons"—to accommodate additive needs. As one might expect, no set of software combinations can meet all functional requirements, particularly with regard to the way functional managers might like to see a specific process solution.

The SCM team undoubtedly will encounter significant pressure to "just get the system installed, and then we can figure out what to do with it." Although this approach is understandable—given the DoD logistics community's degree of frustration with previous system modernization initiatives—the SCM team must resist approving installation of technology solutions just to get *something* working. Private-sector experience indicates that significant performance improvements are unlikely to occur if the selected technology solutions do not specifically enable required business practice improvements. If the team fails to make the proper comparative analysis between required functional improvements and the proposed software solution, the expected performance improvement or cost reduction is unlikely to be achieved.

The operational connectivity node diagram and its accompanying narrative descriptions are a good starting place for reviewing functional requirements. Real improvement will be achieved only if the technological enabler includes required business process and operational changes. At a minimum, the team must express its concerns to management if a proposed software solution does not contribute significantly to necessary process changes to ensure improved performance. Furthermore, this contribution should be documentable through quantitative analysis, simulation, or other empirical means. Experience has shown that investing in new technologies merely because they are fashionable or state-of-the-art is an expensive and often unproductive strategy. As a start, the team may wish to divide the functional characteristics of a proposed technology solution into three categories:

◆ Necessary to improve process operations

◆ Necessary to improve management/oversight of the process

◆ Nice to have.

This simple categorization of the suggested solution's functional attributes helps to create a good high-level perspective of the scope of benefits likely to be attained through adoption of a particular technological solution. Furthermore, by cross-referencing functional requirements to enabling solutions, the SCM team will be better able to assess the potential for actually achieving process improvements and desired results. This comparative analysis will assist management in making the difficult decision of whether to invest in the proposed solution.

## Technology Solutions

Full implementation of SCM in DoD will involve selection and implementation of a wide range of hardware and software technology solutions. Several distinct technologies are involved in the operation of the DoD supply chain, including the following areas:

◆ Automatic identification technology

◆ Materials handling equipment

◆ Packaging technology

◆ Maintenance equipment

◆ Transportation vehicles and equipment

◆ Communications technology

◆ Information storage and retrieval

◆ Computer hardware

◆ Computer software

◆ Others.

Implementing the supply chain requirements we discuss in Chapter 7 undoubtedly will involve the full gamut of the foregoing technology-related areas. This *Guide* cannot fully explore all of the technology applications necessary for full implementation of the SCM concept, however. Furthermore, the SCM team is unlikely to focus its attention beyond a selected subset of hardware-related capabilities such as AIT, databases, or communications systems. Therefore, this *Guide* focuses primarily on software-related capabilities that will be principal enablers for successful SCM implementation in DoD.

## Types of Supply Chain Software

Generally speaking, SCM software applications provide real-time analytical systems that manage the flow of products and information throughout the supply chain network of trading partners and customers. This chain includes many different functions, such as sourcing, requirements and production planning, warehousing, transportation, demand forecasting, order processing, and customer service. The SCM solutions market is fragmented along these functional lines; most vendors sell into specific niches—for example, advanced planning for the manufacturing plant, demand planning for the sales group, and transportation planning for the distribution center. The trend, however, is to consolidate these disparate functions into a comprehensive supply chain planning suite, building on the enterprise resource planning (ERP) platforms. Figure 8-1 is a graphic representation of the current spectrum of supply chain applications.

*Figure 8-1. Supply Chain Management Applications Spectrum*

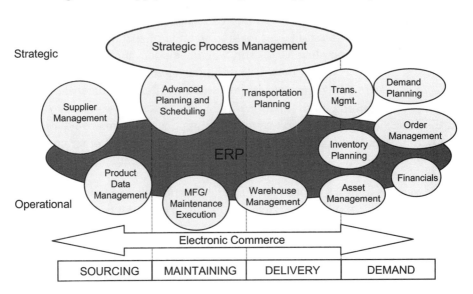

As Figure 8-1 shows, a broad range of commercially available software applications is aimed at satisfying the many functional requirements of the supply chain. Appendix E contains further descriptions of the supply chain software groups pictured in Figure 8-1.

Hundreds of vendors offer software solutions for the supply chain market. Furthermore, the growth of software sales over the next few years is expected to be dramatic. According to AMR Research (a market research firm), there will be a 48 percent compound annual growth in supply chain software sales by 2003. Figure 8-2 shows this significant increase.

*Figure 8-2. Supply Chain Software Sales*

**How hot is SCM software?**

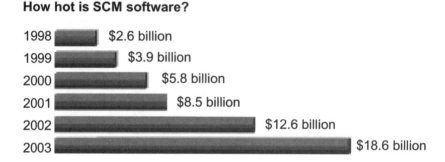

| | |
|---|---|
| 1998 | $2.6 billion |
| 1999 | $3.9 billion |
| 2000 | $5.8 billion |
| 2001 | $8.5 billion |
| 2002 | $12.6 billion |
| 2003 | $18.6 billion |

The rapidly expanding availability of supply chain software solutions presents several challenges to the SCM implementation team. Obviously, the proliferation of software packages makes selection of specific applications for DoD use more complex. Major software developers such as SAP, Oracle, Baan, and others known for their ERP solutions have been working to build suites of software with common architectures and integrated databases for the purpose of putting more functionality into their company's own products. At the same time, these integrators are adopting open-systems conventions that permit seamless operations with software applications of other companies to accommodate a greater scope of functional requirements.

As the various families of products become functionally more comprehensive, the SCM team must take a leadership role in ensuring that the organization's full functional requirements are being addressed by the information technology providers. This important role makes the accuracy and completeness of the SCM team's functional requirements documentation an essential task prior to acquiring the proposed technology solution.

In addition to the emergence of more comprehensive software packages, including broader ranges of functionality, two other trends have been emerging over the past several years. One is the addition of strategic planning software packages into the integrated supply chain environment; the other is the concept of greater collaboration and data sharing with trading partners and suppliers outside the organization. This greater integration requires significantly more sophisticated technology to support collaborative information networks as the supply chain is extended to commercial partners. For DoD applications, the SCM team must recognize that technology solutions must be readily extendable to all segments of the supply chain, including commercial partners and customers. The goal is to develop fully integrated SCM software that performs all key planning and execution functions. There should be an integrated suite of software enablers that minimizes or eliminates the costly and time-consuming transactional or manual interfaces that characterize today's supply chain. From a practical perspective, this degree of integration probably is 4 to 5 years away. Some industry experts contend, however, that the promise of a fully integrated ERP-type system will never be realized as niche systems move ahead by delivering substantially greater functionality and performance improvement—although for more narrow process segments. Thus, for the foreseeable future the SCM team must develop a good working knowledge of many software applications that will be required to interface the full range of DoD's supply chain functional requirements.

SCM software performs essentially two functions. One is planning, including forecasting and scheduling. The other is execution of supply chain functions, such as warehousing, maintenance, and transportation. Another approach to categorizing the software available to accomplish these functions often is described in the following groupings.

*Enterprise Resource Planning*—ERP is the backbone planning and scheduling software system for major corporations today. Standard modules may include financials, purchasing, payroll, human resources, and other administrative functions traditionally handled by the corporate host computer. Newer systems may add warehouse management and other functionality. Central databases are a common component of ERP systems, allowing them to link and manage communications between the planning and execution subsystems.

*Supply Chain Planning (SCP)*—Originally used to plan and schedule manufacturing operations, what used to be called advanced planning and scheduling recently moved into the distribution and warehousing world; now it is known as supply chain planning. This analytical tool is used to deploy inventory at the right price and right time to the right jobs. Modules range from demand and inventory planning to supply chain network design.

*Order Management System (OMS)*—This system essentially manages the relationship between the organization and the customer. It receives, validates, processes, prices, prioritizes, expedites, and even invoices customer orders. An OMS really is a bridge between planning and execution; it acts as the last step in the former and the first step in the latter.

*Customer Relationship Management*—This software automates customer service functions for any industry. Some of the functions are management of customer inquiries; technical support calls; Web inquiries; and requests for service, information, or services, such as order status, asset visibility, or account inquiries.

*Manufacturing Execution System (MES)*—This software integrates the flow of materials and work-in-process with the production process. It does this dynamically in real time, compensating for shifts in production machine availability, inventory levels, order priorities, and labor. The MES accepts data forecasts, costs, and planning information from the ERP and SCP systems. The software then balances these data with what is really happening on the shop floor, making on-the-fly decisions.

*Warehouse Management System (WMS)*—Whereas an MES resides in the world of production, a WMS operates within the four walls of the warehouse or distribution center. The WMS manages inventory, order fulfillment, materials handling equipment, and labor. The software dynamically directs and controls all activities from receiving to shipping. Information collected by the WMS is used to update central databases, initiate billing, and build electronic data interchange status messages for customers.

*Transportation Management Systems (TMS)*—The primary goal of a TMS is to manage a company's transportation network and reduce shipping costs. Primary functions include labor management in the shipping department, load planning and building, and shipment scheduling. The software manages inbound, outbound, and intra-company shipments with an eye on the lowest possible cost without sacrificing customer service or trading partner requirements.

# The Role of the SCM Team in Technology Application

For most DoD activities today, a professional integration contractor will fill the role of system integrator with appropriate technical expertise. For the DoD logistics community, the central design activities owned by the Services and DLA no longer have the personnel or level of expertise required to provide technical design and implementation support for the installation of large, new computer software systems developed in-house. Conversely, many integration contractors are technically focused or have functional knowledge that is oriented principally to private-sector logistics processes. Although applying commercial best practices in DoD whenever appropriate is desirable, large-scale initiatives to transition to SCM concepts must take into account a significant range of DoD-unique functional requirements that are driven by legal or military-specific circumstances. In many cases, the SCM implementation team will be the primary (or only) source of these DoD-unique functional requirements.

The SCM team should be aware that there are two basic practical approaches to selection and implementation of SCM software: the integrated ERP approach and the "best-of-breed" solution. In practice, a third alternative—in the form of a hybrid of the two strategies—often emerges. For the near future, no single vendor's software package is likely to fully satisfy a DoD supply chain's entire functional requirement. A single vendor's package may well dominate the proposed solution, however—to the point that it becomes the major driver of hardware, communications, and personnel training requirements.

For the SCM team, selection of an ERP, best-of-breed, or hybrid solution should center on the issue of which approach best satisfies documented functional requirements. This strategy puts great pressure on the SCM team because, from the viewpoint of the technical provider, any of the three approaches is viable (i.e., they will work technically). From a technical manager's view, the objectives of the prospective supply chain solution are threefold:

- To collect information on each product from production to delivery and provide complete visibility for all parties involved

- To access any data in the system from a single point of contact

- To analyze, plan activities, and make tradeoff decisions on the basis of information from the entire supply chain.

As we have stressed, the SCM team's objectives are quite different. It aims to achieve higher levels of process performance and/or reduced costs while supporting customer requirements. The important task for the SCM team is to analyze each significant proposed technical process improvement component and assess its potential individual and collective contribution to enterprise performance and cost metrics relative to investment costs. Although each major component of the proposed technical solution should be assessed on its own merits, the matrix in Table 8-1 may be of some benefit in an overall comparison of the single-vendor ERP approach, the best-of-breed solution, and the traditional in-house or proprietary development method.

*Table 8-1. Single Vendor ERP Approach Best-of-Breed Solution and the Proprietary Method*

| Implementation issue | Best-of-breed | Single vendor (ERP) | Proprietar, (in-house) |
|---|---|---|---|
| Length of time | 2-4 Years | 1-2 Years | Not known |
| Cost | Higher | Lower | Depends on expertise |
| Flexibility | Higher | Lower | Highest |
| Complexity | Higher | Lower | Highest |
| Quality of solution | Higher | Lower | Uncertain |
| Fit to enterprise | Higher | Lower | Highest |
| Staff training | Longer | Shorter | Shortest |

The SCM team should not become bogged down with the inevitable debate about the merits of one technology solution versus another. The relative benefits of a particular radio frequency tag or of one bar-code design over another should be of only passing interest to the SCM team. The team should persistently fall back on the question of how a particular proposed technology solution will help to meet functional requirements. The bridge between the tangible technology capability and the less tangible statement of a functional requirement is not always readily apparent, however. For example, having the capability to store 20 gigabytes of data in an online database does not mean we automatically know what information is necessary to store there to reduce material ordering cycle times.

The SCM team is responsible for assessing the potential for proposed technology solutions to satisfy functional requirements. To accomplish this task, the team should recognize several technology-related characteristics that are required to support the supply chain process of the future. The logistics functional community needs these *technological enablers* to achieve process improvement objectives:

- ◆ Information is created once, is updated, and is universally available to authorized users throughout a product's life cycle. In the shared data environment, sharing or reusing existing data is the norm. Source data are prepared or acquired one time.

- ◆ Information is managed as an asset to ensure its quality and increase its value. The notion of information ownership by an individual, organization, or information system is superseded by the view that information is a valuable asset, to be treated like other enterprise assets.

- ◆ Information assurance protects information assets and enables information sharing between business partners. Information access and aggregation are governed by strict adherence to protocols that provide security and assurance and mitigate the potential for information contamination and compromise. The information architecture and IT infrastructure ensure that authorized users are not prevented from accessing and processing required data.

- ◆ Electronic business capabilities streamline the logistics process and secure transactions between trading partners and customers. The ability to transact and conduct business partnerships with industry efficiently depends on the use of commercial interface standards and protocols that facilitate electronic communications and data sharing.

- ◆ An integrated data environment (IDE) extends logistics functionality and enables life-cycle weapon system management by the military services, DLA, and the commercial sector. Contractors initially prepare most product data for weapon system and material acquisition in a digital electronic format. The IDE is accessible by all authorized supply chain participants.

- ◆ AIT facilitates asset identification and tracking. The logistics requirement for AIT is a mix of technologies that allows users to capture, aggregate, and transfer data and information efficiently and effectively. User data and information are integrated with DoD systems, technologies, software, and encoding formats, as well as international commercial applications.

◆ Commercial and international EDI standards are used to enable automated information exchanges with customers, the commercial sector, and allied nations.

◆ Product data consist of drawings and specifications in various media and formats and—in a related but often independently stored configuration—records. Logical product data repositories or access to commercial product databases enables integrated logistics support. Product data include all information about the design, manufacture, and support of an item, equipment, assembly, or system of assemblies.

◆ A Common Operating Environment (COE) ensures interoperability and enables rapid development of applications—as opposed to the current DoD environment of stovepipe systems. A COE specifies hardware and software that ensure that the logistics process is interoperable with capabilities developed by independent organizations within and outside the Department.

The foregoing list is not necessarily all-inclusive with regard to potential technological enablers, but it should assist the SCM team in reviewing the types of overall technical capabilities required to support future supply chain functional requirements as discussed in Chapter 7. In summary, information systems that support the future supply chain process will be based on an open architecture that separates applications, data, and presentations and enables changes to be incorporated rapidly. Logistics functional users should have electronic, real-time access to applications. This corporate functionality includes a COE and a common user interface that promote process integration and provide access to information wherever it resides in the logistics process. AIT should be used to identify and track physical assets throughout the supply chain.

This chapter completes our discussion of a strategy for implementation of the SCM concept in the DoD logistics process. As with many dramatic changes, the transition to a true supply chain environment in DoD will, of necessity, be evolutionary; there will be a significant number of false starts, misdirection, and setbacks. In the environment of the 21st century, however, the DoD logistics process inevitably will succumb to the reality that even in an environment as structured and controlled as military logistics, the highly competitive nature of market forces has become a driving factor in the way organizations do business. The customer of the DoD logistics process will no longer tolerate—nor be able to afford—a "take it or leave it" support system.

In the past two decades, the dramatic development of a world-class logistics process in the private sector has spawned a fierce competitor to the once totally dominant government-operated logistics structure. We have presented several strategies and actions that can guide and assist DoD managers in implementing an SCM approach for the military logistics process. In the final chapter of this *Guide*, we discuss a high-level perspective for the "start-up" phase of operating the newly reengineered process.

# Chapter 9
# Managing DoD Supply Chains

Implementation of the SCM concept in DoD will entail overcoming many obstacles. This effort will require establishment of common objectives across multiple organizations with significantly different current processes, systems, and cultures. In some respects, Chapters 1 through 8 of this *Guide* imply that SCM implementation is a mechanical process that can be achieved by accomplishing several predetermined actions. Although the tasks suggested in this *Guide* are essential for implementation, they are not the only elements that are necessary for long-term success.

To reap full benefits from the substantial amounts of time and resources required to implement SCM, DoD must institutionalize the transition to the new way of doing business in the day-to-day management and operation of the end-to-end logistics process. The military services and DLA will spend large sums of money and devote significant amounts of time just to acquire the hardware and software infrastructure needed to operate a minimally effective supply chain. Achieving notably improved performance and cost benefits will require even more resources and commitment over an extended period. This long-term commitment, particularly on the part of higher-level management, is so critical to success that proceeding without such assurances is tantamount to dooming the effort to failure.

If the organization's key management personnel are truly committed to implementing an SCM approach for the logistics process, there should be a significant change in the way the process is managed. Logistics managers at all levels typically feel trapped by the problems of day-to-day operations, coupled with the continued downward pressure of resource reductions. Managers often are unable to effect the changes needed to relieve near-term problems. Breaking this vicious cycle requires a new approach to managing the process.

Today's logistics managers focus largely on overseeing operation of their assigned functional segments of the process. For example, managers may be primarily concerned with materiel management, maintenance, transportation, budgeting, order processing, or other functional areas. Cross-functional issues are raised only at the highest levels of the organization.

In 1995, researchers at Michigan State University (MSU) developed an approach for logistics managers that facilitates a more corporate or universal perspective on a customer- or performance-oriented logistics process. The

MSU approach outlines a new way to address an organization's objective of achieving world class status. Although not all elements of the proposed approach are directly applicable to DoD logistics organizations, the model is broad enough to suggest a workable strategy to effect and ultimately manage required changes.

The MSU research advanced the idea that to attain world-class status in logistics, an organization must move toward a high level of competency in several areas. Competency is defined as "a state of being sufficient to gain and maintain selected customers."[1] There are four essential competencies, as shown in Figure 9-1.

*Figure 9-1. Logistics Competency Model*

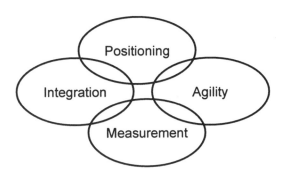

*Positioning.* The positioning competency involves creation and implementation of strategies and process approaches to achieving supply chain objectives. Effective supply chain managers focus directly on building these competencies and allocating resources to implement approved strategies.

*Integration.* This competency relates to establishing and maintaining all of the necessary mechanisms (rules, processes, and infrastructure) across the supply chain to implement desired strategies.

*Agility.* This competency entails establishing an organization's ability to identify and satisfy customer requirements through accommodation and flexibility.

---

[1] Global Logistics Research Team, Michigan State University, *World Class Logistics: The Challenge of Managing Continuous Change*, Oak Brook, Illinois: Council of Logistics Management, 1995.

*Measurement.* This competency involves focusing management's attention on establishing quantitative measures of actual and desired achievement, using functional assessment, benchmarking, and quantification of results.

Effective management of a DoD supply chain requires managers at all organizational levels to embrace these competencies as critical factors for accomplishing their responsibilities for particular supply chain elements. In their day-to-day activities, logistics managers must continuously assess ongoing and proposed individual activities, projects, and initiatives in the context of their relevance to one or more of these competencies. Clearly, this effort will require a significant cultural change on the part of many managers. In the future, simply having a good understanding of assigned functional processes will not be sufficient for effective management of the supply chain. In addition to subject matter knowledge and expertise, the logistics manager must fully understand and work toward enterprise-wide objectives by tracking actual progress in attaining increasing degrees of improvement in supply chain competencies.

To help identify required actions, the MSU researchers identified 17 specific capabilities that represent activities required to attain world-class levels of performance.[2] Although no organization can be expected to achieve perfect success in all of these capabilities, the collective grouping of these factors provides an excellent shopping list of target objectives and guidelines for managing the operation of the total supply chain. Table 9-1 outlines these 17 capabilities in DoD terms.

*Table 9-1. World-Class Logistics Model—Implementing Capabilities*

| Capability | Description |
|---|---|
| **Positioning** | |
| Strategy | Set customer-oriented goals and objectives and put in place implementing processes/enablers |
| Supply chain | Create working partnerships with all supply chain participants |
| Network | Implement physical infrastructure and facilities to manage total supply chain |
| Organization | Structure, relationships, and application of human resources to support supply chain operation |

---

[2] Ibid., p. 28.

*Table 9-1. World-Class Logistics Model—Implementing Capabilities*
*(Continued)*

| Capability | Description |
|---|---|
| **Integration** | |
| Unification | Promote establishment of working, effective interfaces among supply chain participants |
| Information technology | Evaluate and select technical enablers to permit effective supply chain process results |
| Information sharing | Build and operate automated capability to share all logistics and related management information required by all supply chain participants |
| Connectivity | Implement capability for data exchange interoperability among supply chain partners |
| Standardization | Establish common support conventions and responsibilities across organizations |
| Simplification | Streamline procedures and eliminate unneeded or redundant process elements |
| Discipline | Enforce adherence to approved policies and procedures |
| **Agility** | |
| Relevancy | Understand and satisfy customer-generated requirements |
| Accommodation | Ensure that supply chain process is designed to respond to changing customer requirements |
| Flexibility | Manage supply chain on the basis of providing timely response to dynamic customer requirements |
| **Measurement** | |
| Functional assessment | Implement comprehensive measures of performance of discrete process elements or logical functional groupings |
| Process assessment | Implement comprehensive quantification of performance against customer-oriented metrics |
| Benchmarking | Compare and assess organizational performance against specific measures of world-class supply chain organizations |

Table 9-1 provides a good supply chain operational checklist for logistics managers at all organizational levels of DoD. Coincidentally, there is a significant resemblance between the competency list developed by the MSU researchers and the DoD supply chain guiding principles discussed in Chapter 2. The similarities are understandable even though the lists were developed independently. The MSU researchers concluded that there is a universality of required supply chain capabilities not only in North America but throughout the developed world.[3] If this conclusion is correct, and if most of the findings of research conducted for this *Guide* are in agreement, implementation and long-term management of the supply chain in DoD must follow the same pattern and exhibit the same characteristics as in private-sector experiences. Clearly, implementation of SCM on a large scale in DoD will require a significant reevaluation of management approaches in most logistics organizations. In addition to developing an effective SCM strategy, DoD logistics managers require a more comprehensive and accurate way of determining and assessing the costs of the logistics process.

## Activity-Based Costing

In the financial management area, DoD organizations traditionally have focused primarily on budget development and execution. GAO and Congressional committees often have criticized the Department for lacking an effective cost accounting process. In Chapter 4 we suggest that the SCM implementation team explore the possibility of building an ABC capability concurrent with its analysis of SCM implementation requirements.

Although cost accounting is not a principal responsibility of the SCM implementation team, cost assessment—and, ultimately, allocation of financial resources—is of direct interest to supply chain managers. For the foreseeable future, DoD logistics processes and organizations can expect to be considered "bill-payers" in support of the Department's weapons and equipment modernization programs. Faced with continuing reductions in available resources, logistics business managers need greater visibility and analytical understanding of where scarce resources are being expended. The need for changing processes and systems to accomplish SCM provides a unique opportunity to promote concurrent implementation of ABC capabilities in logistics processes.

A workflow model is designed to represent a business process as a set of activities that flow horizontally across the organizational structure. This approach for viewing business processes allows the manager to understand the sequence of "how work gets done" in the organization and how products and services are produced for the customer. In the same manner, understanding and analyzing the costs incurred by these activities is necessary for optimizing the cost-effectiveness of an organization's business processes. Association of costs with specific activities is known as ABC.

---

[3] Ibid., p. 13.

ABC requires a shift in thinking away from the historical assignment of costs to departments or organizations. (Such thinking associated monthly or annual costs with the production department, the finance department, the sales and marketing department, etc.) Cost-containment efforts in the past requested a lowering of expenses in an organization such as the production department. This request was based on an assumption of inefficiencies, but it provided no direction about how to achieve the cost reduction targets.

ABC requires cost analysis to go beyond typical operation and maintenance (O&M) expenses such as salaries, materials, depreciation, travel, and facilities. Traditional cost accounting methods assign overhead costs to products or services by using allocation calculations that are based on irrelevant labor or material costs. ABC identifies actual costs incurred by a business process's component activities as they are being performed. ABC provides that information by using multiple sources to assign costs on the basis of consumption of resources. Instead of lumping logistics costs into standardized categories, ABC breaks the accounting general ledger into homogeneous resource categories and assigns those costs to the specific activities performed, such as purchasing, receiving, warehousing, and order processing.

Because ABC can assign activity costs to the consuming customer, commodity, or supply chain activity, ABC information can provide considerable insight into how different customers or products affect the operation of logistics activities and drive total costs. Coupling ABC with process simulation can provide a useful tool in analyzing how proposed logistics process changes may affect the performance of services or activities provided to the customer, as well as how these changes will alter resource consumption.

An extension of ABC called activity-based management (ABM) has emerged recently. This process analysis methodology uses the cost data aspects of ABC to help assess the quantitative impacts of process improvement activities.

ABC enables activity costs to be examined and assists in optimizing costs individually and across the supply chain. Once changed, the model of the business process is reanalyzed to determine the effects on the entire process. As a result, a true picture of the cost of doing business is produced. The cost of doing business may be calculated for specific products, services, business processes, market segments, distribution channels, projects, and so forth. The uses for ABC are many and varied. The following list provides typical efforts in which ABC has been successfully employed:

◆ Developing benchmarks of current process/product/service costs

◆ Identifying areas that are not cost-effective in current processes

◆ Analyzing value-added versus non–value-added costs

◆ Determining the cost impact of outsourcing decisions

◆ Supporting redeployment, cost-cutting, and right-sizing decisions

◆ Determining costs for improved or redesigned business processes

◆ Verifying the cost-effectiveness of business process improvement efforts

◆ Determining cost targets and budgets for business processes.

Experience in DoD logistics management has shown that using subjective judgments in efforts such as those listed above often has been inadequate, misleading, and extremely costly. ABC provides a quantitative means for evaluating process change when the objective is meaningful improvement in cost-effectiveness. By following a structured approach to analyzing expenditures, ABC can support the essential analysis needed to make key decisions.

The cost and staffing required to implement ABC is the most common reason for not considering ABC or deciding not to implement it. In DoD, obtaining approval for ABC implementation on a stand-alone basis may be very difficult. DoD managers traditionally have given only lip service to the requirement for a comprehensive, modern accounting process. Not only is such an implementation costly, the need for it is obscured by the fact that government organizations are not bound by the requirement to maintain tax records; nor are they concerned with accurately quantifying an annual profit and loss balance sheet.

One approach to ABC implementation involves combining adoption of ABC with the supply chain process reengineering initiative. This approach begins with diagramming logistics activities the organization performs in the operational node connectivity diagram. Then the ABC effort attempts to assign costs to each of the detailed activities identified during the process charting.

Compared with a pure costing approach, a reengineering-linked approach requires significantly more time, effort, and funding to implement because it requires a much larger number of cost drivers for the assignment of resource costs to a very large number of activities. It also must determine how each activity is actually "consumed" to allow assignment of the activity costs. Yet reengineering approaches provide considerably more insight into the elements driving process costs. The chief drawback is the amount of time required to obtain cost information and link it to actual process activities.

For the SCM team, an ABC implementation strategy initially may have to focus on a small-scale pilot project to determine the viability and value of a cost analysis capability for logistics activities. For the long term, the team should press for acquisition of commercial software packages that have imbedded ABC modules or accommodate ABC bolt-on capability.

Besides building a more effective approach to evaluating logistics costs, using ABC would support the need for future supply chain managers to increase their focus on the performance of the total supply chain.

## Performance Measurement

In the future, the effective supply chain manager must have a customer-centered view of the logistics process. The manager also must have a holistic perspective that comprehends the end-to-end process, regardless of the manager's specific niche in the supply chain. Therefore, up-to-date and accurate information on the operational status of all segments of the supply chain must be readily available to all process participants. The importance of supply chain managers having ready access to performance metrics information cannot be overemphasized. In addition, overall performance metrics reports for all participants in a supply chain, regardless of their functional responsibilities, should be consistent, timely, and accurate.

Although many of today's metrics provide useful information, they generally do not provide senior managers with a sense of how well the overall supply chain is performing. In summary, current metrics

♦ Do not measure *total supply chain performance*. Many metrics measure only wholesale performance. Others simply measure the implementation of an initiative without any link to performance metrics that should indicate resulting supply chain improvement.

◆ Are *not linked or correlated* to one another so managers can consider important supply chain relationships. For example, reducing inventory to save money may not be beneficial if readiness rates are declining.

In Chapter 5 we propose implementation of measures designed to portray the results of total supply chain performance as an essential part of the SCM strategy. Traditionally, DoD logistics managers assess performance metrics individually, with little regard to causative relationships between metrics. Furthermore, some metrics are measures of size rather than performance. For example, inventory turnover measures performance, whereas value of inventory measures size. Using size or capacity measures as surrogates for performance often is misleading and in some instances results in establishment of initiatives that have little relevance to—or can even be counterproductive to—achieving performance objectives.

Supply chain managers must operate with full understanding of the applicability and utility of the metrics they are tracking.

Figure 9-2 shows three levels of DoD performance measurement.[4] The top level of the pyramid is the enterprise level. This level should encompass the comprehensive supply chain metrics. The next level of the pyramid is the functional level (e.g., supply, maintenance, and transportation). The bottom level of the pyramid is the process level.

*Figure 9-2. Three Levels of DoD Performance Measures*

---

[4] Logistics Management Institute, *Logistics Functional Requirements Guide*, Report LG806S2, James Reay and Jim Kimberley, August 1998, pp. 5-13.

Enterprise metrics measure the overall effectiveness of the supply chain. In this architecture, the metrics are linked. The metrics selected for the enterprise level typically are cross-functional and measure overall performance. Functional metrics are linked to at least one enterprise metric and measure a major function's performance. Through analysis, logistics managers should recognize that successful attainment of valid performance goals at each level of the pyramid should contribute to accomplishment of performance goals at higher levels of the pyramid. Process (e.g., warehousing, requirements planning) metrics are related to one or more functional metrics and are diagnostic in nature. Process metrics are used to monitor day-to-day effectiveness or to assess problems of individual segments of the supply chain but should not be the primary focus when managers review overall supply chain performance.

As the SCM team constructs the organization's supply chain design, mechanisms to collect, summarize, and evaluate the enterprise metrics data must be fully integrated into the process, and the management information capability to provide metrics performance reporting to all levels of management must be fully operational.

To be successful, future DoD supply chain managers must adopt an end-to-end strategy for managing the supply chain and continuously focusing on customer requirements. They also must acquire and use the tools necessary to manage supply chain costs and assess progress toward performance objectives. Finally, an effective supply chain manager must recognize where his or her organization is in the path toward the goal of implementing a world-class supply chain operation. This perspective is essential because supply chain managers must recognize that implementation of SCM will be accomplished over time as required changes to current processes are put into place.

Several studies focusing on SCM implementation in the private sector have concluded that there are definable and distinctive stages of evolution in organizations that adopt the SCM approach. Charles Poirier of Computer Sciences Corporation has articulated one of these perspectives.[5]

---

[5] Charles C. Poirier, *Advanced Supply Chain Management*, San Francisco: Berrett-Koehler Publishers, 1999, p. 24.

After conducting a long-term review of several hundred companies engaged in SCM implementation, Poirier concluded that the stages or "levels" of progression are as follows:

◆ *Level 1: Sourcing and logistics stage.* At this level, the focus is on individual process improvement initiatives in various areas of logistics management. The objective usually is to redesign or modernize certain segments of the supply chain or to reduce corresponding costs. Projects tend to concentrate on improving internal operations in the organization. Performance metrics tend to be fragmented or not directly related to process improvement efforts. Substantial emphasis is on technological modernization. There may be no overall master plan. Improvement results tend to be marginal.

◆ *Level 2: Internal excellence stage.* In this stage, improvement initiatives often are prioritized and tied to improvements in performance metrics. Initiatives are more integrated, and the concept of continuous process improvement is introduced. An overall strategic plan is developed. Cost savings remain a primary emphasis. Improvement initiatives are still largely aimed at individual processes rather than customer satisfaction. Little attention is given to the total supply chain network. Only limited development of long-term partnerships outside the organization is pursued. Training is largely process or technology oriented.

◆ *Level 3: Network construction stage.* This stage represents a major transition in the organizational objectives, culture, and focus of improvement activity. Customer-centered enterprise performance metrics are implemented throughout the supply chain. Partnerships and alliances are developed with external suppliers and customers. Initiatives focus on adding value rather than technological modernization. Process elements are coordinated across all supply chain activities and aim at network performance and total cost reduction. Core competencies are reviewed and evaluated on the basis of maximizing customer satisfaction and contributing to overall supply chain performance. Activity-centered cost models are implemented. Process improvement initiatives are cross-functional, targeting enterprise metrics improvements. Shared data is a common capability. Supply segments of the chain are linked more closely and directly to demand elements to minimize cycle times, increase accuracy of requirements, and eliminate non–value-added activity.

◆ *Level 4: Industry leadership stage.* At this stage, the organization becomes the supplier of choice to the vast majority of its customers. World-class performance is identified through benchmarking, and the supply chain moves significantly closer to meeting these high levels of performance and value. Traditionally compartmentalized and narrowly focused attitudes are changed through value-oriented training programs. The global communications network and integrated databases extend from supplier to customer organizations and encompass all supply chain elements. Cultural values are modified to promote innovation and imaginative thinking at all levels. Customer support is highly customized.

Nearly all DoD logistics organizations now operate at level 1 or, to a minimal degree, level 2. The transition from level 2 to level 3 is by far the most difficult in an organization's progression toward fully implementing SCM at level 4. In fact, relatively few private-sector companies have made this transition successfully. The SCM team and the managers of the logistics organization should make an objective and realistic appraisal of the status of their supply chain transformation program as soon as possible. Unfortunately, in any organization there often is a strong tendency to set lower targets to assure success. Sometimes, political realities or other factors require such machinations. As Abraham Lincoln said, however, "You can fool some of the people all of the time; all of the people some of the time; but you cannot fool all of the people all of the time." Nor should DoD logistics managers fool themselves.

The road to implementation of SCM in DoD promises to be long and challenging. An unbiased assessment of the location of the starting point is essential for responsible logistics managers to make rational and effective decisions regarding the major investment in time and resources required to implement SCM. In the private sector, only a small number of leadership companies have reached the pinnacle of success in the supply chain hierarchy. Clearly, there is still plenty of room at the top.

# Appendix A
# Key Principles for Project Management Success

This Web-published article by Michael Greer is an excerpt from Chapter 6, "Planning and Managing Human Performance Technology Projects," in *Handbook of Human Performance Technology* (San Francisco: Jossey-Bass, 1999).[1]

1.  Project managers must focus on three dimensions of project success. Simply put, project success means completing all project deliverables on time, within budget, and to a level of quality that is acceptable to sponsors and stakeholders. The project manager must keep the team's attention focused on achieving these broad goals.

2.  Planning is everything—and ongoing. On one thing all PM texts and authorities agree: The single most important activity that project managers engage in is planning—detailed, systematic, team-involved plans are the only foundation for project success. And when real-world events conspire to change the plan, project managers must make a new one to reflect the changes. So planning and replanning must be a way of life for project managers.

3.  Project managers must feel, and transmit to their team members, a sense of urgency. Because projects are finite endeavors with limited time, money, and other resources available, they must be kept moving toward completion. Since most team members have lots of other priorities, it's up to the project manager to keep their attention on project deliverables and deadlines. Regular status checks, meetings, and reminders are essential.

4.  Successful projects use a time-tested, proven project life cycle. We know what works. Standard Models can help ensure that professional standards and best practices are built into our project plans. Not only do these models typically support quality, they help to minimize re-work. So when time or budget pressures seem to encourage taking short cuts, it's up to the project manager to identify and defend the best project life cycle for the job.

---

[1] Further information may be obtained at http://www.michaelgreer.com/.

5.  All project deliverables and all project activities must be visualized and communicated in vivid detail. In short, the project manager and project team must early on create a tangible picture of the finished deliverables in the minds of everyone involved so that all effort is focused in the same direction. Avoid vague descriptions at all costs; spell it out, picture it, prototype it, and make sure everyone agrees to it.

6.  Deliverables must evolve gradually, in successive approximations. It simply costs too much and risks too much time spent in rework to jump in with both feet and begin building all project deliverables. Build a little at a time, obtain incremental reviews and approvals, and maintain a controlled evolution.

7.  Projects require clear approvals and sign-off by sponsors. Clear approval points, accompanied by formal sign-off by sponsors, subject matter experts (SMEs), and other key stakeholders, should be demarcation points in the evolution of project deliverables. It's this simple: anyone who has the power to reject or to demand revision of deliverables after they are complete must be required to examine and approve them as they are being built.

8.  Project success is correlated with thorough analyses of the need for project deliverables. Our research has shown that when a project results in deliverables that are designed to meet a thoroughly documented need, then there is a greater likelihood of project success. So managers should insist that there is a documented business need for the project before they agree to consume organizational resources in completing it.

9.  Project managers must fight for time to do things right. In our work with project managers we often hear this complaint: "We always seem to have time to do the project over; I just wish we had taken the time to do it right in the first place!" Projects must have available enough time to "do it right the first time." And project managers must fight for this time by demonstrating to sponsors and top managers why it's necessary and how time spent will result in quality deliverables.

10. Project manager responsibility must be matched by equivalent authority. It's not enough to be held responsible for project outcomes; project managers must ask for and obtain enough authority to execute their responsibilities. Specifically, managers must have the authority to acquire and coordinate resources, request and receive SME cooperation, and make appropriate, binding decisions which have an impact on the success of the project.

11. Project sponsors and stakeholders must be active participants, not passive customers. Most project sponsors and stakeholders rightfully demand the authority to approve project deliverables, either wholly or in part. Along with this authority comes the responsibility to be an active participant in the early stages of the project (helping to define deliverables), to complete reviews of interim deliverables in a timely fashion (keeping the project moving), and to help expedite the project manager's access to SMEs, members of the target audience, and essential documentation.

12. Projects typically must be sold, and resold. There are times when the project manager must function as salesperson to maintain the commitment of stakeholders and sponsors. With project plans in hand, project managers may need to periodically remind people about the business need that is being met and that their contributions are essential to help meet this need.

13. Project managers should acquire the best people they can and then do whatever it takes to keep the garbage out of their way. By acquiring the best people—the most skilled, the most experienced, the best qualified—the project manager can often compensate for too little time or money or other project constraints. Project managers should serve as an advocate for these valuable team members, helping to protect them from outside interruptions and helping them acquire the tools and working conditions necessary to apply their talents.

14. Top management must actively set priorities. In today's leaner, self-managing organizations, it is not uncommon for project team members to be expected to play active roles on many project teams at the same time. Ultimately, there comes a time when resources are stretched to their limits and there are simply too many projects to be completed successfully. In response, some organizations have established a Project Office comprised of top managers from all departments to act as a clearinghouse for projects and project requests. The Project Office reviews the organization's overall mission and strategies, establishes criteria for project selection and funding, monitors resource workloads, and determines which projects are of high enough priority to be approved. In this way top management provides the leadership necessary to prevent multi-project logjams.

# Appendix B
# Focused Logistics Desired Operational Capabilities for Supply Chain Management

Desired operational capabilities (DOCs) are concept-based statements of operational capabilities required to satisfy a Joint Force Commander's needs in 2010 and beyond and meet 21st Century Challenge requirements. Table B-1 contains current logistics-related DOCs that have been developed and validated by the Joint Staff, Services, DoD agencies, and CINCs through a collaborative process. These logistics DOCs may be used as basic building blocks and primary information categories for more specific supply chain requirements contained in this document.

*Table B-1. Focused Logistics DOCs*

| No. | DOC | Description |
|-----|-----|-------------|
| FL-01 | Provide unimpeded access to operational and logistics information for all who need it. | Provides an operating architecture that allows any user access to operational and logistics data worldwide from a single terminal. Includes logistics policies, procedures, protocols, standards, access control, and security. Will result in *better information* and *improved interoperability*. Requires a reliable and robust interactive command and control network that links operational and tactical combat and support forces information systems. Relies on a communications backbone with redundant communications hardware, software, links, redundancy, survivability, and maintenance. Architecture will allow support activities access to commanders' directions, orders, and execution status. It also will allow commanders access to support requirements, capabilities, and status. Information fusion architecture and information superiority infrastructure will provide means for interoperability across and between logistics and operational functions, as well as expanded availability of logistics information to commanders and their staffs. This DOC conceptualizes the foundation or "operating environment" for information fusion. |

## Table B-1. Focused Logistics DOCs (Continued)

| No. | DOC | Description |
|---|---|---|
| FL-04 | Provide timely and accurate enhanced asset visibility, control, and management. | Provides a fully synchronized means to collect and access continuous real-time information on the location; movement; status; and identity of units, personnel, equipment, and supplies; includes the ability to act on that information. Visibility, control, and management extend to assets in process, in storage, and in transit. Requires collection and integration of *better information* from all echelons, *improved modeling and simulation* tools to optimize logistics plans and operations, and improved *interoperability* among logistics applications and command and control systems to disseminate information and decisions to all who require them. Includes logistics automation policies, procedures, software, equipment, and systems architecture. Also includes a fused operational and logistical picture that annotates units according to their state of logistical readiness—units fully supplied, units requiring supplies, units depleted and combat ineffective. The fused picture predicts the time before resupply at current/predicted rates of expenditure; time to accomplish resupply; and at-a-glance status of each unit's personnel, fuel, and munitions disposition. Requires J-7/J-3 to implement a fully integrated command and control system and J-6 to establish a robust communications infrastructure. This DOC depicts the fusion of logistics applications into powerful, predictive, decision support and execution tools. |
| FL-05 | Provide fully enabled mobility system to optimize rapid joint force projection, delivery, and hand-off of forces and sustainment assets worldwide. | *Improves the joint deployment and distribution process.* Provides a fully integrated process to deploy forces and sustainment worldwide. Includes concepts, doctrine, technological material, and process changes necessary to *use transportation assets more effectively and efficiently.* Also provides a flexible process to receive and transfer units and support to responsible tactical commander. Depending on the extent to which forces have been tailored, equipped, and loaded prior to deployment, the traditional steps of reception, staging, onward movement, and integration may be streamlined or eliminated. May be conducted independently of fixed infrastructure. Incorporates modernized and tailorable prepositioned equipment that is strategically and operationally flexible. |

*Table B-1. Focused Logistics DOCs (Continued)*

| No. | DOC | Description |
|---|---|---|
| FL-06 | Deploy and distribute required forces and sustain at the place and time required. | Provides assets to deploy and distribute forces and sustainment worldwide. Includes airlift and sealift assets, afloat prepositioning assets, and en route support. Effective, efficient use of assets requires improved deployment and distribution processes, communications, command and control, information systems, and decision support tools. |
| FL-07 | Support rapid force maneuver within joint operations area. | Provides a fully integrated capability to sustain and support maneuver in the battlespace. Focuses on alternative uses of transportation assets, including strategic assets and Joint Logistics Over-the-Shore, to support maneuver and sustainment of widely dispersed forces within a nonlinear battlespace. Requires transportation assets and improved communications, command and control, information systems, and decision support tools. Leverages information, logistics, and transportation technologies to plan and execute support of joint operations. Integrates support to provide rapid crisis response, tracking and shifting assets while en route to deliver tailored logistics packages with minimal footprint and early initiation of sustainment directly at strategic, operational, and tactical levels of operation. |
| FL-08 | Provide joint health services support. | Protects forces from all health threats across the full spectrum of conflict. |
| FL-17 | Provide effective, efficient, and responsive infrastructure and logistics support to meet CINC/warfighter operational requirements. | Provides, maintains, and coordinates optimum levels of logistics forces, materials, and consumables necessary to support the national military strategy; provides logistics support to sustain the force in the execution of theater strategy, campaigns, and joint operations. Maximizes logistics support to deployed forces through direct deployment and rapid integration of tailored logistics forces and pinpoints delivery of tailored logistics packages into the battlespace. Includes coordination of the wholesale base and acquisition of material, facilities, and services. Minimizing the need for logistics forces and material in the battlespace depends on a restructured logistics infrastructure outside the theater that can rapidly source and deliver supplies and services. Also includes reduction of supply and maintenance requirements through highly reliable, low-maintenance combat, combat support, and combat service support systems, as well as |

## Table B-1. Focused Logistics DOCs (Continued)

| No. | DOC | Description |
|---|---|---|
| FL-17 contd. | | maintenance capability for "self diagnostics" and "advanced notice failure sensors linked to supply/maintenance activities" for quick resolution or preemptive action. Requires full integration of multinational support; command, control, and communications; automated decision support systems; and systemic restructuring to achieve direct delivery from source to user. |
| FL-20 | Provide capability to synchronize, prioritize, direct, integrate, and co-ordinate common user and cross-Service logistics functions. | Coordinates logistics support to sustain the force in the execution of theater strategy, campaigns, and joint operations. Effectively employs the logistics capability of each Service in theater to support common requirements and general support missions. Exploits emerging logistics enablers and reduces the size of the logistics footprint. Requires full integration of component support capability; robust command, control, and communications; and reliable automated decision support systems. |
| FL-33 | Tailor health care in theater. | Tailors units to provide essential care in theater and enhanced care during evacuation to definitive care. |
| FL-35 | Optimize logistical operations across and between all echelons, coalitions, and host nations. | Provides sustainment support from sources other than the U.S. military. Includes harmonizing the logistics approaches of different national forces; increasing interoperability; and improving command, control, and command relations. Accomplished through in-place bilateral logistics agreements and improved capability to conduct multinational operations within established organizations such as the UN and NATO. Requires optimizing multinational logistics and information-sharing capability. Provides a common logistics picture for member forces, tailored to their requirements and consistent with disclosure policies. Includes policies, procedures, agreements, protocols, standards, access control, security, communications links, hardware and software, maintenance, redundancy, and survivability. |
| FL-36 | Provide responsive engineering support. | Provides effective, efficient, responsive engineering support to meet CINC/warfighter operational requirements and time frames. |

DOCs that relate to health services and engineering are included in the logistics group, but only supporting requirements for those areas that relate to mobility deployment and provision of material support to the joint warfighter are incorporated into the specific requirements list in Chapter 7.

# Appendix C
# Logistics Model

This appendix includes a high-level listing of the DoD logistics process elements, including the three major DoD components: conducting warfighting, acquiring technical capabilities, and managing readiness. Two logistics elements—providing force structure support and maintaining quality of life—that reside in the managing readiness portion of the model are the focus of this guide. (See Figure C-1.) DoD's supply chain management (SCM) responsibilities are embedded in these two elements; they support the "conducting warfighting" and "acquiring technical capability" areas. DoD will continue to require the supply chain-related areas portrayed as a part of managing readiness; they are principal targets, however, for substantial reengineering and alternative, competitive sourcing. A graphical version of this model is published in the *DoD Logistics Functional Requirements Guide.*[1]

*Figure C-1. The DoD Process*

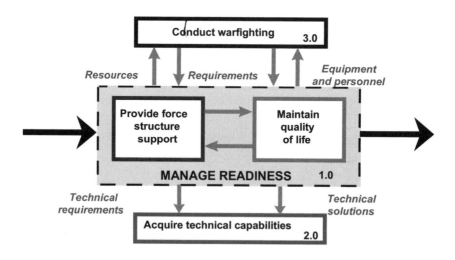

---

[1] U.S. Department of Defense, Deputy Under Secretary of Defense (Logistics), *DoD Logistics Functional Requirements Guide*, August 1998, Appendix C.

1.0 Manage Readiness

   1.1 Plan Strategies

      1.1.1   Analyze Threats

      1.1.2   Analyze Constraints

      1.1.3   Establish Vision and Direction

   1.2 Plan Contingencies

      1.2.1   Conduct Simulations

      1.2.2   Establish Force Levels

      1.2.3   Position Forces

   1.3 Plan Operations

      1.3.1   Establish Objectives

      1.3.2   Design Exercises

      1.3.3   Direct Operations

   1.4 Develop Program

      1.4.1   Identify Deficiencies

      1.4.2   Assess Technical Risks

      1.4.3   Identify Requirements

      1.4.4   Program Resources

   1.5 Manage Personnel

      1.5.1   Recruit Resources

      1.5.2   Manage Placement

      1.5.3   Provide Payroll

      1.5.4   Manage Records

   1.6 Conduct Tactical Training

      1.6.1   Conduct Exercises

      1.6.2   Evaluate Performance

      1.6.3   Identify Deficiencies

1.7 Provide Technical Training

    1.7.1    Establish Standards

    1.7.2    Develop Curriculum

    1.7.3    Schedule Courses

1.8 Provide Force Structure Support

    1.8.1    Manage End Items

        1.8.1.1  Maintain End Items and Equipment

            1.8.1.1.1    Plan Maintenance

                1.8.1.1.1.1  Develop Strategic Plans

                1.8.1.1.1.2  Develop Contingency Plans

                1.8.1.1.1.3  Develop Capabilities and Modernization Plans

                1.8.1.1.1.4  Plan Resources

                1.8.1.1.1.5  Plan Workload

            1.8.1.1.2    Arrange Repair

                1.8.1.1.2.1  Select Sources

                1.8.1.1.2.2  Negotiate Workload

                1.8.1.1.2.3  Award Contracts

                1.8.1.1.2.4  Issue Orders

                1.8.1.1.2.5  Monitor Orders

                1.8.1.1.2.6  Accept Orders

                1.8.1.1.2.7  Close Contracts

            1.8.1.1.3    Plan Production

                1.8.1.1.3.1  Manage Products and Projects

                1.8.1.1.3.2  Plan Authorized Jobs

                1.8.1.1.3.3  Develop Schedules

                1.8.1.1.3.4  Manage Personnel Skills

                1.8.1.1.3.5  Manage Facilities

1.8.1.1.3.6  Manage Tools and Test Equipment

1.8.1.1.3.7  Manage Material

1.8.1.1.3.8  Audit Physical Configuration

1.8.1.1.4  Manage Resources

1.8.1.1.4.1  Develop Budgets

1.8.1.1.4.2  Perform Financial Management

1.8.1.1.5  Execute Maintenance

1.8.1.1.5.1  Develop Operations Packages

1.8.1.1.5.2  Assign Workload

1.8.1.1.5.3  Perform Maintenance

1.8.1.1.5.4  Manage Production Problems

1.8.1.1.5.5  Perform Preventive Maintenance

1.8.1.1.6  Support Operations

1.8.1.1.6.1  Manage Quality and Performance

1.8.1.1.6.2  Manage Environmental Compliance

1.8.1.1.6.3  Manage Information and Systems

1.8.1.1.6.4  Manage Calibration Compliance

1.8.1.2  Sustain Engineering

1.8.1.2.1  Control Configuration

1.8.1.2.1.1  Manage Product Baselines

1.8.1.2.1.2  Review Engineering Change Proposals

1.8.1.2.1.3  Issue Technical Directives

1.8.1.2.1.4  Manage Modifications

1.8.1.2.1.5  Coordinate Interface Control Documents

1.8.1.2.2  Analyze Reliability, Maintainability, and Availability

1.8.1.2.2.1  Review Maintenance Data

1.8.1.2.2.2  Revise Maintenance Plans and Procedures

1.8.2.1.6    Manage Resources

    1.8.2.1.6.1  Develop Budgets

    1.8.2.1.6.2  Account for Finances

    1.8.2.1.6.3  Account for Costs

    1.8.2.1.6.4  Certify Funds Availability

    1.8.2.1.6.5  Pay Bills

1.8.2.2  Procure Spares and Repair Parts

    1.8.2.2.1    Plan Acquisition

    1.8.2.2.1.1  Determine Capital Resources

    1.8.2.2.1.2  Plan Workload

    1.8.2.2.1.3  Determine Organization Size and Structure

    1.8.2.2.2    Manage Resources

    1.8.2.2.2.1  Develop Budgets

    1.8.2.2.2.2  Account for Finances

    1.8.2.2.2.3  Account for Costs

    1.8.2.2.2.4  Certify Funds Availability

    1.8.2.2.2.5  Pay Bills

    1.8.2.2.3    Identify Spares and Repair Parts

    1.8.2.2.3.1  Screen Parts Lists

    1.8.2.2.3.2  Assign Item Manager

    1.8.2.2.3.3  Establish Management Method

    1.8.2.2.3.4  Establish Acquisition Method

    1.8.2.2.3.5  Establish Application Data

    1.8.2.2.3.6  Determine Initial Spares

    1.8.2.2.3.7  Develop Item Description

    1.8.2.2.4    Compute Requirements

    1.8.2.2.4.1  Validate Input Data

    1.8.2.2.4.2  Compute Demand Rates

1.8.2.3  Store Spares and Material

    1.8.2.3.1    Plan Workload

        1.8.2.3.1.1  Develop Strategic Plans

        1.8.2.3.1.2  Develop Contingency Plans

        1.8.2.3.1.3  Develop Capability Modernization Plans

        1.8.2.3.1.4  Plan Resources

        1.8.2.3.1.5  Plan Workload Facilities

    1.8.2.3.2    Arrange Storage

        1.8.2.3.2.1  Determine Sources

        1.8.2.3.2.2  Negotiate Workload

        1.8.2.3.2.3  Award Contracts

        1.8.2.3.2.4  Issue Orders

        1.8.2.3.2.5  Monitor Orders

        1.8.2.3.2.6  Accept Material

        1.8.2.3.2.7  Close Contracts

    1.8.2.3.3    Manage Resources

        1.8.2.3.3.1  Develop Budgets

        1.8.2.3.3.2  Perform Financial Management

    1.8.2.3.4    Receive Material

        1.8.2.3.4.1  Check Material In

        1.8.2.3.4.2  Inspect Material

        1.8.2.3.4.3  Prepare Material for Storage and Shipment

        1.8.2.3.4.4  Stow Material

    1.8.2.3.5    Manage Storage

        1.8.2.3.5.1  Maintain Inventory Records

        1.8.2.3.5.2  Perform Physical Inventories

        1.8.2.3.5.3  Perform Inspections

        1.8.2.3.5.4  Control Special Materials

1.8.3.3 Manage Infrastructure

    1.8.3.3.1    Manage Ports

    1.8.3.3.2    Manage Other Assets; Containers, Rail Fleet

    1.8.3.3.3    Maintain Lift Assets

1.8.3.4 Manage Transportation Operations

    1.8.3.4.1    Determine Short-Term (Current) Requirements

    1.8.3.4.2    Allocate Strategic Assets

    1.8.3.4.3    Arrange Shipments

        1.8.3.4.3.1  Select Mode

        1.8.3.4.3.2  Select Carrier

        1.8.3.4.3.3  Prepare Shipment

        1.8.3.4.3.4  Prepare Documentation

        1.8.3.4.3.5  Bookings and Reservations

    1.8.3.4.4    Conduct Operations

    1.8.3.4.5    Track Shipments

    1.8.3.4.6    Divert, Reconsign, Transship Shipments

    1.8.3.4.7    Process Claims

1.9 Maintain Quality of Life

1.9.1    Provide Facilities

1.9.1.1 Identify Requirements

1.9.1.2 Provide Housing

1.9.1.3 Manage Transportation of Household Goods

1.9.1.4 Provide Education

1.9.1.5 Provide Family Services

1.9.1.6 Operate Exchanges

1.9.1.7 Provide Travel Services

1.9.1.8  Maintain Operating and Support Facilities

    1.9.1.8.1    Determine Material and Repair Requirements

    1.9.1.8.2    Acquire Support Material and Equipment

    1.9.1.8.3    Store and Distribute Material and Equipment

    1.9.1.8.4    Maintain Property Records

    1.9.1.8.5    Maintain Equipment and Real Property

    1.9.1.8.6    Dispose of Excesses

1.9.1.9  Close and Dispose of Excess Facilities

1.9.2    Provide Medical Services

1.9.2.1  Acquire and Train Medical Personnel

1.9.2.2  Operate Hospitals and Clinics

1.9.2.3  Manage Financial Support and Records

1.9.2.4  Acquire Medical Supplies and Equipment

    1.9.2.4.1    Identify Items

    1.9.2.4.2    Compute Requirements

    1.9.2.4.3    Determine Sources

    1.9.2.4.4    Arrange Agreements

    1.9.2.4.5    Analyze Product Data

    1.9.2.4.6    Purchase Materials

    1.9.2.4.7    Monitor Orders

    1.9.2.4.8    Accept Materials

    1.9.2.4.9    Position Inventories

1.9.2.5  Store and Distribute Medical Supplies and Equipment

    1.9.2.5.1    Receive Material

    1.9.2.5.2    Issue Material

    1.9.2.5.3    Manage Inventory

    1.9.2.5.4    Consolidate Material and Orders

    1.9.2.5.5    Process Returns

1.9.2.6  Test Products and Services

1.9.2.7  Provide Theater Medical Support

1.9.2.8  Dispose of Waste and Excess

    1.9.2.8.1   Compute Requirements

    1.9.2.8.2   Manage Reutilization

    1.9.2.8.3   Condemn Assets

    1.9.2.8.4   Evaluate Contents

    1.9.2.8.5   Conduct Sales

    1.9.2.8.6   Dispose of Waste

1.9.3    Provide Subsistence

1.9.3.1  Identify Requirements

1.9.3.2  Procure Subsistence

    1.9.3.2.1   Identify Items

    1.9.3.2.2   Compute Requirements

    1.9.3.2.3   Determine Sources

    1.9.3.2.4   Arrange Agreements

    1.9.3.2.5   Analyze Product Data

    1.9.3.2.6   Purchase Subsistence Products

    1.9.3.2.7   Monitor Orders and Deliveries

    1.9.3.2.8   Accept Delivery of Product

    1.9.3.2.9   Manage Product

1.9.3.3  Store and Distribute Subsistence

    1.9.3.3.1   Receive Material

    1.9.3.3.2   Manage Inventory

    1.9.3.3.3   Ensure Quality and Shelf Life

    1.9.3.3.4   Consolidate Materials and Orders

    1.9.3.3.5   Issue Product

    1.9.3.3.6   Process Returns

1.9.4.5  Store and Distribute Clothing and Equipment

    1.9.4.5.1    Receive Material

    1.9.4.5.2    Manage Inventory

    1.9.4.5.3    Consolidate Materials and Orders

    1.9.4.5.4    Issue Clothing and Equipment

    1.9.4.5.5    Process Returns

1.9.4.6  Test Products

1.9.4.7  Dispose of Excesses

    1.9.4.7.1    Compute Requirements

    1.9.4.7.2    Manage Reutilization

    1.9.4.7.3    Condemn Assets

    1.9.4.7.4    Conduct Sales

    1.9.4.7.5    Dispose of Waste

2.0  Acquire Technical Capabilities

2.1  Explore Concepts

    2.1.1    Research Technology

    2.1.2    Determine Sources

    2.1.3    Demonstrate Technology

2.2  Design Material

    2.2.1    Develop Specifications and Drawings

    2.2.2    Initiate Configuration

    2.2.3    Conduct Failure Mode and Criticality Analysis

    2.2.4    Design Maintenance

    2.2.5    Perform Tasks and Skills Analysis

    2.2.6    Determine Tools and Test Equipment

    2.2.7    Design Facilities

2.3  Manage Program

    2.3.1   Prepare Acquisition Strategy

    2.3.2   Solicit Bids and Offers

    2.3.3   Award Contracts

    2.3.4   Manage Contracts

    2.3.5   Modify Contracts

    2.3.6   Accept Materials and Services

    2.3.7   Close Contracts

2.4  Manage Resources

    2.4.1   Develop Budgets

    2.4.2   Account for Finances

    2.4.3   Account for Costs

    2.4.4   Certify Funds Availability

    2.4.5   Pay Bills

2.5  Produce Material

    2.5.1   Manufacture End Items and Products

    2.5.2   Develop Technical Manuals

    2.5.3   Develop Training Plans

    2.5.4   Provision Spares and Repair Parts

2.6  Test and Evaluate

    2.6.1   Develop Test and Evaluation Master Plan

    2.6.2   Conduct Design Tests

    2.6.3   Conduct Operational Test

2.7  Modify Material

    2.7.1   Revise Specifications and Drawings

    2.7.2   Revise Technical Manuals

    2.7.3   Revise Training Plans

    2.7.4   Revise Spares and Repair Parts

3.0 Conduct Warfighting

   3.1 Perform Strategic Theater Tasks

      3.1.1    Deploy and Sustain Theater Forces

         3.1.1.1 Deployment and Sustainment Execution

            3.1.1.1.1    Plan Deployment and Sustainment

            3.1.1.1.2    Validate Requirements and Sourcing

            3.1.1.1.3    Identify Transportation Assets and Channels

            3.1.1.1.4    Prepare and Load Assets

            3.1.1.1.5    Move to Port of Embarkation (POE)

            3.1.1.1.6    Depart to Port of Debarkation (POD)

         3.1.1.2 Reception Staging, Onward Movement, and Integration

            3.1.1.2.1    Receive Assets at POD

            3.1.1.2.2    Consolidate Unit Requirements

            3.1.1.2.3    Move Assets Forward

            3.1.1.2.4    Ensure Arrival at Destination

         3.1.1.3 Theater Distribution

            3.1.1.3.1    Receive Assets

            3.1.1.3.2    Manage Movement in Theater

            3.1.1.3.3    Determine Process Sustainment Requirements

            3.1.1.3.4    Store Theater Assets

            3.1.1.3.5    Maintain Asset Visibility

            3.1.1.3.6    Accomplish In-Theater Repair

            3.1.1.3.7    Issue Assets to Units

            3.1.1.3.8    Process Returns and Retrogrades

            3.1.1.3.9    Manage Third-Party Logistics

      3.1.2    Develop Theater Intelligence and Reconnaissance

      3.1.3    Employ Theater Strategic Firepower

      3.1.4    Provide Theater Command and Control

3.1.5    Provide Theater Protection

3.1.6    Establish Theater Force Requirements and Readiness

3.1.7    Develop and Maintain Alliance and Regional Relations

3.1.8    Conduct Course-of-Action Analysis

3.1.9    Redeploy and Reconstitute Theater Forces

    3.1.9.1  Execute Redeployment

        3.1.9.1.1    Plan Redeployment

        3.1.9.1.2    Prepare and Load Assets

        3.1.9.1.3    Move to Assembly Areas

        3.1.9.1.4    Accomplish Final Staging

        3.1.9.1.5    Move to POE

        3.1.9.1.6    Outload Assets

        3.1.9.1.7    Depart POE

    3.1.9.2  Perform Reconstitution, Regeneration, and Integration

        3.1.9.2.1    Receive at POD

        3.1.9.2.2    Move to Destination

        3.1.9.2.3    Process Personnel and Equipment

        3.1.9.2.4    Prepare for New Mission

3.2  Perform Operational Level Tasks

    3.2.1    Conduct Operational Movement and Maneuver

    3.2.2    Provide Operational Intelligence and Reconnaissance

    3.2.3    Employ Operational Firepower

    3.2.4    Provide Operational Support

    3.2.5    Exercise Operational Command and Control

    3.2.6    Provide Operational Protection

# Appendix D
# SCOR Model

This appendix outlines the concept and structure of the SCOR process model[1] and related performance metrics. A process model frequently is used to describe a supply chain to make it understandable. The Supply Chain Council created the SCOR model to allow organizations to

◆ communicate by using common terminology and standard descriptions;

◆ leverage metrics and benchmarking to determine performance goals, set priorities, and quantify the benefits of process changes;

◆ understand practices that yield the best performance;

◆ understand the supply chain management (SCM) process and evaluate overall performance; and

◆ identify the best software tools for their process requirements.

Figure D-1 depicts the SCOR model supply chain thread. Each link in the supply chain is made up of a SCOR level 1 (L1) process (plan, source, make, or deliver).

*Figure D-1. SCOR Model Supply Chain Thread*

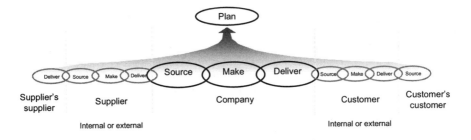

---

[1] Larry Klapper, et al. Logistics Management Institute, *DoD Supply Chain Management; A Recommended Performance Measurement Scorecard,* Report LG803R1, March 1999. This report was based on information from the Supply Chain Council.

Table D-1 depicts level 2 (L2) processes which are the next level of the SCOR model. Column L1 is included to show the relationship between the L1 and L2 processes

*Table D-1. SCOR Level 2 Processes*

| L1 | L2 | Name | Definition |
|----|----|------|------------|
| P | 0 | Plan infrastructure | |
| P | 1 | Plan supply chain | Development and establishment of courses of action that represent projected appropriation of supply chain resources to meet supply chain requirements. |
| P | 2 | Plan source | Development and establishment of courses of action that represent projected appropriation of material resources to meet supply chain requirements. |
| P | 3 | Plan make | Development and establishment of courses of action that represent projected appropriation of production resources to meet production requirements. |
| P | 4 | Plan deliver | Development and establishment of courses of action that represent projected appropriation of delivery resources to meet delivery requirements. |
| S | 0 | Source infrastructure | |
| S | 1 | Source stocked material | Procurement, delivery, receipt, and transfer of raw material and subassemblies. |
| S | 2 | Source make-to-order material | Procurement and delivery of material built to design, or configured on the basis of the requirements of a customer order. |
| S | 3 | Source engineer-to-order material | Negotiation, procurement, and delivery of engineer-to-order assemblies that are designed and built on the requirements or specifications of a customer order or contract. |
| M | 0 | Make infrastructure | |
| M | 1 | Make to stock | The process of manufacturing products. (Make-to-stock products are intended to be shipped from finished goods or "off the shelf," completed before receipt of a customer order, and generally produced in accordance with a sales forecast.) |

*Table D-1. SCOR Level 2 Processes (Continued)*

| L1 | L2 | Name | Definition |
|----|----|------|------------|
| M | 2 | Make to order | The process of manufacturing products. (Make-to-order products are intended to be completed after receipt of a customer order and are built or configured only in response to a customer's order.) |
| M | 3 | Engineer to order | The process of manufacturing distinct items (e.g., parts that retain their identity through the transformation process) that are intended to be completed after receipt of a customer order. (Although make-to-order includes standard products built only in response to a customer order or products configured in response to a customer order, engineer-to-order includes custom products that are designed, developed, and manufactured in response to a customer request.) |
| D | 0 | Deliver infra-structure | |
| D | 1 | Deliver stocked product | The process of delivering a product maintained in a finished goods state before receipt of a firm customer order. |
| D | 2 | Deliver make-to-order products | The process of delivering a product that is manufactured, assembled, or configured from standard parts or subassemblies; manufacture, assembly, or configuration begins only after receipt and validation of a firm customer order. |
| D | 3 | Deliver engineer-to-order products | The process of delivering a product that is designed, manufactured, and assembled from a BOM that includes custom parts; design begins only after receipt and validation of a firm customer order. |

SCOR level 2 processes are used to display supply chain threads, as in Figure D-2.

## Figure D-2. SCOR Process Map

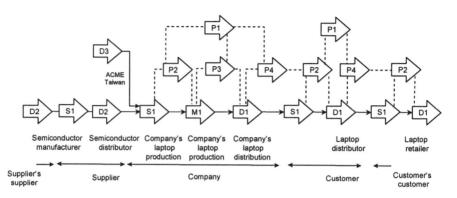

Level 3 (L3) of SCOR further divides level 2 processes into sub-processes. Figure D-3 is an example of this division. It represents Deliver Stocked Product (D1).

## Figure D-3. SCOR Level 3 Sub-processes for Deliver Stocked Product

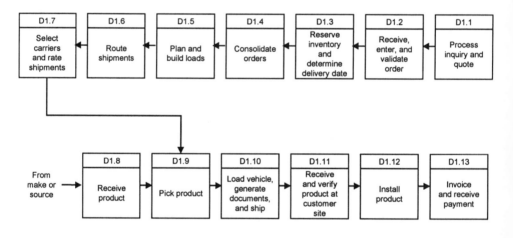

Table D-2 identifies SCOR level 3 processes. Columns L1 and L2 are included to show the relationship among all three SCOR level processes.

## Table D-2. SCOR Level 3 Processes (Continued)

| L3 | Name | Definition |
|---|---|---|
| 2 | Issue material | Physical movement of material (e.g., raw material, fabricated components, manufactured subassemblies, required ingredients, or intermediate formulations) from a stocking location (e.g., stockroom, a location on the production floor, a supplier) to a point of use. (Issuing material includes the corresponding system transaction; the BOM, routing information, or recipe-production instructions determine the material to be issued to support manufacturing operations.) |
| 3 | Manufacture and test | Activities to convert material from the raw or semifinished state to a state of completion and greater value; processes associated with validation of product performance to ensure conformance to defined specifications and requirements. |
| 4 | Package | Activities that containerize completed products for storage or sale to users; packaging in some industries includes cleaning or sterilization. |
| 5 | Stage product | Movement of packaged products to a temporary holding location to await movement to a finished goods location. (Products made to order may remain in the holding location to await shipment per the associated customer order; the actual move transaction is part of the deliver process.) |
| 6 | Release product to deliver | Activities (e.g., assembly of batch records for regulatory agencies, laboratory tests for potency or purity, creating certificate of analysis, sign off by the quality organization) associated with post-production documentation, testing, or certification before a product is delivered to a customer. |
| 1 | Schedule manufacturing activities | Scheduling of operations to be performed in accordance with plans for the manufacture of parts, products, or formulations in quantities; and planned availability of required material. (Scheduling includes sequencing and, depending on factory layout, standards for setup and run; intermediate manufacturing activities generally are coordinated before scheduling operations performed in producing a finished product.) |

## Table D-2. SCOR Level 3 Processes

| L1 | L2 | L3 | Name | Definition |
|---|---|---|---|---|
| P | 1 | 1 | Identify, prioritize, and aggregate supply chain requirements | The process of identifying, prioritizing, and considering all sources of demand, as a whole with constituent parts, in the supply chain of a product or service. |
| P | 1 | 2 | Identify, assess, and aggregate supply chain resources | The process of identifying, prioritizing, and considering all sources of demand, as a whole with constituent parts, in the supply chain of a product or service. |
| P | 1 | 3 | Balance supply chain resources with supply chain requirements | The process of developing a time-phased course of action that commits supply chain resources to meet supply chain requirements. |
| P | 1 | 4 | Establish supply chain plans | Establishment of courses of action that represent projected appropriation of supply chain resources to meet supply chain requirements. |
| P | 2 | 1 | Identify, prioritize, and aggregate material requirements | The process of identifying, prioritizing, and considering all sources of demand, as a whole with constituent parts, for material in the supply chain of a product or service. |
| P | 2 | 2 | Identify, assess, and aggregate material resources | The process of identifying, evaluating, and considering all material, as a whole with constituent parts, used to add value in the supply chain of a product or service. |
| P | 2 | 3 | Balance material resources with material requirements | The process of developing a time-phased course of action that commits material resources to meet material requirements. |
| P | 2 | 4 | Establish detailed sourcing plans | Establishment of courses of action that represent projected appropriation of supply chain resources to meet sourcing plan requirements. |
| P | 3 | 1 | Identify, prioritize, and aggregate production requirements | The process of identifying, prioritizing, and considering all sources of demand, as a whole with constituent parts, in the production of a product or service. |
| P | 3 | 2 | Identify, assess, and aggregate production resources | The process of identifying, evaluating, and considering all aspects, as a whole with constituent parts, that add value in the production of a product. |

## Table D-2. SCOR Level 3 Processes (Continued)

| L1 | L2 | L3 | Name | Definition |
|----|----|----|------|-----------|
| P | 3 | 3 | Balance production resources with production requirements | The process of developing a time-phased course of action that commits production resources to meet production requirements. |
| P | 3 | 4 | Establish detailed production plans | Establishment of courses of action that represent projected appropriation of supply chain resources to meet production plan requirements. |
| P | 4 | 1 | Identify, prioritize, and aggregate delivery requirements | The process of identifying, prioritizing, and considering all sources of demand, as a whole with constituent parts, in the delivery of a product or service. |
| P | 4 | 2 | Identify, assess, and aggregate delivery resources | The process of identifying, evaluating, and considering all aspects, as a whole with constituent parts, that add value in the delivery of a product. |
| P | 4 | 3 | Balance delivery resources with delivery requirements | The process of developing a time-phased course of action that commits delivery resources to meet delivery requirements. |
| P | 4 | 4 | Establish detailed delivery plans | Establishment of courses of action that represent projected appropriation of delivery resources to meet delivery requirements. |
| S | 1 | 1 | Schedule material deliveries | Scheduling and managing deliveries of material for a contract or purchase order. (Requirements for material releases are based on the sourcing plan or other types of material pull signals.) |
| S | 1 | 2 | Receive and verify material | Receipt and acceptance of material deliveries, including all activities associated with receiving, verifying, and accepting material deliveries. |
| S | 1 | 3 | Transfer material | Transfer of accepted material to the appropriate stocking location in the supply chain (including all activities associated with re-packaging, staging, transferring, and stocking material). |
| S | 2 | 1 | Schedule material deliveries | Scheduling and managing deliveries of material for the contract; requirements for deliveries are based on the sourcing plan; this function includes all aspects of managing the contract schedule, including prototypes and qualifications. |

## Table D-2. SCOR Level 3 Proce...

| L1 | L2 | L3 | Name | |
|----|----|----|------|--|
| S | 2 | 2 | Receive and verify material | Receipt and... for contract... ties associa... verifying, an... |
| S | 2 | 3 | Transfer material | Transfer of a... priate stocki... (including all... packaging, s... material). |
| S | 3 | 1 | Identify sources of supply | Identification... capable of de... that meets al... |
| S | 3 | 2 | Select final suppliers and negotiate | Identification... evaluation of... qualifications,... that defines c... material avail... |
| S | 3 | 3 | Schedule material deliveries | Scheduling an... rial for the con... eries are base... function includ... contract sched... qualifications.) |
| S | 3 | 4 | Receive and verify material | Receipt and ac... for contract req... ties associated... verifying, and a... |
| S | 3 | 5 | Transfer material | Transfer of acc... priate stocking l... (including all ac... packaging, stag... material). |
| M | 1 | 1 | Schedule manufacturing activities | Scheduling of o... accordance with... parts, products,... and planned ava... (Scheduling inclu... pending on the fa... setup and run; in... activities general... scheduling opera... ing a finished pro... |

| L1 | L2 |
|----|----|
| M | 1 |
| M | 1 |
| M | 1 |
| M | 1 |
| M | 1 |
| M | 2 |

## Table D-2. SCOR Level 3 Processes (Continued)

| L1 | L2 | L3 | Name | Definition |
|----|----|----|------|------------|
| M | 2 | 2 | Issue material | Physical movement of material (e.g., raw material, fabricated components, manufactured subassemblies, required ingredients, or intermediate formulations) from a stocking location (e.g., stockroom, a location on the production floor, a supplier) to a point of use. (Issuing material includes the corresponding system transaction; the BOM, routing information, or recipe-production instructions determine the material to be issued to support manufacturing operations.) |
| M | 2 | 3 | Manufacture and test | Activities to convert material from the raw or semifinished state to a state of completion and greater value; processes associated with validation of product performance to ensure conformance to defined specifications and requirements. |
| M | 2 | 4 | Package | Activities that containerize completed products for storage or sale to users; packaging in some industries includes cleaning or sterilization. |
| M | 2 | 5 | Stage product | Movement of packaged products to a temporary holding location to await movement to a finished goods location. (Products made to order may remain in the holding location to await shipment per the associated customer order; the actual move transaction is part of the deliver process.) |
| M | 3 | 1 | Finalize engineering | Engineering activities after acceptance of order, but before the product can be manufactured; may include generation and delivery of final drawings, specifications, formulas, and part programs. (Generally the last step in completing preliminary engineering work as part of the quotation process.) |
| M | 3 | 2 | Schedule manufacturing activities | Scheduling of operations to be performed in accordance with plans for manufacture of parts, products, or formulations in quantities and planned availability of required material. (Scheduling includes sequencing and, depending on the factory layout, standards for setup and run; intermediate manufacturing activities generally are coordinated before scheduling operations performed in producing a finished product.) |

## Table D-2. SCOR Level 3 Processes *(Continued)*

| L1 | L2 | L3 | Name | Definition |
|----|----|----|------|------------|
| M | 3 | 3 | Issue material | Physical movement of material (e.g., raw material, fabricated components, manufactured subassemblies, required ingredients, or intermediate formulations) from a stocking location (e.g., stockroom, a location on the production floor, a supplier) to a point of use. (Issuing material includes the corresponding system transaction; the BOM, routing information, or recipe-production instructions determine the material to be issued to support the manufacturing operations.) |
| M | 3 | 4 | Manufacture and test | Activities to convert material from the raw or semifinished state to a state of completion and greater value; processes associated with validation of product performance to ensure conformance to defined specifications and requirements. |
| M | 3 | 5 | Stage product | Activities that containerize completed products for storage or sale to users; packaging in some industries includes cleaning or sterilization. |
| M | 3 | 6 | Release product to deliver | Movement of packaged products to a temporary holding location to await movement to a finished goods location. (Products made to order may remain in the holding location to await shipment per the associated customer order; the actual move transaction is part of the deliver process.) |
| D | 1 | 1 | Process inquiry and quote | Actions to receive and respond to customer inquiries and requests for quotes. |
| D | 1 | 2 | Receive, enter, and validate order | Actions to receive orders from a customer and enter them in a company's order processing system (orders may be received via phone, fax, or electronic media); examine orders "technically" to ensure orderable configuration and provide accurate price; and check customer's credit. |
| D | 1 | 3 | Reserve inventory and determine delivery date | Actions to identify and reserve inventory (on-hand and scheduled) for orders and schedule a delivery date. |
| D | 1 | 4 | Consolidate orders | Process of analyzing orders to determine groupings that result in least cost and best service fulfillment and transportation. |

## Table D-2. SCOR Level 3 Processes (Continued)

| L1 | L2 | L3 | Name | Definition |
|----|----|----|------|------------|
| D | 1 | 5 | Plan and build loads | Actions to select transportation modes and build efficient loads. |
| D | 1 | 6 | Route shipments | Actions to consolidate and route loads by mode, lane, and location. |
| D | 1 | 7 | Select carriers and rate shipments | Actions to select carriers by lowest cost per route, rate, and tender shipments. |
| D | 1 | 8 | Receive product | Activities (e.g., receiving product, verifying, recording product receipt, determining put-away location, putting away, and recording location) that a company performs at its warehouses; sometimes includes quality inspection. |
| D | 1 | 9 | Pick product | Activities (including retrieving orders to pick, determining inventory availability, building the pick wave, picking the product, recording the pick, and delivering product to shipping) in response to an order. |
| D | 1 | 10 | Load vehicle, generate shipping documents, and ship | Tasks involved in placing product on vehicles; generating documentation to meet internal, customer, carrier, and government needs; and sending the product to the customer. |
| D | 1 | 11 | Receive and verify product at customer's site | The process of receiving the shipment at the customer's site, and verifying that the shipped order is complete and the product meets quality requirements. |
| D | 1 | 12 | Install product | The process of preparing and installing the product at the customer's site. (Product is fully functional after completion.) |
| D | 1 | 13 | Invoice and receive payment | Actions to send a signal to the financial organization that the order has been shipped and the billing process should begin. (Payment is received from the customer within the payment terms of the invoice.) |
| D | 2 | 1 | Process inquiry and quote | Actions to receive and respond to customer inquiries and requests for quotes. |

## Table D-2. SCOR Level 3 Processes (Continued)

| L1 | L2 | L3 | Name | Definition |
|----|----|----|------|------------|
| D | 2 | 2 | Receive, config-ure, enter, and validate order | Actions to receive orders from a customer and enter them in a company's order proc-essing system (orders may be received via phone, fax, or electronic media); configure product to the customer's needs, based on standard available parts or options; examine order to ensure orderable configuration and provide accurate price; and check customer's credit. |
| D | 2 | 3 | Reserve re-sources and de-termine delivery date | Actions to identify and reserve inventory or planned capacity for orders, and schedule a delivery date. |
| D | 2 | 4 | Consolidate orders | The process of analyzing orders to determine groupings that result in least-cost and best-service fulfillment and transportation. |
| D | 2 | 5 | Plan and build loads | Actions to select transportation modes and build efficient loads. |
| D | 2 | 6 | Route shipments | Actions to consolidate and route loads by mode, lane, and location. |
| D | 2 | 7 | Select carriers and rate shipments | Actions to select carriers by lowest cost per route and rate and tender shipments. |
| D | 2 | 8 | Pick staged product | Activities (including retrieving orders to pick, verifying inventory availability, building the pick wave, picking the product, recording the pick, and delivering product to shipping) per-formed in the distribution center in response to an order. |
| D | 2 | 9 | Load vehicle, generate shipping documents, and ship | Tasks involved in placing the product on ve-hicles; generating documentation to meet internal, customer, and government needs; and sending the product to the customer. |
| D | 2 | 10 | Receive and verify product at cus-tomer's site | The process of receiving the shipment at the customer's site and verifying that the shipped order is complete and the product meets quality requirements. |
| D | 2 | 11 | Test and install product | The process of preparing, testing, and in-stalling the product at the customer's site; the product is fully functional after completion. |

## Table D-2. SCOR Level 3 Processes (Continued)

| L1 | L2 | L3 | Name | Definition |
|----|----|----|------|------------|
| D | 2 | 12 | Invoice and receive payment | Actions to send a signal to the financial organization that the order has been shipped and that the billing process should begin. (Payment is received from the customer within the payment terms of the invoice.) |
| D | 3 | 1 | Obtain and respond to request for proposals and request for quotes | The process of delivering a product that is designed, manufactured, and assembled from a BOM that includes custom parts. (Design begins only after receipt and validation of a firm customer order.) |
| D | 3 | 2 | Negotiate and receive contract | The process of negotiating order details (e.g., price, schedule, product performance) with customers and finalizing the contract. |
| D | 3 | 3 | Enter order, commit resources, and launch program | The process of entering and finalizing the customer order, approving planned resources (e.g., engineering, manufacturing), and officially launching the program. |
| D | 3 | 4 | Schedule installation | The process of evaluating design and build schedules relative to customer's requested installation date to determine installation schedule. |
| D | 3 | 5 | Plan and build loads and shipments | The process of scheduling simultaneous and consolidated shipments, and planning and building loads. |
| D | 3 | 6 | Route shipments and select carrier | The process of consolidating and routing shipments by mode, lane, and location. (Carriers are selected and shipments are rated.) |
| D | 3 | 7 | Pick staged product | Retrieving orders to pick, verifying inventory availability, building the pick wave, picking the product, recording the pick, and delivering product to shipping. (Performed in the distribution center in response to an order.) |
| D | 3 | 8 | Load vehicle, generate shipping documents, and ship | Tasks involved in placing product on vehicles; generating documentation to meet internal, customer, and government needs; and sending product to the customer. |
| D | 3 | 9 | Receive and verify product at customer's site | The process of receiving the shipment at the customer's site and verifying that the shipped order is complete and the product meets quality requirements. |
| D | 3 | 10 | Test and install product | The process of preparing, testing, and installing a product at the customer's site; product is fully functional after completion. |

## Table D-2. SCOR Level 3 Processes (Continued)

| L1 | L2 | L3 | Name | Definition |
|----|----|----|------|------------|
| D | 3 | 11 | Invoice and receive payment | Actions to send a signal to the financial organization that the order has been shipped and that the billing process should begin. (Payment is received from the customer within the payment terms of the invoice.) |

For each SCOR process, the model provides several performance measures (Table D-3).

## Table D-3. SCOR Performance Measures

| Term | Definition | Process category and process element numbers |
|------|------------|----------------------------------------------|
| Actual-to-theoretical cycle time | Term not defined by SCOR model. | P1.2, P3, P3.4 |
| Asset turns | Total gross product revenue divided by total net assets. | M1, M1.3, M1.4, M2, M2.3, M2.4, M3, M3.4, M3.5 |
| Average plant-wide salary | Total payroll for salaried employees divided by total headcount. | M1, M2, M3 |
| Build cycle time | Average cycle time for build-to-stock products, calculated as average number of units in process divided by average daily output in units. | |
| Build-to-ship cycle time | Average time from when a unit or product is deemed shippable by manufacturing until the unit or product is shipped to a customer. | M1.4, M1.5, M2.4, M2.5, M3.5, M3.6 |
| Capacity utilization | A measure of how intensively a resource is used to produce a good or service that considers several factors (e.g., internal manufacturing capacity, constraining processes, direct labor availability, and key components and material availability). | P1, P1.3, M1, M1.1, M1.3, M1.4, M2, M2.1, M2.3, M3, M3.1, D2.3 |
| Cash-to-cash cycle time | Inventory days of supply (DOS) plus days sales outstanding minus average payment period for material (time for funds to flow back into a company after being spent for raw material). | P1, M1.2, M2.2, M3.3, D2.12, D3.11 |

*Table D-3. SCOR Performance Measures (Continued)*

| Term | Definition | Process category and process element numbers |
|---|---|---|
| Commodity management profile | Number of distinct part numbers (purchased commodities) sourced in the following areas: within 200 miles, country, continent, and offshore. | P2, P2.2, P2.4 |
| Complete manufacture to order ready for shipment time | Time to pick, pack, and prepare for shipment time, in calendar days. | D2.8, D2.9 |
| Create customer order costs | Costs for creating and pricing configurations to order and preparing order documents. | D1.2, D2.2, D3.2 |
| Cross-training | Training or experience provided in several areas (e.g., training an employee on several machines rather than one); cross-training provides workers in case primary operator is unavailable. | M3.2 |
| Cumulative source and make cycle time | Cumulative external and internal lead-time to build a shippable product (begun with no inventory on hand, no parts on order, and no prior forecasts with suppliers), in calendar days. | P1, P2, P3, P3.3, P3.4 |
| Customer invoicing and accounting costs | Costs for invoicing, processing customer payments, and verifying customer satisfaction. | D1.13, D2.12, D3.11 |
| Customer receipt of order to installation complete | Time for product installation, acceptance, and initiation of operations, in calendar days. | D2.10, D2.11, D3.9, D3.10 |
| Customer signature and authorization to order receipt time | Time, in calendar days, order from authorization by customer to order receipt by customer. | D1.2, D2.2, D3.2 |
| Days sales outstanding | Five-point annual average of gross accounts receivable divided by total gross annual sales (divided by 365). | D1.13, D2.12, D3.11 |
| Delivery performance to customer request date | Percentage of orders fulfilled on or before customer's requested date. | P1, P1.3, P4, P4.3, P4.4, M1, M2, M3, D1.10, D2, D2.9, D3, D1.3, D3.8 |

## Table D-3. SCOR Performance Measures (Continued)

| Term | Definition | Process category and process element numbers |
|---|---|---|
| Delivery performance to scheduled commit date | Percentage of orders fulfilled on or before original scheduled or committed date. | M1, M2, M3, M3.1, D1.10, D2, D2.9, D3, D3.8 |
| Demand and supply planning costs | Costs associated with forecasting, developing finished goods or end-item inventory plans, and coordinating demand and supply process across entire supply chain, including all channels (but excluding Management Information System [MIS] related costs). | P1 |
| Distribution costs | Costs for warehouse space and management, finished goods receiving and stocking, processing shipments, picking and consolidating, selecting carriers, and staging products and systems. | D1.8, D1.9, D2.4, D2.5, D2.6, D2.7, D2.8, D3.5, D3.6, D3.7 |
| Engineering change order (ECO) cost | Cost incurred from revisions to blueprint or design released by engineering to modify or correct a part. (Request for the change may be from customer, production quality control, or another department.) | M3, M3.1 |
| End-of-life inventory | Inventory on hand that will satisfy future demand for products no longer in production at an entity. | D1.8 |
| Faultless invoices | Number of invoices issued without error; examples of invoice defects are:<br>• Change from customer purchase order without proper customer involvement<br>• Wrong customer information (e.g., name, address, telephone number)<br>• Wrong product information (e.g., part number, product description)<br>• Wrong price (e.g., discounts not applied)<br>• Wrong quantity, terms, or date. | D1.13, D2.12, D3.11 |
| Field finished goods inventory | Inventory kept at locations (e.g., distribution center, warehouse) outside manufacturing plant. | D2.9, D2.11, D3.10 |
| Fill rates | Percentage of ship-from-stock orders shipped within 24 hours of order receipt. | P1, P1.3, P4, P4.4, M1.3, D1, D1.3, D1.9, D2 |

## Table D-3. SCOR Performance Measures (Continued)

| Term | Definition | Process category and process element numbers |
|---|---|---|
| Finished goods inventory carrying costs | Costs (e.g., opportunity cost, shrinkage, insurance and taxes, total obsolescence, channel obsolescence, and field sample obsolescence) associated with finished goods inventory. | P4, P4.3 |
| Finished goods inventory DOS | Gross finished goods inventory divided by average daily value of transfers. | P4, P4.4, D1, D1.8, D2, D3, D3.8 |
| Finished goods shrinkage | Costs associated with breakage, pilferage, and deterioration of finished goods inventories. | P4 |
| Forecast accuracy | Forecast sum (sum of units or dollars forecast to be shipped each month, based on forecast generated 3 months earlier) minus sum of variances (sum of absolute values, for forecast line item, of differences between each month's forecast and actual demand for the month), divided by forecast sum (forecast accuracy calculated in units and dollars by shippable end product for each distribution channel). | P1, P1.1, P2.1, P3.1, P4, P4.1, P4.2 |
| Forecast cycle | Time between forecast regenerations that reflect true changes in marketplace demand for shippable end products; only valid "bottom-up" forecasts are counted (e.g., weekly or monthly updates to the forecast that merely shift dates for forecast to avoid changing annual dollar-based forecast should not be considered forecast regenerations). | P1.1, P2.1 |
| Incoming material quality | Number of received parts that fail inspection divided by total number of parts received. | D1.8 |
| Indirect-to-direct labor headcount ratio | Ratio of number of employees to support production in general, without being related to a product (indirect labor), to number of employees applied to product being manufactured or used in performance of the service (direct labor). | M1, M2, M3 |
| In-process failure rates | Term not defined by SCOR model. | M3.4 |

## *Table D-3. SCOR Performance Measures (Continued)*

| Term | Definition | Process category and process element numbers |
|---|---|---|
| Installation costs | Costs for verifying site preparation, installing, certifying, and authorizing billing. | D2.11, D3.10 |
| Intra-manufacturing replan cycle | Time between acceptance of a regenerated forecast by locations that produce end product and reflection of revised plan in master production schedule of all affected plants, excluding external vendors. | M1.3, M2.3, M3.4 |
| Inventory accuracy | Absolute value of the sum of variances between physical inventory and perpetual inventory. | P2.2, M1.2, M2.2, M3.3 |
| Inventory aging | Percentage of total gross inventory (based on value) covered by expected demand within time periods. | M1, M2, M3 |
| Inventory carrying costs | Sum of opportunity cost; shrinkage; insurance and taxes; total obsolescence for raw material, work-in-process (WIP), and finished goods inventory; channel obsolescence; and field sample obsolescence. | P1 |
| Inventory cycle-counting accuracy | Absolute value of sum of variances between physical inventory and perpetual inventory. | P1.2 |
| Inventory DOS | Total gross value of inventory at standard cost before reserves for excess and obsolescence (includes inventory on company books only; future liabilities should not be included), calculated by using five-point annual average of sum of all gross inventories (e.g., raw material, WIP, plant finished goods, field finished goods, field samples) divided by cost of goods sold (divided by 365). | P1, P1.3, S1, S2, S3, M1.1, M2.1, M3.2 |
| Inventory obsolescence as a percentage of total inventory | Annual obsolete and scrap reserves taken for inventory obsolescence, expressed as percentage of annual average gross inventory value. | P1, P3, P3.3, P3.4, M1, M1.2, M2.1, M2.2, M3.3, D1.8, D2 |
| Machine wait time | Term not defined by SCOR model. | M1.1, M2.1 |

## Table D-3. SCOR Performance Measures *(Continued)*

| Term | Definition | Process category and process element numbers |
|---|---|---|
| Make cycle time | Sum of the following average times: order release to start actual build, total build cycle, and end build to leave plant (i.e., moves to on- and off-site distribution or goes to customer). For continuous and mixed processes, manufacturing cycle time is calculated as average number of units (e.g., doses, kilos, pounds, gallons) in process divided by average daily output in units. | M1.2 |
| Make flexibility | Time to implement a sustainable un-planned increase in end product supply of 20 percent if one of the following factors is the only constraint:<br>• Internal manufacturing capacity<br>• Direct labor availability<br>• Constraining processes<br>• Key components and material avail-ability<br>• Direct labor availability. | P3, P3.3 |
| Material acquisition costs | Costs for production material (material management and planning, supplier qual-ity engineering, inbound freight and du-ties, receiving and material storage, in-coming inspection, and material process engineering and tooling costs). | S1, S2, S3, D1.8 |
| Materiel man-agement and planning costs as a percentage of material acquisition costs | Costs associated with supplier sourcing, contract negotiation, and qualification, as well as preparation, placement, and tracking of purchase order, expressed as percentage of material acquisition costs; category includes all costs related to buy-ers and planners'. | P2.3, S1.1, S2.1, S3.2, S3.3 |
| Material over-head cost per dollar of material expenditure | Term not defined by SCOR model. | P3 |
| Material process engineering as a percent of mate-rial acquisition costs | Costs associated with tasks to document and communicate material specification, as well as reviews to improve manufac-turability of purchased item, expressed as percentage of material acquisition costs. | S3.1 |

## Table D-3. SCOR Performance Measures (Continued)

| Term | Definition | Process category and process element numbers |
|------|-----------|---------------------------------------------|
| Material requisition cycle time | Term not defined by SCOR model. | M1.2, M2.2, M3.3 |
| Number of call backs as a percent of total inquiries | Number of callbacks divided by total inquiries. | D1.1, D2.1 |
| Number of ECOs | Number of revisions to blueprint or design released by engineering to modify or correct a part. (Request for change may be from customer, production quality control, or another department.) | M3, M3.1 |
| Number of end products and stock-keeping units | Number of end item offerings individually planned and managed. | P3, P3.2 |
| Number of orders not delivered complete | Number of orders for which all items on order are not delivered in the quantities requested. | D2.8 |
| Number of orders with complete and accurate documentation | Number of orders with correct documentation supporting the order, including packing slips, bills of lading, and invoices. | D2.8 |
| Number of supply sources | Number of internal and external direct production material suppliers used. | P2, P2.2, P2.4 |

*Table D-3. SCOR Performance Measures (Continued)*

| Term | Definition | Process category and process element numbers |
|---|---|---|
| Order consolidation profile | Consolidation consists of activities associated with filling a customer order by bringing together all line items ordered by the customer (some items may come directly from the production line; others may be picked from stock); the following profiles are captured:<br><br>• Shipped direct to customer's dock from point of manufacture (no consolidation)<br>• Shipped direct to customer with consolidation completed local to customer by organic transport company<br>• Moved to on-site staging location for consolidation and shipment direct to customer<br>• Moved to on-site stockroom for later pick, pack, and ship<br>• Shipped to different locations for consolidation or later pick, pack, and ship. | D1.4 |
| Order entry and maintenance costs | Costs for maintaining customer database, checking credit, accepting new orders, and adding them to the order system, as well as later order modifications. | D1.2, D2.2 |
| Order entry complete to order ready for shipment time | Release to manufacturing, order configuration verification, production scheduling, build, pick-pack, and prepare for shipment time, in calendar days. | D1.4, D1.5, D1.6, D1.7, D1.9, D1.10, D3.5, D3.6, D3.7 |
| Order entry complete to start manufacture time | Time from completion of order entry to release to manufacturing, in calendar days. | D2.4, D2.5, D2.6, D2.7, D3.4 |
| Order fulfillment costs | Costs for processing order, allocating inventory, ordering from internal or external supplier, scheduling shipment, reporting order status, and initiating shipment. | D1.3, D2.3, D3.3, D3.4 |

### Table D-3. SCOR Performance Measures (Continued)

| Term | Definition | Process category and process element numbers |
|------|------------|--------------------------------------------|
| Order fulfillment lead-times | Average actual lead-times consistently achieved, from customer signature and authorization to order receipt, order receipt to order entry complete, order entry complete to start build, start build to order ready for shipment, order ready for shipment to customer receipt of order, and customer receipt of order to installation complete. | M3, M3.1, D1, D2, D3 |
| Order management costs | Aggregation of the following cost elements:<br>• Create customer order costs<br>• Order entry and maintenance costs<br>• Contract, program, and channel management costs<br>• Installation planning costs<br>• Order fulfillment costs<br>• Distribution costs<br>• Transportation costs<br>• Installation costs<br>• Customer invoicing and accounting costs. | P1, P4, P4.1, P4.2, D1, D1.1, D2, D2.1, D3, D3.1 |
| Order management cycle time | Term not defined by SCOR model. | P4, P4.1, P4.2 |
| Order ready for shipment to customer receipt of order time | Includes total transit time (all components to consolidation point), consolidation, queue time, and additional transit time to customer receipt of order, in calendar days. | D1.11, D2.9, D3.8 |
| Order receipt to order entry complete time | Time, in calendar days for order revalidation, configuration check, credit check, and scheduling of received orders. | D1.2, D1.3, D2.2, D2.3, D3.3 |
| Overhead cost | Costs of operating business that cannot be directly related to products or services produced; costs (e.g., light, heat, supervision, and maintenance) are grouped in several pools and distributed to units of product or service by standard allocation method (e.g., direct labor hours, direct labor expenses, or direct material expenses). | M1, M2, M3 |

*Table D-3. SCOR Performance Measures (Continued)*

| Term | Definition | Process category and process element numbers |
|---|---|---|
| Percentage defective | Term not defined by SCOR model. | S1, S1.1, S3 |
| Percentage of Electronic Data Interchange (EDI) transactions | Percentage of orders received via EDI. | S1.1, S2.1, S3.3 |
| Percentage of faultless installations | Number of faultless installations divided by total number of units installed. | D1.12, D2.11, D3.10 |
| Percentage of orders scheduled to customer request | Percentage of orders with delivery scheduled within agreed time frame of the customer's requested delivery date. | M2.1, M3.2, D2.3 |
| Percentage of parts delivered to point of use | Percentage of material receipts delivered directly to production, consolidation point or point of use. Includes receipts with no inspection or only minor visual and paperwork inspection. | M1.2, M2.2, M3.3 |
| Perfect order fulfillment | Orders that meet all of the following standards:<br>• Delivered complete; all items on order delivered in quantities requested<br>• Delivered on time, using customer's definition of on-time delivery<br>• Complete and accurate documentation (including packing slips, bills of lading, and invoices) to support the order<br>• Delivered in perfect condition, correct configuration, customer-ready, no damage, and faultlessly installed (as applicable). | D1.10, D1.11, D2, D2.2, D2.9, D2.10, D3, D3.8, D3.9 |
| Planing stability | Term not defined by SCOR model. | P1.4 |
| Plant cost per hour | Term not defined by SCOR model. | M1, M2 |
| Plant finished goods inventory DOS | Gross plant finished goods inventory divided by average daily value of transfers. | M1.5, D2.8, D3.7 |

## Table D-3. SCOR Performance Measures (Continued)

| Term | Definition | Process category and process element numbers |
|------|-----------|----------------------------------------------|
| Plant-level order management costs | Aggregation of the following cost elements, for which manufacturing is the central focal point of orders:<br><br>• Create customer order costs<br>• Order entry and maintenance costs<br>• Contract, program, and channel management costs<br>• Installation planning costs<br>• Order fulfillment costs<br>• Distribution costs<br>• Transportation costs<br>• Installation costs<br>• Customer invoicing and accounting costs. | M2.1, M3.2 |
| Product and grade change-over time | Term not defined by SCOR model. | M1, M1.3, M2, M2.3 |
| Product and process data accuracy (e.g., BOMs, routings, planning factors) | Term not defined by SCOR model. | P1, P1.2 |
| Production flexibility | Upside flexibility—number of days to achieve an unplanned, sustainable, 20 percent increase in production.<br><br>Downside flexibility—percentage of order reduction sustainable at 30 days before delivery with no inventory or cost penalties. | M1.1, M2.1, M3.2 |
| Production plan adherence | Term not defined by SCOR model. | P3, P3.4 |
| Published delivery lead-times | Standard lead time (after receipt of order) published to customers by sales organization for typical orders only (not standing and resupply orders). | D1, D2 |

## Table D-3. SCOR Performance Measures (Continued)

| Term | Definition | Process category and process element numbers |
|---|---|---|
| Purchased material by geography | Number of distinct part numbers of raw material, externally manufactured components, manufactured finished products, packaging material, and labeling material sourced in the following areas: within 200 miles, country, continent, and offshore. | S3.1 |
| Quality levels | Term not defined by SCOR model. | M1.3, M2.3 |
| Quarantine time | Time for setting items aside from availability for use or sale until required quality tests have been performed and conformance certified. | M1.6, M2.6 |
| Ratio of actual to theoretical cycle time | Term not defined by SCOR model. | M1.3, M1.4, M2.3, M3.4 |
| Raw material and WIP inventory DOS | Gross raw material and WIP inventory divided by average daily value of transfers. | P2, P3, D2, D3 |
| Raw material DOS | Gross raw material inventory divided by average daily value of transfers. | P2, P2.3, M1.2, S1.1, S2.1, S3.2, S3.3 |
| Raw material inventory carrying costs | Costs associated with raw material inventory (e.g., opportunity cost, shrinkage, insurance and taxes, and obsolescence). | P2 |
| Raw material shrinkage | Costs associated with breakage, pilferage, and deterioration of raw material inventories. | P2 |
| Receiving and material storage costs as a percentage of material acquisition costs | Costs associated with taking possession of and storing material; includes warehouse space and management, material receiving and stocking, processing work orders, pricing, and internal material movement, but does not include incoming inspections. | S1.3, S2.3, S3.5 |
| Receiving and put away cycle time | Term not defined by SCOR model. | M3.3 |
| Receiving costs as a percentage of material acquisition costs | Costs associated with taking possession of material (excluding inspection), expressed as a percentage of material acquisition costs. | S1.2, S2.2, S3.4 |

### Table D-3. SCOR Performance Measures (Continued)

| Term | Definition | Process category and process element numbers |
|------|-----------|------------------|
| Replan cycle time | Time between initial creation of regenerated forecast and its reflection in master production schedule of production facilities for end product. | P1, P1.1, P1.3, P1.4, P2.3, M1, M2 |
| Responsiveness lead-time | Term not defined by SCOR model. | M1.1, M2.1, M3.2 |
| Return on assets | Financial measure of income-producing value of an asset, calculated as net income divided by total assets. | P1 |
| Routing data accuracy | Term not defined by SCOR model. | P0 |
| Schedule achievement | Percentage of time that a plant achieves its production schedule, based on number of scheduled end items or volume for a period (overshipments do not make up for undershipments). | M1.1, M2.1, M3.2 |
| Scrap expense | Expense incurred from material being outside specifications and possessing characteristics that make rework impractical. | M1.3, M2.3, M3.4 |
| Shrinkage | Costs associated with breakage, pilferage, and deterioration of inventories. | P4 |
| Source cycle time | Cumulative lead-time (total average combined inside-plant planning, supplier lead-time [internal or external], receiving, and handling from demand identification at factory until material is available in production facility) to source 95 percent (chosen to eliminate outlying data) of value of material from internal and external suppliers. | S1.2, S2.2, S3.4 |
| Source flexibility | Term not defined by SCOR model. | P2, P2.3 |
| Supplier cycle time | Term not defined by SCOR model. | P2, P2.4 |
| Supplier fill rate | Term not defined by SCOR model. | P2, P2.4 |
| Supplier on-time delivery performance | Percentage of orders fulfilled on or before customer's requested date. (Supplier's performance measured by customer.) | P2, P2.3, P2.4, S1.2, S2.2, S3.4 |

## Table D-3. SCOR Performance Measures (Continued)

| Term | Definition | Process category and process element numbers |
|---|---|---|
| Supply chain finance costs | Costs associated with paying invoices, auditing physical counts, performing inventory accounting, and collecting accounts receivable. (Does not include customer invoicing and accounting costs.) | P1.3 |
| Total build time | Average time for build-to-stock or configure-to-order products, from when production begins on the released work order until build is completed and unit is deemed shippable. | M1.3, M2.3, M3.4 |
| Total logistics costs | All supply chain-related MIS, finance and planning, inventory carrying, material acquisition, and order management costs. | P4 |
| Total manufacturing employment | Term not defined by SCOR model. | M1.3, M2.3, M3.4 |
| Total source lead-time | Cumulative lead time to source 95 percent of value of material from internal and external suppliers. | S1, S1.1, S2, S2.1, S3, S3.1, S3.2, S3.3 |
| Total WIP inventory DOS | Gross WIP inventory divided by average daily value of transfers. | P3, P3.3, P3.4 |
| Training and education | Term not defined by SCOR model. | M1.3, M2.3 |
| Transportation costs | Company-paid freight and duties from point of manufacture to end customer or channel. | D1.4, D1.5, D1.6, D1.7, D2.9, D3.8 |
| Unit cost | Total labor, material, and overhead cost for one unit of production (e.g., part, gallon, pound). | M2, M3 |
| Value-added employee productivity | Total product revenue minus total material purchases, divided by total employment (in full-time equivalents). | P1, M1, M1.3, M2, M2.3, M3, M3.4 |
| Warranty and returns | Number of returns in warranty period. (A warranty is a commitment, expressed or implied, that a fact regarding the subject matter of a contract is or will be true). | M1.3, M1.4 |
| Warranty costs | Costs associated with material, labor, and problem diagnoses for product defects. | M1, M1.3, M1.4, M2, M2.3, M2.4, M3, M3.4, M3.5 |

## Table D-3. SCOR Performance Measures (Continued)

| Term | Definition | Process category and process element numbers |
|---|---|---|
| WIP shrinkage | Costs associated with breakage, pilferage, and deterioration of WIP inventories. | P3 |
| WIP inventory carrying costs | Costs associated with WIP inventory (e.g., opportunity cost, shrinkage, insurance and taxes, and total obsolescence). | P3, P3.4 |
| Yield | Ratio of usable output from a process to its input. | M1, M1.3, M2, M2.3, M2.4, M3.4 |
| Yield variability | Condition that occurs when output of a process is not consistently repeatable in quantity or quality. | M1.3, M2.3, M3.4 |

# Current Supply Chain Management Applications

*Table E-1. Supply Chain Management Applications' Functionality*

| Application | Function |
|---|---|
| Enterprise resource planning (ERP) | Automate and synchronize day-to-day operations (e.g., finance, human resources, maintenance, inventory management, warehousing). |
| Advanced planning and scheduling | Create production plans and schedules in maintenance facility. Use constraints and business rules to optimize schedules. |
| Demand planning | Forecast demand and measure forecast accuracy through analytical algorithms. |
| Demand content | Provide additional information such as point-of-sale or information to facilitate forecasting of customer requirements. |
| Inventory planning | Plan inventory in each distribution point to satisfy demand. |
| Manufacturing execution systems | Manage shop floor activities in maintenance or manufacturing facility. |
| Warehouse management systems | Manage inventory control, product placement, and stowing/picking in warehouse. |
| Transportation planning | Optimize freight movement, select modes, plan routes, and select carriers. |
| Transportation content | Provide information to help optimize distribution network. |
| Transportation execution | Automate transportation operations such as dispatch, shipment reconciliation, and shipping documentation. |
| Order management | Automate customer-centered order fulfillment process. |
| Component and supplier management | Administer data on identification, configuration of component parts, suppliers, and purchasing process. Source assemblies, parts, and material. |
| Product data management | Categorize and store product data. Manage visibility and exchange of data from design and repair processes. |
| Strategic management | Help assess, model, and evaluate supply chain to make sourcing, maintenance, distribution, and infrastructure decisions. |
| Customer assistance management | Manage customer support life cycle, including logistics workforce support. |

# Appendix F
# Abbreviations

| | |
|---|---|
| ABC | activity-based costing |
| ABM | activity-based management |
| ADP | automated data processing |
| AIT | automatic identification technology |
| ASCET | Achieving Supply Chain Excellence through Technology |
| AWG | Architecture Working Group |
| BOM | bill of material |
| C3I | Command, Control, Communications and Intelligence |
| C4ISR | Command, Control, Communications, Computers, Intelligence, Surveillance, and Reconnaissance |
| CINC | commander-in-chief |
| CLM | Council of Logistics Management |
| CLS | contractor logistics support |
| COA | course-of-action |
| COE | Common Operating Environment |
| CONUS | continental United States |
| COTS | commercial off-the-shelf |
| CPFR | collaborative planning, forecasting, and replenishment |
| CSP | customer service pyramid |
| CWT | customer wait time |

| | |
|---|---|
| DLA | Defense Logistics Agency |
| DOC | desired operational capability |
| DoD | Department of Defense |
| DOS | days of supply |
| DPTR | delivery performance to request |
| DRI | Defense Reform Initiative |
| ECO | engineering change order |
| EDI | Electronic Data Interchange |
| EFT | Electronic Funds Transfer |
| ERP | enterprise resource planning |
| FL | focused logistics |
| FY | fiscal year |
| FYDP | Fiscal Year Defense Program |
| GPRA | Government Performance and Results Act |
| IDE | integrated data environment |
| IT | information technology |
| JTF | joint task force |
| JV | Joint Vision |
| JV2010 | Joint Vision 2010 |
| JV2020 | Joint Vision 2020 |
| LAN | local area network |
| LMI | Logistics Management Institute |

| | |
|---|---|
| MES | Manufacturing Execution System |
| MIS | Management Information System |
| MRPII | Manufacturing Resources Planning II |
| MSU | Michigan State University |
| NMC | not mission capable |
| O&M | operations and maintenance |
| OIL | open issues list |
| OMS | Order Management System |
| OSD | Office of the Secretary of Defense |
| OV-1 | Operational View-1, High-Level Operational Concept Graphic |
| OV-2 | Operational View-2, Operational Node Connectivity Description |
| PC | personal computer |
| PFD | process flow diagram |
| PMG | Performance Measurement Group |
| POA&M | plan of action and milestones |
| POD | Port of Debarkation |
| POE | Port of Embarkation |
| PRTM | Pittiglio Rabin Todd & McGrath |
| SC | supply chain |
| SCC | Supply-Chain Council |
| SCM | supply chain management |
| SCOR | Supply Chain Operational Reference |

SCP    Supply Chain Planning

SME    subject-matter expert

SPS    Segmented Purchasing Strategy

TAV    total asset visibility

TMS    Transportation Management Systems

U.S.    United States

WIP    work-in-process

WMS    Warehouse Management System

WWII    World War II

# Index

Functional Requirements Guide · 14, 18, 68, 79, 128, 182
functions · 13, 15, 17, 23, 24, 26, 27, 33, 34, 42, 44, 45, 56, 59, 74, 77, 90, 93, 94, 96, 103, 106, 110, 126, 144, 147, 150, 152, 154, 158, 165, 167, 168

## G

gap analysis · 103, 105, 115
General Accounting Office · 49, 127
global economy · 9
Government Performance and Results Act · 27
guiding principles · 5, 17, 18, 27, 49, 54, 177

## I

implementation actions · 5, 21, 28, 75, 76, 100
implementation focal point · 23
implementation phase · 43
implementation plan · 27, 28, 30, 61
implementation strategy · 6, 64, 95, 98
implementation team · 20, 21, 22, 23, 25, 26, 27, 29, 30, 31, 33, 34, 35, 39, 40, 41, 43, 45, 46, 47, 48, 49, 50, 54, 55, 56, 58, 59, 64, 67, 68, 69, 72, 73, 77, 83, 86, 93, 94, 96, 102, 104, 106, 116, 117, 162, 166, 169, 178
implementation tools · 55
initial focus areas · 55, 64
innovation · 9, 19, 94, 185
integrated data environment · 171
Integrated Definition (IDEF) modeling · 56
integrated supply chain · 12, 25, 44, 54, 64, 88, 98, 106, 167
integration contractor · 169
integration strategy · 25

## J

Joint Vision 2010 (JV2010) · 9, 10, 11, 21
Joint Vision 2020 (JV2020) · 9, 21

## L

leadership · 4, 22, 23, 26, 98, 99, 162, 166, 185
local area network · 55
logistics community · 1, 4, 21, 22, 40, 41, 104, 161, 162, 163, 169
Logistics Competency Model · 175
Logistics Management Institute · 70, 72
logistics network · 16
Logistics Strategic Plan · 10, 12, 21
logistics vision · 12, 17

## M

Managing Supply Chains · 174
market demand · 16
metrics · 17, 30, 31, 33, 39, 55, 60, 67, 68, 69, 70, 71, 72, 75, 76, 92, 94, 95, 96, 103, 105, 107, 108, 110, 111, 114, 115, 116, 118, 120, 121, 122, 124, 125, 170, 177, 181, 182, 183, 184

## N

Naval Supply Systems Command · 23

## O

open issues list · 62
operational concept graphic · 34, 35, 49, 95, 107, 110, 116
operational customers · 86
operational implementation · 43
operational node connectivity description · 35, 36, 94
organizational resistance · 22, 104

## P

performance measurement · 6, 29, 68, 129, 182
Performance Measurement Group (PMG) · 119